THE DAY OF
ISLAM

ADVANCE PRAISE

"Paul Williams's meticulously researched and shocking exposé is the mother of all wake-up calls for America, politicians and citizens alike. If Americans do not respond in a significant way to these warnings, I'm not sure what can be done to save them."

Carol A. Taber
President of FamilySecurityMatters.org
and former publisher of *Working Woman*

"Dr. Williams substantiates the hidden truth about militant Islam's menacing nuclear threat to 'dar al-Harb'—our homeland. He clearly underscores how unbridled political correctness has done much to undermine our nation's resolve and lessen our ability to confront this evil in earnest."

Jeffrey M. Epstein
President of America's Truth Forum

"Dr. Paul Williams brilliantly exposes the threat Islam poses to the Western world. He presents the readers with undeniable facts and a well-researched investigation revealing a catastrophic demise if the Western world fails to act."

Robert S. Turk
Chairman of B'nai Elim

PAUL L.
WILLIAMS

THE DAY OF
ISLAM

THE ANNIHILATION OF AMERICA AND THE WESTERN WORLD

Prometheus Books

59 John Glenn Drive
Amherst, New York 14228-2197

Published 2007 by Prometheus Books

Inquiries should be addressed to
Prometheus Books
59 John Glenn Drive
Amherst, New York 14228–2197
VOICE: 716–691–0133, ext. 207
FAX: 716–564–2711
WWW.PROMETHEUSBOOKS.COM

11 10 09 08 07   5 4 3 2 1

Library of Congress Cataloging-in-Publication Data

Williams, Paul L., 1944–
    The day of Islam : the annihilation of America and the Western World / by Paul L. Williams.
        p. cm.
    ISBN 978–1–59102–508–5 (alk. paper)
    1. Qaida (Organization) 2. Terrorism—United States—Forecasting. 3. Nuclear terrorism—United States—Forecasting. 4. Islamic fundamentalism. I. Title.

HV6432.5.Q2W547 2007
363.325—dc22

                                                                        2007001601

Printed in the United States of America on acid-free paper

For Jeffrey Epstein,
founder of America's Truth Forum,
my great friend, and an intrepid American patriot

Allah bears witness that the love of jihad and death in the cause of Allah has dominated my life and the verses of the sword permeated every cell in my heart, "and fight the pagans all together as they fight you all together." How many times did I wake up to find myself reciting this holy verse?

O women kinfolk! Do not use cosmetics or imitate the whores and mannish women of the West.

O [my] wives! You were, after Allah, the best support and the best help: from the first day you knew that the road was full of thorns and mines. You left the comforts of your relatives and chose to share the hardships next to me.

As to my children, forgive me because I have given you only a little of my time since I answered the jihad call. I have chosen a road fraught with dangers and for this sake suffered from hardships, embitterment, betrayal, and treachery. I advise you not to work with al Qaeda and the Front (The Islamic Front for Fighting the Crusaders and the Jews).

Osama bin Laden, October 2002

CONTENTS

ACKNOWLEDGMENTS

I could not have completed this work without the help of the following individuals: Dr. Hugh Cort; Private Investigator Douglas Hagmann of the Northeast Intelligence Network; Private Investigator Laurice Tatum; Judy McLeod of Canada Free Press; my steadfast secretary, Mary Riggall; my Polish colleague David Dastych; and my wonderful wife, Patricia, who remains the love of my life. They deserve considerably more credit from me than this brief note of acknowledgement.

THE NUCLEAR SOLUTION

Abu Shihab el-Kandahari
Al Qaeda Commander

I n the name of Allah the most merciful. Thus, you are not mistaken in reading this text. This is the only way to kill the greatest possible number of Americans. The Americans have never experienced a threat like this one. During World War II, America used this [nuclear] weapon twice in three days following the successful Japanese attack on Pearl Harbor. Today, the United States uses the most powerful and advanced weapons of destruction against the peaceful citizens of Iraq and Afghanistan, and it proudly supports the war that Russia is waging against Chechnya, not out of affection for Russia, but rather from its hatred of Muslims.

America has bombed Iraq with weaponry that will pollute the soil and underground water with radiation for thousands of years. It also enhances its bombs with depleted uranium to cause even greater harm to the people and the environment. This, so that no one should think that after they leave the island of [the Prophet] Muhammad [the Arabian Peninsula], which they have transformed into a restricted area, just to return to the same place [because of the pollution perpetrated by them]. It seems, in fact, that the wild beasts in the White House have forgotten or have tried to forget one very important thing, which is, in all pride—the al Qaeda organization. This organization, which strikes fear in the hearts of the infidel West, turns youth into people who have nothing in this world but their devotion to Allah and to His Prophet Muhammad, and who are the tormentors of the sons of whores [i.e., the West], and who are shining examples of estrangement from the sins of this world . . . and of selling their souls to Allah. . . . Therefore, an eye for an eye, a tooth for a tooth. Even though the Americans have bombs possessing enormous power, al Qaeda is even more powerful than they, and it has in its possession bombs which are called "dirty bombs," and bombs with deadly viruses, which will spread fatal diseases throughout American cities. . . .

The coming days will prove that Kaedat el-Jihad [the al Qaeda organization] is capable of turning America into a sea of deadly radiation, and this will prove to the world that the end is at hand. . . . Yes, we will destroy America and its allies, because they have used their power for evil against the weak.

And now, the end approaches at the hand of the enlightened [Islamic] youth astride their horses [fighting the war against the infidels]; they will dismount either as victors or vanquished [i.e., fall in holy war for Allah].

CHAPTER ONE

THE FORGOTTEN TESTIMONY

Praise be to Allah and peace be upon the Master of Messengers, his family, and his companions. We ask for His forgiveness, seek His guidance, and seek refuge from Him for our sins and evil actions. We pray to Allah, praise and glory be to Him, to accept us with the martyrs and the virtuous ones among His worshippers and to make us die Muslims.
Osama bin Laden, December 2001

On September 5, 1996, a day after Osama bin Laden issued his declaration of war against the United States, Jamal Ahmed al-Fadl walked into the US embassy in Kenya, presented his bona fides as a senior member of the *mujahadeen* ("holy warriors"), and began to provide information to US intelligence officials on the origin, organization, and objectives of the mysterious organization known as "al Qaeda" ("the base").

Al-Fadl's information, later corroborated by a wealth of sources, proved to be so telling and important that he became known as Confidential Source One.[1]

Within forty-eight hours of his appearance in the embassy, al-Fadl was whisked away to the United States. He was placed on the highest level of security within the witness protection program, and he remained under wraps in hotel suites and government safe houses throughout the Washington, DC, area for the next four and a half years.

Little was known about al-Fadl, not even his name, until he appeared in federal court on February 6, 2001, as a key witness in *The United States of America v. Osama bin Laden, et al.*

Confidential Source One turned out to be a small, skinny, deeply tanned native of Sudan with a scruffy black beard, a sharply sloped forehead, and deep-set eyes. He wore an Islamic skullcap, the traditional *shalwat jameez* (long loose tunic), and (what appeared to be) a perpetual scowl. On the witness stand, he seemed about as comfortable as a sand crab in a snowstorm.

Although he had resided for several years in New York, al-Fadl's command of English was limited. His statements were often ungrammatical and confusing and his voice barely audible to the judge and jury despite the microphone that had been placed before him. In the midst of the hearing, Denise Nasar, an interpreter, was asked to convey to the court what the witness was saying.[2]

A MATTER OF MONEY

Jamal al-Fadl's bone of contention against bin Laden was straightforward and understandable. The guy had been stiffed. He had worked for years as a front man for al Qaeda in cooking deals with black market arms agents, including those who sold high-end goods, but he had received little financial reward. He had received less pay at five hundred dollars per month than the lowest-ranking Arab in bin Laden's employ, who received a monthly salary of twelve hundred.[3]

One of al-Fadl's assignments was particularly dangerous. He was asked to negotiate the terms of the sale of nuclear materials from a lieutenant colonel in the Sudanese army and former government minister. The slightest slipup could have resulted in his head being on a stake in the marketplace of Hilat Koko. The negotiations were successful. Bin Laden got his nuclear material at the rock-bottom price of $1.5 million per kilo.[4] And what did al-Fadl receive for his efforts that served to make the great jihad against the United States a reality? A measly ten thousand dollars!

When the uranium was sent to a laboratory in Cyprus for testing, bin Laden said that he had no further need of al-Fadl's services. And when the emir boarded his private jet to head back to Afghanistan with his family, friends, and fellow jihadists, al-Fadl, the faithful servant, was left behind to fend for himself without a parting gift or even a pat on the back for good luck.

Al-Fadl was irate. And to display the full measure of his extreme displeasure, he pilfered over one hundred thousand dollars from bin Laden's holdings and hightailed it to the nearest US embassy for sanctuary.

Bilking the bucks proved to be an easy task since al-Fadl, as the al Qaeda paymaster, had access to the emir's accounts in Bank Shami, Bank Tadaman Islami, Bank Faisal Islami, and the Bank of Almusia.[5]

THE BROOKLYN STOREFRONT

Jamal al-Fadl had been born and raised in the squalid village of Ruffa, south of Khartoum. In 1986 he obtained a student visa and moved to Brooklyn, where he attended night school, worked as a clerk at a grocery store, and became an active member of the Farouq Mosque.[6]

Located at 554 Atlantic Avenue, a street lined with Islamic stores and shops, the Farouq Mosque is a far cry from such opulent Muslim places of worship as the six-million-dollar Dar al-Hijrah Islamic Center, replete with minarets, in Falls Church, Virginia. A passerby could easily mistake the mosque for a rundown social club, a cut-rate *halal* hash joint, or a dingy bookstore that specializes in secondhand editions of Arabic pornography. The only indication that the nondescript storefront is a mosque comes from the inscription that is inscribed above the doorway: *Ashhadu an la ilaha ilaha illa Llah, wa ashhadu anna Mohammad rasulu Llah* ("There is no God but Allah, and Muhammad is his prophet").

Few realize that this seedy establishment has served as a central recruiting station for the jihad, a shelter for al Qaeda operatives, and a fund-raising establishment that has supplied millions of dollars to cells of radical Islam throughout the world.[7]

THE AL-KIFAH REFUGEE CENTER

By the time Jamal al-Fadl became an active member of the congregation, the Farouq Mosque had served as the headquarters of the Al-Kifah Refugee Center, a front for al Qaeda, with branch offices in Atlanta, Boston, and Tucson, and recruiting offices in twenty-six states.[8]

Founded by Abdullah Azzam, bin Laden's mentor and the cofounder of al Qaeda, the Al-Kifah Refugee Center acted as a CIA front for transferring funds, weapons, and recruits to the anti-Soviet *mujahadeen* in Afghanistan. It represented the Reagan administration's way of bringing about the collapse of "the evil empire" and the end of the cold war. In exchange for this service, the Brooklyn mosque—unbeknownst to most Americans—began receiving annual stipends in excess of two million dollars from Uncle Sam.[9] The stipends continued until 1993, when the leaders of the mosque, including blind Sheikh Omar Abdel Rahman, were implicated in the bombing of the World Trade Center in lower Manhattan.

From 1982 to 1988, Abdullah Azzam was a frequent visitor to the Farouq Mosque. In a 1988 videotape, he can be seen and heard telling a large crowd that "blood and martyrdom are the only way to create a Muslim society."[10] His remarks are punctuated by rapturous cries of "Amen" and "Right on, brother" from the congregation. The call to arms was echoed by Mustafa Shalabi, the volatile imam and Azzam's protégé, who was murdered on March 1, 1991, by unknown assassins.[11]

THE AFGHAN CAMPAIGN

Among several others in attendance, al-Fadl took the call to heart, and, with the support and blessing of Shalabi and the Farouq flock, he packed his belongings, boarded a plane, and headed off to Peshawar, the Pakistani border town that served as home to hundreds of thousands of Afghan refugees.

After a few weeks in Azzam's guesthouse, al-Fadl was sent to a military training camp on the outskirts of the Afghan city of Khost, where he learned how to handle a Russian-made Kalashnikov rifle, how to fire US-supplied Stingers and other surface-to-air rockets, and how to pack explosives, including C-4, in suitcases and duffel bags.[12]

In addition to the military training, al-Fadl and the other recruits attended a madrassah (religious school), where they studied the Hadith (the collection of sacred teachings) and committed surahs (chapters) of the Koran to memory.[13]

After forty-five days of basic training, al-Fadl was summoned to a meeting with Osama bin Laden, the billionaire deputy emir of the Afghan Service Bureau (Maktab al-Khidamat, or MAK), who was known among the *mujahadeen* by such aliases as Abu Abdallah and al Qaqa.[14] They met in a two-story villa in the university district of Peshawar that served as the MAK headquarters.

After the meeting, al-Fadl was sent to the frontline of the fighting at Jaji and other sites, where he distinguished himself in battle and became known among his comrades as "the Sudanese."[15]

THE FLAME OF JIHAD

In 1989, after ten years of warfare, the Soviets retreated from Afghanistan. More than a million Afghans—8 percent of the population—had been killed and millions more were maimed or seriously wounded. Out of the thirteen million who survived the conflict, almost half were refugees.[16]

Many of the victorious Muslims returned to their native lands, carrying the torch of Islamic revolution. In the Balkans, ethnic hostility among Muslims, Croats, and Serbs resulted in the secession of Bosnia-Herzegovina from Yugoslavia, which sparked a three-year conflict that resulted in the loss of 150,000 lives.[17] In November 1991 the Muslims of Chechnya declared independence from Russia, resulting in a conflict that cost forty million dollars a day, killed 35 to 140 people per week, and made Grozny one of the most devastated cities on earth.[18] In 1992 civil war erupted in Algeria when the government postponed elections to prevent the Islamic Salvation Front, a party intent upon turning the country into a theocratic *shariah* (Islamic law) state, from taking power. By 2005 the insurgency had resulted in the deaths of 120,000 Algerians in a conflict characterized by a brutality that exceeded the bloodiest of African civil wars. Entire villages had been massacred with the help of truck-mounted guillotines.[19] In Egypt the Islamic Group *al-Gama'a al-Islamiyya* initiated a campaign against tourism and Western culture by bombing and burning theaters, bookstores, banks, and commercial outlets, and killing Christians and Jews by organized pogroms.[20]

THE BIRTH OF AL QAEDA

The Arabs who remained in Afghanistan were confronted with the question of the future of the jihad. A meeting was held in Khost. It was attended by a group of twelve leading figures of the *mujahadeen*. Abu Ayoub, the chairman of the gathering, proposed the formation of an organization that would wage war beyond the borders of Afghanistan until the dawning of the Day of Islam, when all of creation will fall in submission before the throne of Allah.[21] Some dispute arose about the name until the group settled on al Qaeda, or "the Base." The Base was to serve as a loose confederation of radical Islam—dominated by the Egyptian Islamic Jihad.[22] The leader by unanimous decision was Osama bin Laden. The choice was inevitable: Osama held the checkbook.

All members of the organization were asked to sign an agreement that they would devote their lives to the cause of al Qaeda and the Day of Islam. Jamal Ahmed al-Fadl was the third to sign. He and the others who signed the document became involved in a ritual of fasting and prayer, self-castigation with a whip made of dangling chains, and the recitation of vows over the Koran. The ritual culminated in the recitation of the following blood oath (*bayat*) to bin Laden:

> *The pledge of God and his covenant is upon me to listen and obey the superiors who are doing this work in energy, early-rising, difficulty and easiness and for his superiority upon us so that the word of God will be the highest and his religion victorious.*[23]

The requirements for joining were spelled out in the following manner:

- A binding commitment
- Good listening skills
- Obedience
- Good manners
- Reference from members
- Recitation of the pledge[24]

THE IRAQI FOUNDERS

When al-Fadl provided details of the formation of al Qaeda in federal court on that cold day in February 2001, many intelligence analysts and national news commentators noted that four of the founders were Egyptians with ties to the Egyptian Islamic Jihad. Overlooked by practically everybody was the testimony that an even greater number were Kurds from Iraq. The Kurdish Iraqis included Abu Ayoub, the organizer of the event, along with Abu Burhan, Abu Fadl al-Iraqi, Abu Ubaidah al-Iraqi, and Mamdouh Mahmud Salim (Abu Hajer al-Iraqi).

A transcribed portion of al-Fadl's broken English testimony regarding the formation of al Qaeda is as follows:

> *Q. Did there come a time when you attended a meeting with Abu Ayoub al-Iraqi?*
> *A. Yes. At that time I was in Farook Camp in Khost.*
> *Q. Can you tell us what happened at the meeting you attended in the Farook Camp in Khost, Afghanistan?*
> *A. He came with—Abu Ayoub and his brother Yasin—they came to the camp and they got meeting about we going to make group training people and we don't want to stop after Russia left Afghanistan.*
> *Q. Can you tell us what Abu Ayoub al-Iraqi said?*
> *A. He said we going to make group and this is group that under Farook, and it's going to be one man for the group and it's going to be focused in jihad and we going to use the group to do anything out of Afghanistan.*
> *Q. Can you tell the jury what the name of the group was?*
> *A. Al Qaeda.*[25]

Upon their return to northern Iraq, many Kurds with ties to al Qaeda joined the Islamic Movement of Kurdistan and, in 1991, took part in a rebellion that Saddam Hussein brutally repressed with the use of chemical weapons. The al Qaeda Kurds under Abu Ayoub went on to form Ansar al-Islam ("Soldiers of God"), which continued the resistance.

Few US intelligence officials paid the slightest attention to this development. Even in the wake of al-Fadl's court appearance, the attacks of 9/11, and the US-led invasion of Iraq, no leading member of the Bush administration bothered to ask about Abu Ayoub and his whereabouts. The man who organized al Qaeda was not even mentioned in *The 9/11 Commission Report*—an oversight that is truly mind-boggling.

Moreover, despite his prominence, Abu Ayoub is scarcely mentioned in books by noted authors concerning radical Islam and international terrorism. Neither he nor the other Kurds mentioned by al-

Fadl have been the subjects of investigative reports by the national media. If asked "Where is Abu Ayoub?" leading news commentators and national security figures inevitably will respond with the query "Who is Abu Ayoub?"

When Saddam Hussein was toppled from power in April 2003, al Qaeda operatives, including Abu Musab al-Zarqawi, found a base of support for terrorist attacks against the occupation forces among the hundreds of Kurds who comprised Ansar al-Islam.[26] If the question concerning Abu Ayoub had been adequately addressed by military force, the lives of countless Iraqis, two thousand American troops, and one hundred and fifty British troops might have been spared since the coalition forces focused on routing out the terrorist insurgents among the Sunnis, who gained scant representation in the general elections, rather than the Kurds, who became the ruling faction.

THE SHURA

Al-Fadl went on to provide the court with information concerning the internal workings of al Qaeda. The organization, under the leadership of an emir, was governed by a *shura*, an Islamic council comprised of mullahs (those who were learned in religious law) and military officials who had commandeered forces against the Soviets in the great jihad. In addition to Abu Ayoub (who served for several years as the deputy emir) and the Iraqis mentioned above, the leading members of the council were identified as follows:

Osama bin Laden—emir. He was born in 1957 and, along with his twenty-five brothers and twenty-nine sisters, was educated in Wahhabist schools. His Yemeni father, Mohammad bin Laden, founded a construction company in Saudi Arabia and, with royal patronage, became a billionaire. His Syrian mother, Alia, was the fourth and least favorite of Mohammad's wives.[27] Osama, which means "young lion" in Arabic, studied economics, physics, and engineering at the King

Abdul Aziz University in Jeddah, where he came under the influence of such prominent teachers of religion as Muhammad Qutb and Abdullah Azzam, the same Azzam who became active in the Brooklyn mosque.

In 1979 Osama headed off to Pakistan to join the Afghan resistance. Along with Azzam, he established Maktab al-Khidamat and used his financial resources to support his fellow holy warriors by building tunnels, roads, and bunkers.[28] Those willing to risk their lives can still visit the huge tunnels that he blasted into the Zazi Mountains of the Bahkitiar Province for use as guerrilla hospitals and ammunition dumps.[29]

Bin Laden also engaged in battle, including hand-to-hand combat against the Red Army in Jaji and Shaban. In one encounter, he lost several toes on his right foot, necessitating the use of a walking stick.[30] He also injured a kidney, a mishap that has resulted in renal failure and a dependency on dialysis.[31]

The emir has been implicated in a host of deadly attacks on the United States and its allies, including the 1993 World Trade Center bombing, the 1998 bombings of the US embassies in Kenya and Tanzania, the 2000 bombing of the USS *Cole* in Yemen, and the attacks of 9/11.

In the wake of the US-led invasion of Afghanistan and the battle at Tora Bora, bin Laden found shelter in the North-West Frontier Province of Pakistan. He presently remains in the small village of Dir, about fifty miles from the Afghan border. His whereabouts may be a mystery to US intelligence, but it is proclaimed in the *shabnamas* or "night letters" that are circulated among Pashtu tribesmen.[32]

Although assumed dead by several prominent US military and intelligence figures, Osama appeared like the Ghost of Christmas Past on January 19, 2006, to deliver the following message:

> *Reality testifies that the war against America and its allies has not remained confined to Iraq, as he claims. In fact, Iraq has become a point of attraction and recruitment of qualified resources. On the other hand, the* mujahadeen, *praise be to God, have managed to breach all the security measures adopted by the unjust nations of the coalition time and again. The evidence of this is the bombings you*

have seen in the capitals of the most important European countries of this aggressive coalition. As for the delay in carrying out similar operations in America, this was not due to failure to breach your security measures. Operations are under preparation, and you will see them on your own ground once they are finished, God willing.[33]

Ayman al-Zawahiri—aka the Doctor, Abu Mohammad, Abu Abdullah, Abu al-Muiz, the Teacher, Ustaz, Abdel Muaz, and Nur. Like Osama bin Laden, al-Zawahiri hails from a very prosperous and highly connected family. His paternal grandfather, Sheikh al-Ahmadi al-Zawahiri, was the Imam of Al-Azhar Mosque, one of the greatest positions of authority in Sunni Islam. His maternal grandfather, Abd al-Wahab Azzam, was president of Cairo University and an ambassador to Pakistan, Saudi Arabia, and Yemen. His parents, Rabi'a al-Zawahiri and Umayma Azzam, were pillars of society in modern Egypt.[34]

Upon his graduation from Cairo University's Faculty of Medicine with a degree in surgery and the mark of *gayyid giddan* (the highest mark possible), al-Zawahiri became involved with the Egyptian Islamic Jihad.[35] He first came to public attention in 1981 when he was charged as a conspirator in the assassination of Egyptian president Anwar Sadat. He was sentenced to three years in prison for illegal possession of weapons.

Upon his release, the doctor headed for Afghanistan to take part in the holy war. In 1991 he published *The Bitter Harvest*, a condemnation of the Muslim Brotherhood (for not taking action against such apostates as current Egyptian president Hosni Mubarak and King Fahd of Saudi Arabia) and a call for jihad against the Western world.

In December 2001 al-Zawahiri's wife and children were killed during the US bombing of Tora Bora. In 2002 he married two widows of an Egyptian Islamic Jihad colleague.

Presently, he is believed to be sheltered in a remote location along the Afghan-Pakistan border, moving freely between Khost in Afghanistan and Wana in Pakistan.

In the wake of 9/11, al-Zawahiri began to appear regularly on Arab television, where he delighted Muslim audiences by calling President Bush a "simpleton" and a "warmonger" and by speaking of the imminent demise of the Western world.

Fed up with such taunts and threats, the Bush administration attempted to kill al-Zawahiri in a surprise attack on Damadola, a small village in the Bajaur tribal area of Pakistan, where intelligence sources believed the doctor was having dinner. The intelligence sources were wrong. The bombing killed eighteen people, including women and children, but not the elusive doctor, who was dining elsewhere.

Since the attack had not been authorized by President Pervez Musharraf, more than ten thousand irate Pakistanis took to the streets in Karachi, chanting "Death to America" and "Stop bombing innocent civilians."[36]

On January 20, 2006, al-Zawahiri, wearing white robes and a white turban, appeared again on Arab television to label President Bush a "butcher," to threaten a new attack against the American people, and to speak of the US attempt to assassinate him by air strike as follows: "The American planes raided in compliance with Musharraf the traitor and his security apparatus, the slave of the Crusaders and the Jews. In seeking to kill my humble self and four of my brothers, the whole world has discovered the extent of America's lies and failures and the extent of its savagery in fighting Islam and Muslims."

Muhammad Atef—aka Abu Hafs el-Masry, Abdul Aziz, Abu Sitta, Abu Hafs Taysir, Sheikh Taysir Abdullah, Abu Fatima, Taysir, Abu Khadija, Abu Hafs. Before joining forces with bin Laden, Atef was an Egyptian policeman and member of the Egyptian Islamic Jihad. Implicated in the assassination of Sadat, he fled Egypt to seek refuge in Sudan and later Afghanistan, where he distinguished himself by leading a daring encirclement of Soviet Special Forces at the battle of al-Masada (the Lions' Den).

Described as quiet, resourceful, and noted as a voracious reader, Atef served as the head of al Qaeda's Military Committee and played a leading role in the bombing of the US embassy in Nairobi.[37]

Atef, whose daughter is married to one of bin Laden's sons, was killed in November 2001 during the US bombing of an al Qaeda stronghold. Despite all the hoopla about the elimination of al Qaeda's high command, Muhammad Atef remains the only member of the *shura* to be killed thus far as a result of the war on terror.

Abdullah Ahmed Abdullah—aka Saleh, Abu Mohammed el-Masry, Abu Marium, Abu Mohammed el-Masri Saas al-Sharif. An Egyptian of Saudi origin, this seasoned veteran of the Afghan war tutored the *mujahadeen* in the art of explosives. A member of al Qaeda's Military and Islamic Study Committees, he helped to build the bombs for the 1998 attacks on the US embassies. He was one of the five al Qaeda operatives indicted by a US grand jury on December 20, 2000.

In March 2004 Pakistani intelligence reported that Abdullah Ahmed Abdullah had been killed in South Waziristan. This led to much rejoicing among the Bush administration. The celebration, however, proved to be premature. The slain terrorist turned out to be both still alive and an al Qaeda fugitive of minor significance.[38]

Anas al-Liby—aka Nazih al-Raghie. This Libyan national was the surveillance expert who reconnoitered the US embassy in Nairobi and taught members of the group techniques such as sophisticated map reading, blueprinting, measuring wall thickness, and installing hidden cameras. He helped draft the al Qaeda manuals. Al-Liby, too, was indicted by the grand jury on December 20, 2000.

In 2002 the Bush administration gleefully announced that al-Liby had been captured in Sudan. The announcement, as it turned out, was another short-lived success story, based on false reports from spurious news sources.[39]

In 2003 al-Liby was involved in two attempts to assassinate Pakistani president Pervez Musharraf and was named as Pakistan's most wanted man, with a bounty of $350,000 on his head.[40]

Along with Abdullah Ahmed Abdullah, this al Qaeda operative

stands as a stellar case of flawed US intelligence. In May 2005 President Bush announced yet again that al-Liby had been captured—this time in Pakistan—and hailed the news as "a critical victory in the war on terror." The CIA, however, had not correctly read the report from Pakistani intelligence. The al Qaeda agent who had been captured was not bin Laden's "top general" or "a major facilitator and chief planner for the al Qaeda network."[41] Nor was he the man whom Secretary of State Condoleezza Rice called "a very important figure."[42] The suspect, as it turned out, was Abu Faraj al-Libbi, a low-ranker who, according to one source, was netted "among the flotsam and jetsam" of bin Laden's organization.[43]

What's worse, al-Libbi, despite the similarity in names, bore not even the slightest resemblance to al-Liby. He even lacked the al Qaeda chieftain's distinguishing physical characteristic: a long villainesque scar that runs down the left side of his face. Moreover, the agent in custody suffered from acute psoriasis or leucoderma, while Anas al-Liby never displayed signs of either condition. To make matters worse, the fingerprints of the suspect failed to match al-Liby's prints, which remained on file with the CIA. The prints had been lifted from an apartment that the real "major facilitator and chief planner" for al Qaeda had occupied in the United Kingdom. The fact that President Bush and Secretary Rice could make such statements in the light of such blatant contradictory evidence is remarkable and speaks volumes of the chaotic situation within US intelligence agencies, not to mention the administration itself.

For the record, al-Liby is not under wraps. He remains in a villa, controlled by SAVAMA (the Iranian intelligence service) in southern Iran. He is very comfortable. The villa contains a sauna and a swimming pool.[44]

Saif al-Adel. This mysterious figure turned out to be the nom de guerre of former Egyptian army colonel Muhamad Ibrahim Makkawi, who served in the special forces. He trained the tribal fighters who, in 1993, ambushed eighteen US Army Rangers in Mogadishu (the infamous Black Hawk Down incident). Al-Adel helped plan the 1998 attacks on the US embassies, the attack on the USS *Cole*, 9/11, and the 2003 bombings in Riyadh.[45] He, too, remains safely sequestered within a villa in Iran.[46] In a recent interview with Mohammed al-Shafey of *Asharq Alawsat* (the Saudi daily), al-Adel said that al Qaeda had never sought to establish a connection with Saddam Hussein and that the US invasion of Iraq was "boneheaded."

Abu Ubaidah al-Banshiri—aka Aadil Habib, Galal Fouad Emelify Abdeldaim, Jalal, and Adeel Habib. This Iraqi cofounder of al Qaeda was a police officer in Egypt before he headed off to fight in the great jihad against the Soviets. He took part in the monumental battle at al-Masada, where he was hit in the leg by machine gun fire.[47] He served as the emir of the Military Committee and spent a great deal of time (even for a *mujahadeen*) in fasting and prayer, and gained recognition as a *qaricept* (a scholar who had committed the entire contents of the Koran to memory).[48]

Al-Banshiri was one of a thousand people who drowned in a ferry accident on Africa's Lake Victoria (between Kenya and Tanzania) in May 1996.[49]

Mamdouh Mahmud Salim—aka Abu Hajer. This electrical engineer from Iraq was described by al-Fadl as bin Laden's "best friend."[50] Salim was a religious scholar and a key member of al Qaeda's Islamic Study Committee. He provided the group with the rationale for "collateral damage" by citing the fatwa of Ibn al-Tamiyeh, who called for all-out war against pagan invaders of Muslim lands, even if such a war meant the killing of many civilians. If such victims were indeed innocent, according to al-Tamiyeh, then killing them would be a boon since it would grant them early entrance to heaven.[51]

In Sudan, Salim operated bin Laden's Al Hajira Company, which ostensibly built roads and bridges and possessed a permit to import explosives for demolition and construction. He also became the point man for the acquisition of nuclear weapons and began to comb the world for off-the-shelf nuclear weapons and highly enriched uranium and plutonium for use in the production of atomic bombs.[52] His travels were subsidized, in part, by the Benevolence International Foundation of Chicago, Illinois, a "charity" that raised millions for the jihad.[53]

Salim eventually was arrested in Munich, Germany, on September 16, 1998, while attempting to purchase several kilos of enriched uranium from Russian black market dealers. Extradited to the United States, he was placed on trial with four other al Qaeda agents for the bombings of the US embassies in Kenya and Tanzania on August 7, 1998.[54]

While waiting for trial, Salim was confined to a cell within the Metropolitan Correctional Center in lower Manhattan. On November 1, 2000, he plunged a sharpened Afro comb into the eye of a prison guard, used the same weapon to stab another guard in the stomach, and sprayed hot sauce in the face of other attendants during a failed prison escape.[55] He was charged with attempted murder and removed to a maximum-security facility. At this writing, he has yet to face a judge and jury.

Mamdouh Mahmud Salim, of all the members of the *shura*, merits special comment. He had been (a) identified by the FBI as a member of bin Laden's high command, (b) singled out by al-Fadl as the author of al Qaeda's position on collateral damage, and (c) named in his indictment as the point man for the terrorist group's procurement of nuclear weapons. Yet he never became the subject of a book or a major magazine article (let alone the subject of such network news programs as *60 Minutes* or *20/20*) and received no mention (not even as a footnote) in *The 9/11 Commission Report*, despite the fact that members of the commission had reviewed 2.5 million pages of documents and interviewed more than twelve hundred individuals in ten countries.[56]

FURTHER TESTIMONY

Al-Fadl went on to describe how the *shura* operated through three committees: the Military Committee, which oversaw recruitment, training, and the acquisition of munitions; the Islamic Study Committee, which made rulings on religious law and trained recruits in the teachings of the Koran and the Hadith; and the Finance Committee, which controlled the group's financial holdings and the transfer of funds to the various cells. The cells represented units of al Qaeda within sixty countries throughout the world. Each unit engaged in missions independent of the others. This measure served to safeguard the overall objectives of the organization.

At four in the afternoon of that February in 2001, al-Fadl, sweating and stammering, continued to spill his guts. He spoke of Muaz el-Masry, an interpreter of dreams, who attended all committee meetings and met with bin Laden on a daily basis. He described the headquarters of the organization in Peshawar. He described Ayman al-Zawahiri's pivotal role as the chief counsel to bin Laden and the most distinguished scholar within the group.

The judge repressed a few yawns. The jury became listless. The government officials kept checking the time.

Al-Fadl, however, had more to say—including testimony regarding the laboratory for weapons of mass destruction that had been established in Hilat Koko and the details of bin Laden's purchase of highly enriched uranium from black market sources in Khartoum. Unfortunately, few were listening.

Concerning the appearance of Confidential Source One in federal court, Benjamin Weiser of the *New York Times* in a front-page article wrote:

Before the embassy bombing trial, Osama bin Laden loomed large in the American psyche, a villain of unimaginable evil and sophisticated reach. It was an image fed by destruction done and by American law enforcement eager to drive home the reality of his threat. In some ways, though, it was an image created because so little was known about how he worked.

But the trial, which left many of the details of the bombing uncontested, made clear that while Mr. bin Laden may be a global menace, his group, Al Qaeda, was at times slipshod, torn by inner strife, betrayal, greed, and the banalities of life that one might find in any office.

"To listen to some of the news reports a year or two ago, you would think bin Laden was running a top Fortune 500 multinational company—people everywhere, links everywhere," said Larry C. Johnson, a former deputy director of the State Department's Office of Counterterrorism. "What the evidence at trial has correctly portrayed is that it's really a loose amalgam of people with a shared ideology, but very limited direction."[57]

CHAPTER TWO

THE DAWN OF
DOOMSDAY

We will turn your morning into black night like the face of Con-
doleezza [Rice]. We will ruin your life like her messed-up hair; both
your coming and going will be miserable.
        Abu Musab al-Suri, "Message to the American People," 2006

Is there a sane person who discloses his [WMD] secrets?
                        Muhammad al-Ablaj, *Al Majallah*, 2003

THE $64 QUESTION

Does al Qaeda possess an arsenal of nuclear weapons? No question in the war against radical Islam is more important than that. But some American journalists and scholars think not. They argue that the fact that such weapons haven't been used yet offers proof positive that the terrorist group has been unable to purchase or build them. Such thinking reflects a failure to realize that the distinguishing characteristic of Islamic terrorism is patience. Bin Laden's favorite Islamic verse, repeated five times a day in al Qaeda cells throughout the world, is as follows: "I will be patient until I outpatient Patience." In his fatwas and other writings, he singles out patience as the most important quality of a holy warrior. This is not mere lip service. The *mujahadeen* waited eight years from the first attack on the World Trade Center in 1993 to the second on 9/11.

Most foreign journalists and scholars think otherwise. The Saudis maintain that al Qaeda has an arsenal of forty to seventy tactical nukes—some had been built with the help of SPETSNAZ (Soviet Special Forces) operatives, Chinese scientists, and technicians from the A. Q. Khan Research Laboratories in Pakistan; others were off-the-shelf items that became available in the nuclear black market that began to boom in the wake of the collapse of the Soviet Union. The Russians are more cautious and believe that the arsenal might only contain twelve to fifteen fully assembled nukes.[1]

Well-respected writers, including Peter L. Bergen in *The Osama bin Laden I Know*, dismiss such conjectures as to the availability and number of nukes as idle speculation, arguing that such statements are not supported by documentation or empirical evidence.[2]

But documentation and evidence have been provided. The documentation came with the testimony of Jamal Ahmed al-Fadl in a New York court on February 13, 2001, and the evidence exists as a canceled check in the amount of $1.5 million. This check presently remains within the "Alec file," the CIA's codename for its confidential file on Osama bin Laden.

THE HOMECOMING HERO
AND SADDAM HUSSEIN

After the Soviet withdrawal from Afghanistan, bin Laden went home to Saudi Arabia, where he was greeted as a hero and received invitations to speak at mosques, schools, and community centers. More than 250,000 cassettes of his speeches were produced for sale in shops and marketplaces. In these speeches, bin Laden decried the evidence of Western cultural imperialism and moral decadence that had cropped up throughout the kingdom: women disobeying *shariah* (Islamic law) in their dress and demeanor; men flaunting their business exploits and drinking alcohol at social functions. "When we buy American goods," he maintained in one message, "we are accomplices in the murder of Palestinians. American companies make millions in the Arab world with which they pay taxes to their government. The United States uses that money to send $3 billion a year to Israel, which it uses to kill Palestinians."[3]

While bin Laden was ranting and raving to any Arab who would listen during that fateful summer of 1990, Saddam Hussein ordered the invasion of Kuwait, forcing the al-Sabagh royal family to flee their palaces and seek refuge in Saudi Arabia. The Saudi royal family reacted with great alarm to the invasion, fearing that the madman from Iraq with his dream of a New Babylon might turn his attention to their country, which possessed the largest reserves of crude oil in the world.[4]

BIN LADEN'S PROPOSAL TO THE PRINCES

Bin Laden responded to the threat by rushing to the office of Prince Sultan ibn Abdul Aziz al-Saud, the Saudi minister of defense, with a ten-page proposal in hand. He informed Prince Sultan that the heavy engineering equipment used by large construction companies, including his family's firm, could be used to build fortifications at the border and around the oil fields. He proposed that the *mujahadeen* should be incorporated within the Saudi military since they remained the most formidable military unit on the face of the earth. He himself would serve as their general.

Prince Sultan listened with polite attention—bin Laden's father, after all, had been one of the country's richest men and an esteemed friend of King Fahd—but he declined to take the offer seriously.[5] He arranged for bin Laden to present his proposal to Prince Turki bin Faisal ibn Abdul Aziz al-Saud, the minister of intelligence.

Prince Turki also listened politely as bin Laden explained his plan to unite all Arabs in a jihad against Hussein and as he warned against inviting "infidel" forces into the holy land to protect the interests of the kingdom. Such an invitation, bin Laden insisted, would represent an effrontery to the teachings of the Prophet and would outrage all true believers.[6] As a seasoned diplomat, Prince Turki gave the wide-eyed and ascetic bin Laden a warm smile and a pat on the back as he opened the door and sent him on his way to the offices of governmental officials, until he came to the exit and found himself in the street with the proposal still in hand.

King Fahd and the Saudi princes were convinced that they had too much to lose by placing the fate of their kingdom in the hands of a radical upstart like bin Laden, even though they likely knew that bin Laden and his cohorts possessed a stockpile of hundreds of thousands of weapons, including delayed-timing devices for crates of C-4 plastic explosives, long-range sniper rifles, wire-guided antitank missiles, and more than a thousand shoulder-fired Stinger antiaircraft missiles.[7]

THE OUTRAGE FROM UNCLE SAM

Within a week of the invasion of Kuwait, King Fahd accepted the offer from President George H. W. Bush to protect the interest of his oil-rich kingdom with a coalition of military forces. The offer, which had been presented to him by Secretary of Defense Dick Cheney, seemed reasonable. The Saudis, after all, had always depended on military assistance from the *kafir* (unbeliever) nations of the Western world. When the kingdom was established in 1932, the Saudis were protected by the British, then by the Americans, who established an air base at Dhahran that remained in operation from 1946 to 1962, and finally by the French, who came to the aid of the royal family when, in 1979, a group of fanatics laid seige to the Great Mosque in Mecca and demanded King Fahd's abdication.

But this situation was different—vastly different. The threat from Iraq called not for the maintenance of a peacetime air base or the deployment of force on a weekend mission to suppress a rebellion. This situation called for the establishment of two permanent military installations between the holy cities of Mecca and Medina. And it was to this protective measure that the royal family granted their consent.

Throughout the summer and fall of 1990, giant US C-130 transporters arrived at airstrips throughout Saudi Arabia to discharge hundreds of tanks, trucks, jeeps, and artillery transport vehicles. Satellite dishes suddenly sprouted from the rooftops of hotels and office buildings. And long lines of US soldiers, including women in army fatigues, appeared on highways and byways throughout the kingdom.

Nothing could be more offensive to the *ummah*, the pious community of believers. Bin Laden seethed with rage. "The Arabian Peninsula," he wrote, "has never—since Allah made it flat, created its desert, and encircled it with seas—been stormed by any forces like the Crusader armies now spreading through it like locusts, consuming its riches and destroying its plantations. All of this is happening at a time when nations are attacking Muslims like people fighting over a plate of food."[8]

Bin Laden circulated pamphlets and delivered speeches in Islamic centers to decry the desecration of holy ground. Others joined in the condemnation of the "American invasion." Sheikh Safar ibn Abd al-Rahman al-Hawali, Sheikh Salman bin Fahd al-Awda, and other clerics who joined in the protest were rounded up by the Saudi police and locked in prison cells without the comforts of air-conditioning and running water.[9]

FINDING NEVERLAND WITH OSAMA AND THE *MUJAHADEEN*

In the early fall of 1991, Saudi security uncovered documents that linked bin Laden to an attempt to mount an armed rebellion within the kingdom.[10] King Fahd and the royal princes finally lost patience with the hotheaded rabble-rouser. Despite pleas from bin Laden's friends and family, they ordered his exile and froze his financial assets.

The punishment, though substantial, seemed providential. However, bin Laden cast his sights on Sudan, one of the poorest and most turbulent nations in the world, which beckoned to him and his *mujahadeen* like an Islamic Shangri-la.

In 1989 General Omar Hassan Ahmed al-Bashir staged a coup to overthrow the government of Sadiq al-Mahdi and established one of the most violent and repressive regimes in history. With the help of Hassan al-Turabi, a Sorbonne graduate and leader of the Muslim Brotherhood, he set out to create a purist Islamist state in an arid wasteland plagued by malaria, typhoid, rabies, polio, giardiasis, and guinea worms, and where a decent slave with a full set of teeth could be purchased at the rock-bottom price of two hundred dollars. To achieve this end, millions of Muslims—deemed apostates—were put to death, thousands of Christians were martyred or forced to recant their faith and submit to circumcision, and an uncountable number of political dissidents were subjected to torture that would cause Grand Inquisitor Torquemada himself to shudder.[11]

Bin Laden accepted a personal invitation from al-Turabi to relocate to Sudan in order to take part in the grand theocratic experiment.[12] From a radical perspective, the union of al Qaeda and the al-Bashir regime seemed to have been planned by Allah himself. Bin Laden could operate without restraint and with the protection of the Sudanese government, while the poverty-ravaged country could benefit from the millions he would invest in the economy.

THE MOVE TO SUDAN

In preparation for the relocation, Jamal al-Fadl was sent to Sudan to purchase farms, homes, and businesses for bin Laden. On behalf of bin Laden, he purchased a wide tract of land at Soba, north of Khartoum on the banks of the Blue Nile, for $250,000, where al Qaeda came to establish a Muslim version of a collective farm, as well as a salt-evaporation facility near Port Sudan for $180,000.[13]

By 1991 more than two thousand members of al Qaeda arrived in Khartoum to set up shop. As a welcoming present, they were provided with Sudanese passports so that al Qaeda operatives could travel throughout the world with new identities.[14]

Bin Laden, with his four wives and numerous children, moved into a three-story cream-colored stucco villa within the Riyadh district of the city. A few blocks away he established his corporate headquarters, known as Wadi al-Aqiq (the "mother of all companies," according to al-Fadl) within a modern, glass-fronted office building on McNimr Street. From this location, a host of capitalistic enterprises were established, including Laden International, which traded weak Sudanese pounds for strong US dollars; Al Hajira Construction, which built roads and bridges for the Sudanese government; Al Themar agricultural company, which employed four thousand workers at its one-million-acre Al Damazine farms. The farms produced peanuts, corn, and sunflowers. Other business followed: Taba Investment, Ltd., traded in sugar, bananas, canned goods, and soap; Blessed Fruits grew fruit and vegetables; and Al Qudurat manufactured leather goods. Bin Laden also set up a trucking company, a tannery, a bakery, and a cattle-breeding company, and sank fifty million dollars of his own money into the Al Shamal bank in Khartoum.[15]

TERROR INCORPORATED

Thus al Qaeda gave rise to "Terror Incorporated" and became a player in the global economy. By 1992 bin Laden had his own in-house magazine, the *Newscast*, which was circulated among thousands of his employees. The *Newscast* carried news of Islam throughout the world and developments in the jihad against Christians and Jews. The editor of the paper was dubbed Abu Musa Reuter, after the famous American news service.[16] The *mujahadeen*, as it turned out, possessed a great sense of humor.

Al Qaeda proved to be a much better employer than Wal-Mart and many other US companies. The workers enjoyed full health benefits, paid vacations, and travel reimbursement. At the company store, they received free sugar, tea, rice, and other staples. Salaries ranged from $500 to $1,500 a month, money that went a long way in a country where the average worker labored sixty hours a week and earned less than $50 a month.[17]

Bin Laden's largesse, as it turned out, taught him the most painful lesson of labor relations within a free-enterprise system, namely, whatever you pay and provide to the workers, they inevitably will want more. Al-Fadl was one of the first to complain—even though bin Laden had purchased a very comfortable (by Sudanese standards) home for him in the city's most affluent neighborhood. Disgruntled, he went to the boss and asked to be paid as much as Wadith el-Hage and other top advisors. Al-Fadl relayed the outcome as follows: "He [bin Laden] say some people, they traveling a lot and they do more work, and also they got chance to work in the country. Some people, they got citizenship from another country and they go back over there for regular life, they can make more money than in group. And he says that's why he try to make them happy and give them money."[18]

This reply did not please al-Fadl. In effect, he was told that others worked harder than he did and were more valuable to the cause of the holy war, so he should shut up and get back to work.

In subsequent months, al-Fadl came to serve in the role of a kind of Dilbert for the terror organization. He was dispatched with bags of money to al Qaeda cells in Kenya, Pakistan, Budapest, Croatia, Bosnia, Jordon, and Eritrea.[19]

AN ASSIGNMENT FOR AL-FADL

In 1993 Abu Talal el-Masry, the head of al Qaeda's Financial Committee, gave al-Fadl his most important assignment to date. "He told me," al-Fadl told the court, "we hear somebody in Khartoum, he got uranium, and we need you to go and study that, is that true or not."

Sudan was the ideal place for bin Laden to launch his quest for weapons of mass destruction. The nuclear black market, thanks to the collapse of the Soviet Union, was booming, and Sudan had become a pivotal transshipping location for weapons and materials, including weapons-grade uranium. The goods flowed from Russia to Germany and from Germany to Sudan. From Sudan, the nuclear flow continued to such places as Iran, Libya, and Pakistan.[20]

Al-Fadl's first meeting with the nuclear black market agents took place in an office building on Jambouria Street in the midst of Khartoum. One agent was Salah Abdel al-Mobruk, a lieutenant colonel in the Sudanese army and former government minister; the other was an arms dealer named Basheer. The agents said that the asking price for the uranium was $1.5 million per kilo, plus payments of commissions for their services.[21] They further said that the money had to come from a bank outside of Sudan so that the sale could not be traced by any member of the Sudanese government.

When questioned by Basheer about the serious intent of al Qaeda to purchase the uranium, al-Fadl claimed, "I know people, they [are] very serious, and they want to buy it."[22] He further informed Basheer that bin Laden was more concerned about the quality of the material and the country of origin than the cost.

Al-Fadl's testimony of the involvement of Salah Abdel al-Mobruk in the trafficking of nuclear weapons and supplies should have raised the curiosity of the United Nations and the International Atomic Energy Program. It should have triggered an investigation into al-Mobruk's possible involvement in other transactions regarding weapons of mass destruction. But it sparked little interest from any government agency or international news outlet. Indeed, the Sudanese minister didn't even manage to garner a footnote in *The 9/11 Commission Report.*

ENTER ABU RIDA AL-SURI—
AN AMERICAN FROM MISSOURI

After reporting back to al-Makkee (aka al-Masry), al-Fadl later told the court that he was sent to speak with Abu Rida al-Suri, another member of the al Qaeda high command and a principal player in the story. This meeting took place at the Ikhlak Company in the Baraka building in Khartoum. Al-Suri ordered al-Fadl to return to Basheer in order to relay that the organization had an "electric machine" capable of testing the grade of the uranium.

At this point in the trial, no court official sought the identity of Abu Rida al-Suri or his position within the terror organization. Abu Rida al-Suri is an alias for Mohamed Loay Bayazid, who was born in Syria and raised in Kansas City, Missouri. A naturalized American citizen, he traveled to Afghanistan in 1981 to take part in the holy war. One of the founders of al Qaeda, he came to serve, along with Mamdouh Mahmud Salim, as a point man for al Qaeda's procurement of nuclear weapons and materials and as a key planner of what would be an American Hiroshima—a goal that remains to be fulfilled.

Late in 1993, al-Suri (Bayazid) returned to the United States and became a director of the Benevolence International Foundation (BIF) in Chicago. This so-called Islamic charity served to transfer funds to al Qaeda cells throughout the world; to purchase rockets, mortars, rifles, dynamite, and bombs for the Chechen rebels and Hezb e Islami in Afghanistan; and to provide a cover, including visas, to al Qaeda operatives, including Mahmud Salim. The BIF also allegedly became involved in the development of weapons of mass destruction, including smallpox as an instrument of terror.[23]

Other al Qaeda officials joined Bayazid at the BIF in Chicago, including Mohamad Jamal Khalifa, bin Laden's brother-in-law, and Wali Khan Amin Shah. Both reportedly became involved in an attempt to bomb twelve airliners over American cities and in a plot to assassinate Pope John Paul II.[24]

The BIF established a branch office in Broward County, Florida, where it offered support to José Padilla (who planned to detonate a radiological bomb in midtown Manhattan) and Mandhai Jokhan (who was convicted of attempting to blow up power plants in southern Florida).[25] Another branch office was set up in Newark, New Jersey.

On December 14, 2001, the US State Department froze the assets of the BIF, and the records of the organization were confiscated by federal agents.[26] By that time, Bayazid was long gone, and his present whereabouts remain unknown.

BASHEER PRODUCES THE GLOWING GOODS

Al-Fadl testified that he arranged for a meeting between Basheer and al-Suri (Bayazid) that was held in a small house within the village of Bait al-Mal, several miles north of Khartoum. At the meeting, according to al-Fadl, Basheer produced a metal cylinder approximately three to four feet tall. After jotting down the words on the label and the serial number, al-Suri instructed al-Fadl to take the note to the residence of "Abu Hajer" (Mamdouh Mahmud Salim) in Khartoum. Asked about the contents of the note to "Abu Hajer," al-Fadl said: "It's information, I remember it say 'South Africa' and serial number and quality something. It's all in English. So I don't remember all the what [*sic*] in the paper."[27]

After reading the note, "Abu Hajer" sent al-Fadl back to the office of al-Suri with instructions that they were to inform Basheer that al Qaeda was willing to purchase the cylinder if it passed the test to determine its suitability. Al-Fadl and al-Suri complied with this directive. When questioned by Basheer about the testing, al-Suri said that al Qaeda had secured the necessary equipment from Kenya to grade the quality of the uranium.[28] After arranging a final meeting between al-Suri and al-Mobruk, al-Fadl was handed a check for ten thousand dollars for his time and effort and told that his services were no longer required in the matter.

AL QAEDA'S LABORATORY FOR WMDs IN KHARTOUM

Several days later, according to al-Fadl, Amin Abdel Marouf, a member of the Islamic National Front in Sudan, informed him that the uranium was set to be tested in Hilat Koko, a section of Khartoum. Al-Fadl testified that he did not know if, in fact, the uranium had been tested and that he was not privy to further information about the transaction.[29]

The subject of al Qaeda's laboratory for weapons of mass destruction within the capital of Sudan was raised several times during *The United States v. Osama bin Laden* in New York federal court. On February 6, 2001, it had become the center of this exchange between Assistant US Attorney Patrick Fitzgerald and Jamal al-Fadl:

Q. Did you ever travel to the section of Khartoum called Hilat Koko with any member of al Qaeda?

A. Yes, I did.

Q. Who did you go with?

A. I remember one time I went with Abu Rida al-Suri, and one time I went with Abu Hajer al-Iraqi.

Q. Anyone else?

A. And one time I went with—

Q. We will go through that name. M-U-Q-A-D-E-M. Is that a name or a title?

A. No, a title. He got one eagle and one star.

Q. Does that mean he is an officer?

A. Yes, he is in the army.

Q. In which army?

A. Sudanese army.

Q. His name?

A. Yes. Abu Baset Hamza.

Q. Tell us about the time you went to Hilat Koko with Abu Hajer al-Iraqi, what you discussed.

A. I learn that in this building they try to make chemical weapons with regular weapons.

Q. Can you explain what you mean by chemical weapons with regular weapons?

A. I remember another guy; he explain to me more about this.

Q. Who was that?

A. Amin Abdel Marouf

Q. What did Amin Abdel Marouf explain to you?

A. He say the war between the government and the Sudan and the rebels in south Lebanon, it's like 30 years, and always the rebels during the rain time, they took the Sudanese army to north, and he say if we use weapons like that, it easy for us to win.

Q. Was a war going on in the south of Sudan?

A. Yes.

Q. That was between who and whom?

A. Between Islamic National Front, they run the government, and John Garang group [Sudan People's Liberation Movement].

Q. Returning to your conversation with Abu Hajer al-Iraqi, did he discuss with you who it was that was trying to make these chemical weapons in the area there of Hilat Koko?

A. He tell me the al Qaeda group try to help Islamic National Front to do these weapons, to make these weapons.

The subject of the al Qaeda laboratory in Hilat Koko came up again on February 13, 2001, when al-Fadl was cross-examined by David Stern, the attorney for the defendant Khalifan Mohammed:

Q. There came a time you talked about when you went to Hilat Koko in Khartoum, remember that time?

A. Yes.

Q. And you went there with Salim, didn't you?

A. Yes.

Q. And when you went there, you were going to a place where they were making chemical weapons, right?

A. Yes, that's what I told—they told me.

Q. And that's what you believed?

A. Yes.

Q. Do you know what chemical weapons are used for?

A. No.

Q. Do you know that they're used to kill people?

A. They say they use it with regular weapons, that's what I hear.

Q. What do they mean when they said they use it with regular weapons?

A. I really have no idea what they mean.

Q. Okay. So I'm asking you, do you know that chemical weapons are used to kill people?

A. Yes, that's what I hear from them.

Q. You know that, for example, they use gas to kill people, right?

A. Yes.

Q. And whoever is in the area where that gas goes runs the risk of being killed?

A. Yes.

Q. And when you went there with Mr. Salim— by the way, what year was that?

A. Maybe during '93.

Q. When you went there with Mr. Salim, did you say to him, this is a terrible thing, let's not get involved in chemical weapons production?

A. No, I didn't tell him that.

Q. Did you say, I refuse to get involved in chemical weapons production, I quit al Qaeda?

A. No.

After establishing and reestablishing the existence of the laboratory in Hilat Koko, Stern pressed al-Fadl to speak more about the purchase of nuclear material for al Qaeda and of bin Laden's plans for the use of weapons of mass destruction against the United States. The exchange went as follows:

Q. Now I want to talk to you some about '93 or '94. There came a time when you found out that, according to you, al Qaeda wanted to purchase uranium, correct?

A. Yes.

Q. Did you know what they want uranium for?

A. I remember, yeah, Abu Jaffar al-Tayar, he's Egyptian, and he says it's easy to kill more people with uranium.

Q. You can make a huge bomb with uranium, right?

A. Yes.

Q. And you didn't say, "I don't want any part of anything that will kill a lot of people," right?

A. No.

Q. They asked you to go help get uranium, you said yeah?

A. Yes.

Q. And you tried to get as much information about the uranium as you could?

A. Correct.

Q. You tried to find out if it was enriched or not enriched?

A. What "enriched?"

Q. It was ready to be made into a bomb immediately or had to have something else done to it.

A. The quality, yes.

Q. Try to find out what country it was from?

A. The quality and which land, yes.

Q. But you yourself were not an expert in uranium, were you?

A. No, I just, I got the information and I bring it back to somebody.

Q. Isn't the somebody you brought it back to Salim?

A. Abu Musab al-Suri.

Q. Did you ever talk to Salim about this bomb?

A. I give him the paper.

Q. Salim?

A. Yes, but we didn't talk about it.

Q. But you gave him the paper?

A. Just the paper.

Q. And, according to you, he told you or you were told that he was going to get some kind of machine to test this uranium, right?

A. Not Salim, Abu Musab Suri told me machine going to come from Kenya.

Q. That was to see if this uranium was good enough to build a bomb to kill a whole lot of people?

A. Yes.

DINNERTIME FOR JUDGE SAND

It was drawing near five o'clock. Judge Leonard Sand again was becoming restless and irritable. He looked at his wristwatch and said: "Let me just interrupt, Mr. Stern. Approximately, how much longer do you have?" Stern answered three minutes and switched to a different topic. The matter of al Qaeda's quest for nuclear weapons seemed as inconsequential to the growling stomach of a hungry judge as it was to most in attendance that cold day in February, seven months before the two jet airliners crashed into the World Trade Center towers.

FED POOH-POOHS THE BOOGEYMAN

Of Jamal al-Fadl's testimony concerning the threat of al Qaeda, Larry C. Johnson, a former deputy director of the US State Department's Office of Counterterrorism, penned the following for an op-ed piece that appeared in the *New York Times* on July 10, 2001:

> *Americans are bedeviled by fantasies about terrorism. They seem to believe that terrorism is the greatest threat to the United States and that it is becoming more widespread and lethal. They are likely to think that the United States is the most popular target of terrorists. And they almost certainly have the impression that extremist Islamic groups cause most terrorism.*
>
> *None of these beliefs are based in fact. . . . The overall terrorist trend is down. . . . Nor are the United States and its policies the primary target. . . . The greatest risk is clear: if you are drilling for oil in Colombia—or nations like Ecuador, Nigeria, or Indonesia—you should take appropriate precautions; otherwise Americans have little to fear.*
>
> *Although high-profile incidents have fostered the perception that terrorism is becoming more lethal, the numbers say otherwise, and early signs suggest that the decade beginning in 2000 will continue the downward trend.*[30]

In terms of myopia, it might seem difficult to top Johnson's statements, until one realizes that officials who have replaced Johnson at the State Department have neglected to call for an investigation of the alleged al Qaeda laboratory in Sudan.

Al-Fadl's testimony fell upon deaf ears. Sudan, despite news of a rapprochement between General Bashir and the Bush administration in 2003, continues to serve as the world's biggest terrorist training ground, housing an estimated fifteen thousand fighters from such organizations as Jamaat-e-Islami, Islamic Jihad, Hamas, Hezbollah, and al Qaeda. Many of these camps were built by the United States in the 1980s to train CIA-backed Afghan *mujahadeen*.[31] It's not a stretch to assume that the laboratory in Hilat Koko remains in full operation.

THE NAGGING QUESTIONS

But what of the uranium? Was it uranium-238, the most abundant and stable uranium isotope, which is not fissionable but can be used to produce a fissionable isotope of plutonium? Or was it highly enriched weapons-grade uranium-235, which can be bombarded with light neutrons to produce rapid fission and an atomic blast of energy? Evidence may point to the latter. The uranium in question came from Valindaba, the nuclear manufacturing facility near Pretoria in South Africa. Under the apartheid regime, Valindaba produced enough weapons-grade uranium to build twenty atomic bombs—each with an explosive yield of fifteen to twenty kilotons.[32] In the "Alec file," one still can find a copy of the canceled bank check in the amount of $1.5 million used to pay for the sample kilo from the Sudanese blackmarketeers. Surely, bin Laden would not have made this payment if the uranium had failed to pass the test and was not of suitable "quality," especially after he went through such extraordinary measures to conduct the test. This raises larger questions. If indeed bin Laden acquired uranium-235 from this transaction, then how much more did he acquire in Sudan and elsewhere? And what was his purpose in acquiring such costly, deadly, and volatile material?

CHAPTER THREE

FROM RUSSIA, WITH LITHIUM

It really boggles my mind that there could be 40,000 nuclear weapons, or maybe 80,000, in the former Soviet Union, poorly controlled, and poorly stored, and that the world isn't in a state of near hysteria about the danger.

Former US Senate majority leader Howard Baker
before the Senate Foreign Relations Committee, 2002

Where could they [al Qaeda] get this weapon? Where did they get the material from which it could be made? Well, my list, and I believe that anybody at a meeting at the Defense Department or the White House would have a similar list absent specific evidence: Russia, Russia, Russia, Russia, Russia. The first five slots. Maybe they even deserve more, given the amount of material that's there.

Dr. Graham Allison, director of Harvard University's
Belfer Center for Science and International Affairs,
February 20, 2003

*The liberation of the Caucasus would constitute a hotbed of jihad
. . . and that region would [then] become the shelter of thousands of
Muslim mujahidin from various parts of the Islamic world, particularly the Arab parts. This poses a direct threat to the United States.
. . . If the Chechens and other Caucasian mujahidin reach the shores
of the oil-rich Caspian Sea . . . [t]his will form a mujahid Islamic
belt to the south of Russia that will be connected in the east with
Pakistan, which is brimming with mujahidin movements in Kashmir.*
Ayman al-Zawahiri, 1996

It couldn't have happened at a worse time.

On September 27, 1991, President George H. W. Bush announced that the United States would withdraw all nuclear weapons from its forces throughout the world with the stipulation that Soviet leader Mikhail Gorbachev follow suit in a grand display that the cold war was finally over and that a new age had dawned—the age of peace and reconciliation, of mutual trust (if not, brotherhood) and *perestroika* (the Russian word for "restructuring"). Gorbachev agreed, and the process of nuclear withdrawal got under way.

The process was greatly facilitated by the enactment of the Nunn-Lugar Soviet Threat Reduction Act of 1991, which provided Russia with millions to aid in the movement of its twenty-two thousand nukes to secure locations. It didn't work out as planned. The legislation didn't result in making the world a safer place, but rather in creating a nightmarish specter that presently hovers over planet earth.

To comprehend this development, it's necessary to come to terms with the sorry state of affairs within Russia when the momentous event of nuclear withdrawal took place. Here's an overview of the effects of the Soviet implosion from 1991 to 1995.

1991

The Afghan war is over and the Soviet Union falls from the Berlin wall and shatters into twelve jagged pieces: Armenia, Azerbaijan, Belarus, Georgia, Kazakstan, Kyrgyzstan, Moldova, Russia, Tajikistan, Turkmenistan, Ukraine, and Uzbekistan—with Russia, by far, the largest piece. The great egg has cracked and loses much of its yoke, and all the communist leaders and all the Red Brigade can't put the USSR back together again. Overnight, Mother Russia becomes transformed from a formidable first world power to a miserable third world country on life support.

1992

The inflation rate within the Russian republic soars 2,520 percent as a result of the decontrol of prices.[1] Bread lines form throughout the country. Butcher shops offer blue chickens that have died of malnutrition and pies made from rancid beef and horse meat. Savvy customers learn not to purchase the pies that are surrounded by dead flies. But, at least, there are cabbages and red beets enough to make borscht, albeit without the sour cream. And vodka remains in abundance. It's the only thing that makes life endurable for many during the long winter. But the vodka is hardly top-shelf Stoli. Much of it is bootleg stuff—stolen medical alcohol mixed with tap water and flavored with machine oil and brake fluid.[2] By September, 31.9 percent of Russian workers are unemployed and the suicide rate has doubled.[3]

1993

The crime rate skyrockets. Within Russia, eighty-four murders a day are now being committed. A hit can be arranged for as little as two hundred dollars.[4] It's an ideal time to get rid of a nagging wife or a lazy husband. Seven thousand murders remain unsolved; many have been committed with silencers at close range, using the same hand-guns that have been issued to the police and the military—perhaps a clue to why the criminals remain at large.[5]

The power vacuum created by the disappearance of the commis-sars becomes filled by the *mafiyas*. Suddenly, the swankiest restau-rants and the most opulent hotels in Moscow and St. Petersburg are inhabited by men in pinstriped suits with girlfriends clad in faux leopard skin and red leather.

More than eight thousand crime families pop up.[6] The Lubertskys come from a workers' suburb east of Moscow. They operate from Izmailovsky Park, the Dormodedovo Airport, and storefronts along Shabalovka Street. The Lubertskys specialize in protection and prosti-tution.[7] The Kazan family moves drugs and raids restaurants on the Arbat. The Long Pond *mafiya* hails from a northern dead-end suburb of barrack housing. They fence stolen cargo from the Sheremetyyevo Airport and run the prostitutes at the Minsk Hotel, but their main busi-ness is auto parts from chop shops. The Baumanskayas, from the neighborhood between Lefortovo Prison and the Church of the Epiphany, run the Rizhsky Market and black markets throughout Moscow. At these markets, well-heeled Russians and tourists can pur-chase such "hot" goods as TVs; VCRs; short-wave radios; cartons of Marlboros and Winstons; bottles of Starka, Russkaya, and Kuban vodka; Stechkin machine pistols; choice Number Four heroin from the Golden Crescent; and world-renowned acid (LSD) from the chemists at Leningrad University. The Sointserskaya from the Mosow suburb of Sointsevo represents one of the largest crime families. They corner much of the market in extortion and gun running.[8]

Not all crime families are centered in Moscow. The Tambov syn-dicate controls much of the criminal activity in St. Petersburg.[9] They operate around Gostiny Dvor and the underground passage on Nevsky Prospekt, along with train stations, food stands, and flea markets throughout the city. They single out tourists for their crimes, which they often commit in broad daylight. The robbery rate in St. Petersburg is fifty to a hundred times that of Moscow and the mugging rate is two hundred to four hundred times greater.[10]

But, according to informed sources, the meanest of the mean and the baddest of the bad of all the *mafiyas* are the Chechens. They supervise all the criminal activity in the Russian republic and exact a share of all action. Their major criminal interests center on bank robberies, kidnappings, cigarette smuggling, and white-collar crime.[11] They are different from the other *mafiyas*, not only in brutality and bloodletting, but also in culture and religion. The Chechen people are neither Communists nor Christians, but rather, fundamentalist Muslims who have descended from the Tartars, a Western tide of the Golden Horde of Genghis Khan in the thirteenth century.

The Tartars came to inhabit towns and villages throughout the northern Caucasus Mountains, with Grozny, as in "Ivan Grozny" ("Ivan the Terrible"), as their capital city. Socially, religiously, and ethnically, they are far removed from the Soviet model of atheistic proletarians united in a vision of the stateless state.

The loyalties of the Chechen people have never been to the Kremlin but rather to the one hundred *teips*, or clans, that make up Chechen society. They don't even speak Russian but a unique language known as Nakh, and they uphold a strong sense of national and cultural identity. The Russian officials who doubted the toughness and resolve of the Chechen people never attempted to sing a few bars of "Death or Freedom," the Chechen national anthem:

> *We were born at night when the She-wolf whelped.*
> *In the morning, under lions' howl, we were given our names.*
> *In eagles' nests our Mothers nursed us,*
> *To tame the bulls our fathers taught us.*
>
> *If hunger gets us down—we'll gnaw the roots.*
> *If thirst o'er takes us—we'll drink the grass dew.*
> *We were born at night when the She-wolf whelped.*
> *Nation, native land, and Allah—we serve them only.*[12]

During World War II, many Chechens collaborated with the Nazis. Soviet premier Joseph Stalin executed thousands and shipped more than half a million in boxcars for disposal in northern Kazakstan, where 25 percent died.[13] In 1957 softheaded Nikita Khrushchev, Stalin's successor, allowed them to filter back to their former farms and lands. It was a decision that some Russians will recall with regret.[14]

In 1980 thousands of Chechens rallied to the cause of the *mujahadeen* and fought side by side with Osama bin Laden and his Afghan Arabs against the Soviet forces in Afghanistan.

Now, with the Afghan war at an end, the radical Chechens busy themselves by making preparations for a *gazavat* ("holy war") of independence from Mother Russia. The funding for the struggle will come from wealthy Saudi Wahabbists (including Osama bin Laden) and the lucrative activities of the Chechen *mafiya*. In September the rebels stun the world with a display of SS-20 missiles during a military parade in Grozny. The missiles, stolen from a Soviet arsenal, have a range of 9,500 kilometers and the capability to launch nuclear warheads.[15]

Mother Russia refuses to cut the unruly child from her apron strings. The refusal springs not from maternal affection but rather from the economic fact that Chechnya is located in the midst of a nice fat oil reserve and represents a strategic location for the pipeline that carries the black gold from the fields in Baku on the Caspian Sea to the Ukraine.[16]

1994

The civil war erupts in Chechnya. It will continue to rage unabated throughout the next decade, producing a daily death toll of five to twenty civilians at a daily cost of forty million dollars to Mother Russia. Much of the war is financed by the United States, which seeks to support Russian president Boris Yeltsin against his domestic enemies. President Clinton even hails Yeltin as "Russia's Abraham Lincoln."[17]

Grozny soon becomes the most devastated city on earth (a position once held by Beirut, Lebanon). One hundred thousand civilians lie dead among the rubble.[18] The cost of rebuilding is estimated at thirteen billion dollars.[19]

The Russian army, now dwindled to a feeble force of 1.7 million, is in complete disarray. Ten to twenty soldiers die a day from noncombative factors. Most are driven to suicide by *dedovshcina*, the brutal practice of hazing recruits.[20] Paychecks are scarce since the government remains strapped in debt. Many soldiers are forced to beg for food and shelter at outposts and on the street corners of major cities, including Moscow, Kiev, and St. Petersburg.

The eighty thousand or so Russian troops in Chechnya are a far cry from the tall, robust, and square-jawed members of the Red Army who high-stepped before admiring millions during May Day celebrations. They are mostly small farm boys with bad teeth and scant education. They have been forcefully consigned into the Russian army, beaten to pay protection money to their commanding officers, and sent to combat the rebel forces with Kalashnikovs and very little training in guerrilla warfare.

In December the attack on Grozny ends in a rout as throngs of dirty and unshaven Chechen peasants—many armed with shovels and pitchforks—drive back the invading army of raw recruits. Russian corpses line the streets of the mountain capital.

The experience is totally disheartening. Thousands of Russian troops desert their posts. Many are captured by the insurgent Chechens, who find them wandering the mountainside without maps or food. It is easy for rebels and photojournalists to pass through any Russian roadblock as long as they can provide a loaf of bread, a candy bar, or a pack of Marlboros to the hungry, frightened, and lice-ridden soldiers on patrol.[21]

The only way for many members of the military to eke out a living comes from selling items from the arsenals. And so, everything goes up for grabs—assault rifles, mortars, artillery shells, and RPG-7s—even to the enemy. In the words of one Chechen militant: "Wave some cash at a Russian soldier and he will give you the tank he is sitting in."[22] Things get really crazy. Overnight there are reports of 6,430 stolen weapons from the arsenals, including assault tanks and antiballistic missiles.[23]

The most egregious example of the unchecked thefts is provided by Admiral Igor Khmelov, the commander of the Russian Pacific Fleet, who is charged and convicted of selling sixty-four ships, including two aircraft carriers, to South Korea and India, and keeping the proceeds for himself. Sure, Admiral Khmelov was a crook, but nobody could accuse him of price gouging. His official price for a seaworthy, state-of-the-art aircraft carrier was $5 million, a bargain by even the standards of a backstreet bazaar in Bombay.[24]

But the real bucks come from the weapons capable of producing the biggest bangs. And big bang means nuclear. In the black market, radioactive material suitable only for the production of dirty nukes is worth a small fortune. A kilo of chromium-50, a common form of radioactive material, goes for $25,000; cesium-137 for $1 million; and lithium for $10 million.[25] And the prospective buyers include agents from North Korea, Iran, Libya, and a well-financed group of Muslim terrorists called al Qaeda.

In January 1992 an Egyptian newspaper reports that Iran has purchased three Soviet nuclear warheads from Kazakstan for $150 million. The report is confirmed by Russian intelligence.[26] This is only the beginning of the wholesale theft and proliferation caused by the nuclear threat-reduction act. In November 1993 two nuclear warheads, enough to wipe out New York and Los Angeles, are stolen by two employees from the Zlatoust-36 Instrument Building Plant, a weapons-assembly facility in Chelyabinsk. Fortunately, the weapons are later recovered in a residential garage, and the two workers are taken into custody.[27] Two weeks later, Russian navy captain Alexei Tikhomirov breaks into a nuclear storage facility at the Sevmorput shipyard near Murmansk and steals three segments of a reactor core containing 3.4 kilograms of highly enriched uranium. At the time of Tikhomirov's arrest, the Russian prosecutor says that "potatoes were guarded better" than nuclear material at Murmansk.[28]

Crime continues to skyrocket throughout the Russian republic.

The interior minister now reports that the number of organized crime families has risen from 785 in 1991 to 5,691. Forty percent of private businesses and 60 percent of the public sector remain under the control of the various *mafiyas*.[29] The crime families extort protection money from everyone—from street peddlers to bank officials. They annex many of the Bering Strait fisheries. They transport over half a million hookers to cities throughout Europe. They launder money through business fronts in Israel, where they pose as Jewish refugees in order to gain Israeli passports.[30]

With a booming market in nuclear goods and materials, the Chechen *mafiya* begins using radioactive isotopes to commit unique acts of murder. The first victim is Victor Kaplun, the owner of a meatpacking plant in Moscow. The Chechens plant gamma ray–emitting pellets in Kaplun's office. He is dead of radioactive poisoning within a week.[31] Half a dozen similar cases are reported.

1995

More than seven hundred attempted sales of nuclear material have been reported by Germany. Several of these transactions involve weapons-grade nuclear material—material suitable for use in the construction of a nuclear bomb. Uranium that is enriched with 20 percent or higher U-235 becomes elevated to weapons grade. One kilogram equals 2.2 pounds. One thousand grams equal one kilogram, and one gram is equal to about 0.04 ounce (the weight of a paperclip). To construct a tactical nuke, one would have to amass 15,900 grams of HEU (highly enriched uranium), and thanks to the meltdown in Russia, tracking agencies, such as the Stanford Database on Nuclear Smuggling, Theft, and Orphan Radiation Sources (DSTO), report that over 40 kilograms, enough to make several bombs, have been sold on the black market. The DSTO is careful to note that the real amount may be ten times this amount—enough to wipe out much of the human race. A sampling of sales that have been intercepted by authorities is as follows:

May 1992—1.5 kilotons of HEU from the Luch Scientific Production Association is seized by Russian authorities. The material has been enriched 90 percent.

March 1993—Russian police retrieve 3.05 kilograms of HEU that also has been enriched 90 percent.

May 1993—0.1 kilogram of HEU, enriched 50 percent, is recovered by investigators in Lithuania.

July 1993—Russian police obtain 1.8 kilograms of HEU from an attempted sale outside of Moscow.

November 1993—Russian police seize 4.5 kilograms of HEU, enriched 20 percent, from black market dealers.

May 1994—German police snag .006 kilogram of plutonium-239 from an attempted sale by Russian dealers.

June 1994—In another bust involving Russians, Germans confiscate .0008 kilogram of HEU that has been enriched 87.8 percent.

July/August 1994—The German busts continue as police seize .00024 kilogram of plutonium and .4 kilogram of plutonium from Russian arms dealers.

December 1994—Police in the Czech Republic recover 2.7 kilograms of HEU, enriched 87.7 percent, from an attempted sale involving Russian agents.

June 1995—Czech cops make further busts and confiscate .0004 gram of HEU, enriched 87.7 percent, and .017 kilogram of HEU, enriched 87.7 percent.

June 1995—Back in Russia, police authorities recover 1.7 kilograms of HEU, enriched 21 percent.

In an effort to contain some of the nuclear "leakage," the US government purchases one thousand pounds of HEU from an unprotected site in Almaty, Kazakstan. The nuclear material is transported to Oak Ridge, Tennessee, where it is stored in a secure facility. Such a measure seems tantamount to placing a Band-Aid on a hemorrhage.

The life expectancy for a Russian man is now fifty-eight—fifteen to seventeen fewer years than his European and American counterparts. Russian women average between 2.5 and 4 abortions each, and Russia's death rate now stands 70 percent higher than its birthrate. Even the return of millions of Russians from the former Soviet republics cannot reverse the fact that the country is on a downward spiral.[32]

CHAPTER FOUR

THE CHECHEN CONNECTION

We found that he [Osama bin Laden] *and al Qaeda were involved in an extraordinary sophisticated and professional effort to acquire weapons of mass destruction—in this case, nuclear weapons, so, by the end of 1996, it was clear that this was an organization unlike any other one we had ever seen.*

Michael Scheuer, former CIA operative in charge of the
bin Laden file and author of *Imperial Hubris*

The world stockpiles of nuclear warheads, plutonium, and HEU [highly enriched uranium] *are immense. More than a decade after the Cold War, the world's arsenals still contain some 30,000 assembled weapons. Enough plutonium and HEU exist in the world to make nearly a quarter million nuclear weapons—all of it produced by human beings during the five decades of the nuclear age.*

Matthew Bunn, Anthony Wier, and John P. Holdren,
"Controlling Nuclear Warheads and Materials:
A Report Card," Belfer Center for Science and
International Affairs, Harvard University, March 2003

I n 1991 Dr. John Colarusso, a specialist in Russian affairs at McMaster University, reported that the Chechen rebels came into possession of at least three nuclear warheads. He claimed that the warheads had been sold to them by Pavel Grachev, Russia's former defense minister. Colarusso further testified that the Chechens had discovered two more warheads in an abandoned ballistic missile silo in the Chechen village of Bamut. The silo, he said, had been destroyed by a propellant fire, leaving the two warheads at the bottom of a shaft.[1] Shortly after the publication of this report, Russian vice president Alexander Rutskoi announced that several nuclear weapons were missing, but he did not say what had happened to them.[2]

To investigate the matter of the missing warheads, Fred Cuny, a senior associate at the Carnegie Endowment for International Peace, traveled in 1994 to Bamut, where he and his three traveling companions reportedly were rounded up by the rebels and executed as spies. Their bodies have never been found.[3]

A MODEST PROPOSAL

In November 1994 Dzhokhar Dudayev, the leader of the Chechen rebels, petitioned the United Nations to dispatch troops to protect the weapons of mass destruction within the Chechen arsenal.[4] Some had likened the diminutive Dudayev, whose first name was pronounced "Jokar," to Boris Badenov of *Rocky and Bullwinkle* fame. This unfortunate resemblance may have caused UN officials to dismiss the Chechen leader's petition as a pathetic attempt at grandstanding by a cartoonlike figure, who represented an inconsequential group of Muslim dissidents from a backwater Russian province.

Undaunted by the dismissal, Dudayev issued a warning to the Clinton administration, stating that his government had obtained the warheads and small tactical nuclear weapons that had been manufactured for the KGB. He offered to sell these weapons to the US State

Department with the stipulation of official recognition of Chechnya's independence from Russia. Dudayev added that if the United States rejected the offer, he would sell the weapons to Libya, North Korea, or Iran.

A BLIND EYE

Dudayev provided enough technical information about the tactical nukes that officials from the National Intelligence Council, an umbrella organization for the US analytical community, were dispatched to Chechnya in order to verify the existence of the weapons.[5] The findings were alarming. Upon their return, the officials informed a congressional committee that weapons-grade and weapons-using nuclear materials, including SADMs (small atomic demolition munitions), had been stolen from Soviet stockpiles and could be in the hands of the Chechen rebels. "Of these thefts," the officials said, "we assess that undetected smuggling has occurred, although we do not know the extent or the magnitude."[6] The Center for Nonproliferation Studies at the Monterey Institute of International Studies provided further verification of Dudayev's claims by producing confirmation from a "senior advisor to [Russian president] Boris Yeltsin" that an unspecified number of suitcase nuclear devices had been manufactured for the KGB but had not been listed on the Soviet nuclear inventory.[7]

Despite these findings, the Clinton administration refused to enter into any negotiations with Dudayev and members of his government and continued to believe that the rebels were grandstanding for attention with preposterous claims.

DUDAYEV'S TOLL CALL

The Chechens, in turn, continued to issue more statements about their newly acquired arsenal. Shamil Basayev, commander of the Confederation of the People of the Caucasus (KHK), held a press conference in 1995 in Shali, where he echoed Dudayev's claim that the Chechens were, indeed, in possession of the nuclear warheads.[8] Basayev went further by displaying containers of radioactive materials, including such substances as cobalt-60, cesium-137, and strontium-90.[9] Stunned by this announcement, Russian interior minister Anatoly Kulikov admitted that the rebels might have obtained some isotopes from their raid on the Budyonnorsk medical center and additional radioactive material from the Grozny branch of Russia's Radon Nuclear Waste Facility.[10]

The official Russian response to the demonstration came in October when Dudayev pulled his car to the side of the road in the village of Gekhi-Chu, 180 miles southeast of Grozny, to make a call to one of his compatriots on his newly acquired satellite phone. As soon as the call was made, the Russians used electronic equipment to locate the signal. Within minutes, a Russian helicopter homed in on the target and fired an air-to-surface missile.[11] What remained of the troublesome Chechen leader had to be scraped from the driver's seat of his Neva.

NUCLEAR TERRORISM DAWNS

The assassination of Dudayev spurred the Chechens to make a vivid display that would show the world once and for all that they possessed weapons of mass destruction. This occurred on November 23, 1995, when Basayev directed a Russian television crew to a radiological bomb that his troops had planted in Izmailovsky Park, outside of Moscow.[12] The bomb had been made of seventy pounds of cesium-137 and, if detonated, would have killed hundreds in a matter of minutes and contaminated thousands more. The value of the cesium on the black market was thirty-two million dollars. The incident represented the first deployment of a radiological device as a weapon of terror. Regarding the incident, Basayev said: "Putting uranium in Moscow requires one person. One person gets killed and the city dies."[13]

CIA director John Deutch appeared before Congress to downplay the incident, maintaining that the cesium, if wrapped around a conventional explosive and detonated, would pose only a "minimal health hazard." Nothing could be further from the truth. In the best-case scenario, the blast would kill only a few hundred. But the explosion would distribute particles of cesium over several square miles of Moscow. Within minutes, the microscopic particles would adhere to everything: skin, clothing, cars, buses, buildings, soil, sidewalks, trees, plants, and the soles of shoes.[14]

A single grain of cesium, if inhaled or ingested, is a bone sucker. It goes straight to the marrow, halts the production of platelets, and causes the mutation of cells. Within days of the detonation, those who had been exposed to the particles would display the first symptoms of radiation poisoning: bleeding from the nose and mouth, diarrhea, hair loss, purple fingernails, high fever, and delirium. Several hundred would be dead within a matter of days. Their bodies would have to be placed in lead-lined caskets to prevent further contamination.[15] Within a matter of months and years, thousands more would develop various kinds of malignancies: thyroid cancer, pancreatic cancer, liver cancer, breast cancer, cancer of the reproductive organs, and malignant brain tumors.

The cesium bomb would produce other results as well. The decontamination effort would require that the radioactive particles be removed from every area of the city and countryside. Removing cesium particles is no easy task. The particles cannot be blown away or scrubbed away. The cleanup would require the dumping of mounds of sand over the exposed soil, the uprooting of trees and shrubbery, the removal of all asphalt and concrete from streets and sidewalks, the killing of household pets and park animals (including birds), and the razing of nearly every structure in the city.[16]

ENTER BIN LADEN

The demonstration left little doubt that the Chechen rebels had obtained an arsenal of weapons of mass destruction. But officials from the United

Nations and the Clinton administration continued to ignore the demands of the rebels, to enter into negotiations to retrieve the "broken arrows" (the official term for lost or stolen nukes), or to make a cash offer to buy the Chechen arsenal. This position forced the rebels to make a deal with the next person in line. And that person happened to be a billionaire emir from Saudi Arabia by the name of Osama bin Laden.

For the Chechens, to make a deal with the emir of al Qaeda seemed a matter of kismet. Bin Laden had trained Basayev at his camps in Afghanistan, and the two had developed a close and abiding friendship. After the Soviet withdrawal from Afghanistan, al Qaeda forces and Chechen rebels had fought side by side with the Azeri *mujahadeen* in the Azerbaijan war with Armenia for control of the territorial enclave of Nagorno-Karabakh.[17] When the Chechen rebellion broke out in 1994, bin Laden established a bogus financial firm in Baku to give cover to al Qaeda operations in moving men, money, and munitions to the rebels. The operation was conducted with precision, and bin Laden calculated his total cost of sending an armed fighter to the new theater of jihad to be less than fifteen hundred dollars.[18] At this bargain rate, the emir was able to send many of his elite warriors across the Afghan border into Dagestan and, from there, to the backdoor of Chechnya. By 1996 the six thousand guerrillas fighting the Russian forces for the control of Chechnya included three hundred members of al Qaeda.

DOOMSDAY AND THE DRUG TRADE

Another reason for making the deal with bin Laden sprang from the fact that al Qaeda and the Chechen rebels were partners in a billion-dollar business. Through his friendship with Basayev, bin Laden established the so-called Abkhaz route for the flow of heroin to markets in Europe and the United States.[19] The route led from Afghanistan through Khorog in Tajikistan and Osh in Kyrgyzstan along a treacherous mountain road to the Vedensky Rayon in Chechnya. From this location, Abkhaz trucks and MI-16 helicopters transported the product to the port city of Sukhumi in the breakaway Georgian province of Abkhazia, where it was loaded onto Turkish ships and transported to the port of Famagusta in northern Cyprus. At Famagusta, the heroin was broken down into small packets for international distribution.[20] In America, these small packets, usually measuring a tenth of a gram, became known as "Binnys" (in honor of Osama bin Laden) and sold for twenty dollars on college campuses. "Terrorism, organized crime, and the illegal trade [in narcotics] are one interrelated problem," Abdurakhim Kakharov, a deputy interior minister of Tajikistan, told a congressional committee in Washington on September 6, 2001. "The terror groups and the drugs are exported from the same source—Afghanistan."[21]

MUSLIM TO MUSLIM

There was a third reason why the Chechen rebels opted to sell the nuclear weapons to al Qaeda. Bin Laden had issued a call for all Muslims to engage in a holy war against the United States and Israel. And the Chechens, with many adherents to a Sufi mystic branch of Sunni Islam called Muridism, felt obliged to answer the call.[22] This was in keeping with the teaching of the holy Koran: "Fight those who believe not in Allah nor the Last day, nor hold that forbidden which hath been forbidden by Allah and his Messenger, nor acknowledge the religion of Truth, [even if they are] the People of the Book [Christians and Jews], until they pay the *jizya* [the required tax on non-Muslims who dwell in Islamic lands] with willing submission and feel themselves subdued" (9:29). And how better to offer support than by providing the emir with the weapons that would insure his victory and bring forth the Day of Islam?

To exact the deal, bin Laden dispatched a joint delegation of al Qaeda and Taliban officials to meet with the Chechen rebels' high command outside of Grozny. For $30 million cash and two tons of choice Number Four heroin with a street value of $700 million, the Chechens would deliver twenty portable tactical nukes. The money for the transaction would come, in part, from a mainland Chinese bank in the Quangdong Province. The withdrawal, according to *Al-Watan Al-Arabi* (the Saudi weekly), was eventually made by Dr. Ayman al-Zawahiri.[23]

THE CHECHEN CODICIL

There was a side bar to the agreement. The Chechen rebels received the right to participate in and monitor the production of heroin at the al Qaeda/Taliban laboratories in Kuteh and Peshawar in northern Pakistan near the Russian border and Razani in southern Pakistan near Iran. This arrangement resulted in a meteoric increase in business. The laboratories soon became capable of producing five thousand metric tons of heroin a year, making bin Laden the largest supplier of the new international drug of choice. By the end of 1997, the poppy harvest in Afghanistan soared to 3,276 tons of raw opium. Soon revenues began to pour into the coffers of al Qaeda, the Taliban, and the Chechen Mafia at a rate estimated at between $5 billion and $16 billion a year.[24] By 1998 the National Household Survey discovered 149,000 new heroin users who required treatment for their addiction within the United States. Eighty percent of the new addicts were under the age of twenty-six. The average new addict was spending two hundred dollars a day to maintain his habit.[25]

While the drug trade soared to new heights in the United States, it began to boom beyond belief in Europe. Between 1966 and 2001 Europeans consumed more than fifteen tons of heroin a year—twice the amount that was sold in America. "The drug trade is a triple-pronged weapon for bin Laden and the Taliban," according to Rachel Ehrenfeld, director of the Center for the Study of Corruption. "It finances their activities. It undermines the enemy. And it proves that their enemy is corrupt, which they then use in their own recruiting propaganda."[26]

THE ARREST OF MR. AMIN

Any doubts that al Qaeda was involved in a monumental business transaction with the Chechens should have been put to rest when Russian security police arrested Dr. Ayman al-Zawahiri at the Chechen border in December 1996. Al-Zawahiri, with his beard shaved and his hair cropped, was traveling under the alias of "Mr. Amin." He was accompanied by two al Qaeda operatives and a Chechen guide. At his trial in April 1997, al-Zawahiri purportedly "lied fluently and prayed frequently." When asked about the nature of his business in Chechnya, the good doctor said that he "wanted to know the price of leather, medicine, and other goods."[27] Lacking sufficient evidence of any wrongdoing, the judge ordered his release.

By the time al-Zawahiri returned to Afghanistan, the weapons had arrived in Khost, where they were stored in a laboratory within a subterranean tunnel and placed under the care of five Turkoman nuclear experts.[28] Some of the weapons were transported to laboratories at the Taliban's central secure complex near Kandahar, where maintenance and upgrading were conducted under the supervision of a nuclear physicist from the Iraqi Tammuz reactor—the reactor that had been destroyed by the Israelis in 1981.[29]

Reports of al Qaeda's purchase of the twenty nukes from the Chechens was not only conveyed to the US State Department by Russia's Federal Security Service but also leaked to the press. The story appeared on August 16, 1998, in the *London Times* and, several weeks later, in such publications as the *Jerusalem Report*, *Al-Watan Al-Arabi*, *Muslim Magazine*, and *Al-Majallah* (London's Saudi weekly).[30] Such news failed to capture headlines in the United States since the thought of a group of Islamic fanatics with tactical nukes seemed preposterous.

Bin Laden and company, however, made no secret of their newly acquired nuclear arsenal. In a statement titled "The Nuclear Bomb of Islam," bin Laden said: "It is the duty of Muslims to prepare as much force as possible to terrorize the enemies of God."[31] In a December

1999 interview with journalists from *Time* magazine, the emir let it be known in an oblique way that al Qaeda had secured the nukes. "Acquiring weapons for the defense of Muslims is a religious duty. If I have acquired these weapons, then I thank God for enabling me to do so."[32] Similarly, when asked by ABC News if he had obtained weapons of mass destruction, bin Laden said: "If I seek to acquire such weapons, this is a religious duty. How we use them is up to us."[33]

Eventually, the leader of al Qaeda became more forthright in his statements. In an interview with Hamid Mir two months after 9/11, bin Laden said: "If America uses chemical or nuclear weapons, then we may respond with chemical or nuclear weapons." When the Pakistani journalist asked how he obtained such weapons, the emir said: "It is not difficult, not if you have contacts in Russia with other militant groups. They are available for $10 million and $20 million."[34] At this point in the interview, al-Zawahiri interjected: "If you go to BBC reports, you will find that thirty nuclear weapons are missing from Russia's nuclear arsenal. We have links with Russia's underworld channels."[35]

Bin Laden and al-Zawahiri are devout and earnest Muslims. They mainly speak without guile or duplicity, and they usually do not spew mendacities for the sake of media posturing. What they say they mean. This is evidenced by the attacks on US targets since the issuance of al Qaeda's declaration of war: the bombings of the US embassies in Kenya and Tanzania, the attack on the USS *Cole*, and the events of 9/11.

But there remains a pervasive belief that the statements of these men should not be taken seriously; that they are backward Bedouins without the capacity to launch an attack that could kill millions of Americans; that they purchase nuclear materials only for storage in an Afghan cave; that they are unaware of proper maintenance for such an arsenal; and that they obtained a religious ruling to launch a nuclear attack against American civilians only for storage in bin Laden's filing cabinet.

Such belief fails to take into consideration the fact that bin Laden is a highly trained engineer with a background in physics and one of the most gifted military tacticians in the annals of modern warfare. In an interview with Tim Russert of *Meet the Press*, Michael Scheuer, author of *Imperial Hubris* and the former CIA analyst in charge of the "Alec file," the file on Osama bin Laden, provided the following analysis of the elusive emir:

MR. RUSSERT: Do you believe we're losing the war on terror?

MR. SCHEUER: I think without question we're losing the war on terror, sir, not because they are stronger than us but because we resolutely refuse to recognize [that] the motivation of the enemy is grounded so thoroughly in their religion and their perception that American policies are a threat to annihilate that religion. And that's not to say we should sympathize or empathize with their position, but certainly if you're going to destroy your enemy, you better understand what he's about.

MR. RUSSERT: Do you think Osama is still fully in control of al Qaeda?

MR. SCHEUER: I think it's wishful thinking to think that he isn't, sir. The one example is the tremendous sophistication and spontaneity of his media machine. There has to be some command and control there. And to imagine that it doesn't—that he's unable to do it is just absolutely incorrect. He's really a remarkable man, a great man in many ways, without the connotation positive or negative. He's changed the course of history. You just have to try to take your fourth-grader's class to the White House visitors' center...

MR. RUSSERT: When you say "great man," people cringe.

MR. SCHEUER: Yes, sir. Absolutely they cringe, but a great man is someone—a great individual is someone who changes the course of history. And certainly in the last five or six years, America has changed dramatically in the way we behave, in the way we travel. Certainly he's bleeding us to death in terms of money. Look at the budget deficit now. Much of that goes against Osama bin Laden.

MR. RUSSERT: Do you see him as a very formidable enemy?

MR. SCHEUER: Tremendously formidable enemy, sir, an admirable man. If he was on our side, he would be dining at the White House. He would be a freedom fighter, a resistance fighter. It's—and again, that's not to praise him, but it is to say that until we take the measure of the man and the power of his words, we're very much going to be on the short end of the stick.[36]

Some in the media and the government refused to believe that the Chechens ever came to acquire off-the-shelf nukes, arguing that, if they had the weapons, they would have used them. Such thinking failed to take into account the fact that a nuclear attack by the Chechens against Russia would have resulted in nuclear retaliation against Chechnya—a retaliation that would have transformed the homeland of the rebels into an uninhabitable desert since Russia possesses not only tactical but also strategic atomic devices.

Still, the doubts about the deal and al Qaeda's nuclear arsenal persisted, even as reports of additional nuclear buys by bin Laden began to surface, including twenty nuclear warheads from Kazakstan, Turkmenistan, Russia, and the Ukraine.[37] These accounts were verified by Israeli, British, Russian, Saudi, and Pakistani intelligence, but were greeted with skepticism and indifference by the many counterintelligence officials in Washington, DC.

"If bin Laden had these weapons, he would have used them," one FBI official said. "You can say what you will but the accounts, in my opinion, are bullshit."

This statement shows that even members of America's premier intelligence agency remain unaware that proof of the existence of al Qaeda's nuclear arsenal already has been provided.

CHAPTER FIVE

OSAMA'S NUCLEAR BABIES

These devices represent probably the greatest threat if they end up in the hands of terrorists due to the combination of small size and full-scale nuclear explosion effects. Interception of "suitcase bombs" is difficult along land borders and practically impossible along maritime borders.

Center for Nonproliferation Studies

I gathered the heads of all the national laboratories and asked them a simple question. I said, "I would like you to go back to your laboratory and try to assume for a moment you are a relatively informed terrorist group with access to some nuclear scientists. Could you build, off the shelf, a nuclear device? Not a dirty bomb, but something that would start a nuclear reaction—an atomic bomb." They came back several months later and said, "We built one." They put it in a room and explained how—literally, off the shelf, without doing anything illegal—they actually constructed the device.

Senator Joseph Biden, January 2004

W hen Tom Clancy published *The Sum of All Fears*, his fifth Jack Ryan novel—this one dealing with a small atomic demolition munition (SADM) being detonated at the Super Bowl—he was taken to task by several government officials for leaking confidential information about portable nukes. The criticism prompted him to pen the following for the paperback edition:

> *All the material in this novel relating to weapons technology and fabrication is readily available in any one of dozens of books. . . . I was first bemused, then stunned, as my research revealed just how easy such a project might be today. It is generally known that nuclear secrets are not as secure as we would like—in fact, the situation is worse than even well-informed people appreciate. What required billions of dollars in the 1940s is much less expensive today. A modern personal computer has far more power and reliability, and the "hydrocodes" which enable a computer to test and validate a weapon's design are easily duplicated. The exquisite machine tools used to fabricate parts can be had for the asking. When I asked explicitly for specifications for the very machines used at Oak Ridge and elsewhere, they arrived Federal Express the next day. Some highly specialized items designed specifically for bomb manufacture may now be found in stereo speakers. The fact of the matter is that a sufficiently wealthy individual could, over a period of from five to ten years, produce a multistage thermonuclear device. Science is all in the public domain, and allows few secrets.*[1]

Clancy penned these words in 1992, unaware that a sufficiently wealthy person named Osama bin Laden was in Sudan with plans to manufacture or purchase such a device.

Although *The Sum of All Fears* became an international best seller, it was dismissed by some critics as a work of science fiction with technological explanations that belonged in the realm of the fantastic.

HOLLYWOOD HOOEY?

Five years later, *The Peacemaker* became the first movie from Dream Works, the new studio created by Steven Spielberg, Jeffrey Katzenberg, and David Geffen. It was produced on location at such places as Sarajevo, the Ural Mountains, Vienna, Turkey, and midtown Manhattan, and starred George Clooney and Nicole Kidman. The story concerned a group of Russian terrorists, who steal nine suitcase nukes from a train that is transporting them to a military center to be defused in accordance with the Nunn-Lugar Soviet Threat Reduction Act. "I didn't join the Russian Army to dismantle it for the Americans," one soldier grumbles. The train is destroyed by a nuclear blast to make it appear that all the bombs have been destroyed by an unfortunate accident—a mix-up in signals at a switching station. Clooney as a macho intelligence officer with Army Special Forces joins Kidman, "the acting head of the White House Nuclear Smuggling Group," to hunt down the thieves and uncover the weapons. After a series of hair-raising chases, they manage to recover all but one of the suitcase nukes—one that has been purchased by a radical Muslim, who takes the weapon to New York City in order to attempt to detonate it at the United Nations.

The movie was a box-office dud, in part because some critics thought that the idea of a suitcase nuke being transported to Manhattan and detonated by a single agent was "improbable"—"a premise lifted straight out of the James Bond franchise."[2]

But are the premises of both the Clancy novel and the Clooney movie simply fiction—preposterous notions that pose no possibility of occurring in the immediate future?

Some—including several leading journalists—say yes.

ENTER RICHARD MINITER

In *Disinformation: 22 Media Myths That Undermine the War on Terror*, Richard Miniter, a former reporter for the *Wall Street Journal* and the *Sunday Times* (London), writes that the notion of a small nuclear device that can be deployed and detonated by a single operative has been "authoritatively dismissed" by all authorities on the subject. He says that the only person who ever claimed to see a suitcase-sized nuke was Rose Gottemoeller, a Defense Department official who, in the early 1990s, visited the Ukraine to monitor compliance with disarmament treatises. And these nukes, according to Miniter, were hardly portable devices, but rather weapons that were the size of three footlockers and that would require "a team of several people to detonate."[3] Miniter further insists that the US military possessed only two types of SADMs. Each, he maintains, weighed over 154 pounds, measured thirty-four by twenty-six by twenty-five inches, and had to be transported by three operatives.[4] He writes:

> *For now, suitcase-sized nuclear bombs remain in the realm of James Bond movies. Given the limitations of physics and engineering, no nation seems to have invested the time and money to make them. Both the U.S. and the USSR built nuclear mines (as well as artillery shells), which were small but hardly portable—and all were dismantled by treaty by 2000.*[5]

The fact that a journalist of Miniter's stature can issue such statements without comment from fellow members of the press and "informed" critics speaks volumes of the state of American journalism.

Rose Gottemoeller is far from the only person to see a suitcase-sized nuke. Small tactical nuclear weapons, including lightweight weapons that could neatly fit within a standard Samsonite suitcase, have been in existence since the cold war, and they have been viewed and handled by thousands of US Army, Navy, and Air Force officials. Anyone with a library card or a computer can verify this fact since information concerning the small nukes was declassified by the Department of Energy on December 22, 1997.

Why Miniter and other writers of his ilk would call into question the existence of weapons is mind-boggling. Surely he is not ignorant, since

Miniter has shown himself in such previous works as *Shadow War* and *Losing Bin Laden* to be a knowledgeable and gifted journalist. And the latter seems nonsensical since no rational individual would set out to undermine the gravity of the threat from radical Islam. The author's position, therefore, is quizzical if not incomprehensible.

UNCLE SAM'S SADMs

The tactical nuclear weapons within the US arsenal came in a wide variety of sizes, shapes, and forms. The XM-388 nukes were fashioned to be fired from 120- and 150-millimeter recoilless rifles. They possessed a range of 1.24 to 2.49 miles. The casing was thirty inches long and eleven inches in diameter at the widest point. The weight of these weapons, including the warhead and fin assembly, was seventy-six pounds. They were first tested at Fort Campbell, Kentucky, on May 14, 1962, hardly cutting-edge technology in this day and age.[6]

The W-82 SADMs, developed around the same time, were designed to be carried in backpacks and became known as "rucksack bombs." They measured three feet by six feet and produced an explosive yield in excess of one kiloton. The smallest of the US nukes (known as Davy Crockets) were the W-54s, which were designed at the Los Alamos Scientific Laboratory and built by the Atomic Energy Commission. They were crafted to be parachuted into enemy territory by Navy SEALS. They weighed a mere fifty-one pounds and represented the smallest and lightest fission bomb (implosion-type) ever deployed by the United States.

The development of these weapons is hardly a clandestine secret that remains buried in the bowels of the CIA. Stockpiled W-54 warheads were test-fired at the Nevada Test Site on July 7 and July 17, 1962, and represented the last of the nuclear atmospheric detonations on American soil. The tests were observed by former attorney general Robert Kennedy and General Maxwell D. Taylor and were captured on film.[7] In addition, the United States developed B-54s, which weighed

58.6 pounds and were deployed to destinations in Europe, South Korea, and Guam.[8]

THE RED ARMY ARSENAL

What was good for the goose was good for the gander. Every weapon within the US nuclear arsenal was duplicated by the Soviets and then some. The Soviets, during the cold war, managed to build the mother of nuclear bombs—the Tsar Bomba (King of Bombs), a hundred-megaton device that can be viewed on the Web.[9] They also came up with the baby of all nukes, an artillery shell eighteen inches long and six inches in diameter that remains on display at Chelyabisk-70, Russia's largest nuclear design center.[10]

The Soviet versions of the Davy Crockets were the Red Army's RA-155 (for land usage) and the Red Navy's RA-115-01 (for underwater operations). Each could be detonated by a single agent in ten minutes, producing explosive yields between 0.5 and 2 kilotons.[11] According to Russian sources, bin Laden purchased three RA-115s from the Ukraine. The same sources confirm that these weapons could neatly be fitted in a suitcase.[12] Some of the nukes in the al Qaeda arsenal, therefore, are not devices designed for suitcases but weapons that can be fitted into a piece of luggage.

Other tactical nuclear weapons in the Soviet arsenal included air-defense warheads, atomic land mines weighing 200 pounds, and 120-pound artillery shells capable of wiping out an enemy force at a range of two hundred miles. In total, twenty-two thousand small nukes had been manufactured by the Soviet army and became part of the equipment for Soviet forces stationed in Russia, East Germany, Hungary, Poland, Bulgaria, and Czechoslovakia.[13]

In addition, they developed suitcase-sized weapons for special usage by the KGB.

MORE DISINFORMATION

Richard Miniter quotes the Russian newspaper *Ezhenedelny Zhurnal* to support his contention that only three hundred SADMs in all were produced.[14] This is yet another example of misinformation in *Disinformation*. Thousands of SADMs were produced by the United States and the Soviets. Consider the case of the W-54s, the lightest nukes in the American arsenal. Twenty-one hundred were produced at an estimated cost (excluding the warheads) of $540 million. They were designed and built by the US Atomic Energy Commission. The Soviet small nukes became part of the standard equipment for Red Army forces stationed in Russia, East Germany, Hungary, Poland, Bulgaria, and Czechoslovakia.[15]

IDEMA'S EARLY WARNING

Miniter further argues that all knowledge of the suitcase nukes springs from two sources: (1) the testimony of General Alexander Lebed, former Russian Security Council secretary, who informed a US congressional delegation to Moscow in May 1997 that more than eighty-four small atomic demolition devices were missing from the Russian arsenals and could be in the hands of Muslim extremists; and (2) the comments of Dr. Graham Allison, director of Harvard University's Belfer Center, who claims that suitcase nukes may now be in the hands of al Qaeda. In 1992, Special Forces Sergeant Jonathan "Jack" Keith Idema reported to a congressional committee that weapons-grade nuclear material was pouring into the black market and that a number of suitcase nuclear devices were now in the hands of Chechen rebels.[16] Sergeant Idema offered this testimony in 1992, five years before General Lebed came to the fore.

What's more, Dr. Allison was hardly the only other individual or agency to verify the existence of the suitcase nukes. In 1995 the Center for Nonproliferation Studies at the Monterey Institute of International Affairs received confirmation from a "senior adviser to [Russian president] Boris Yeltsin" that an unspecified number of suitcase nuclear devices had been manufactured for the KGB but had not been listed on the Soviet nuclear inventory.[17] That statement was provided nine years before Dr. Allison's *Nuclear Terrorism: The Ultimate Preventable Catastrophe* was published.

LEBED'S ALARM

General Lebed informed the congressional delegation that he was able to verify the production of 132 small nukes and could only account for 48. When asked about the whereabouts of the missing weapons, Lebed replied: "I have no idea."[18] He went on to admit that he had no idea how many small nukes had been produced by the Soviet Union during the cold war. He also said that some of these small nukes, with explosive yields of one kiloton, had been refined so that they could be carried by one person in a case measuring sixty by forty by twenty centimeters (twenty-four by sixteen by eight inches). Such devices, he concluded, represented "ideal weapons for nuclear terror."[19]

The Russian general repeated these charges in an interview with the CBS newsmagazine *60 Minutes*, which was aired on September 7, 1997. In the interview, Lebed added that the small nukes in question had been designed for use in sabotage operations and lacked the failsafe equipment that had been built into other Soviet nuclear weapons.[20] A portion of the hair-raising exchange between CBS correspondent Steve Kroft and General Lebed is as follows:

> *Kroft: Are you confident that all of the weapons are secure and accounted for?*
> *Lebed: Not at all. Not at all.*
> *Kroft: How easy would it be to steal one?*
> *Lebed: It's suitcase-sized.*
> *Kroft: You could put it in a suitcase and carry it off?*

Lebed: It is made in the size of a suitcase. It is a suitcase, actually. You could carry it. You could put it in another suitcase if you want to.

Kroft: But it's already a suitcase.

Lebed: Yes.

Kroft: I could walk down the streets of Moscow or Washington or New York, and people would think I'm carrying a suitcase?

Lebed: Yes, indeed.

Kroft: How easy would it be to detonate?

Lebed: It would take twenty, thirty minutes to prepare.

Kroft: But you don't need secret codes from the Kremlin or anything like that?

Lebed: No.

Kroft: You are saying there are a significant number that are missing and unaccounted for?

Lebed: Yes, there is. More than a hundred.

Kroft: Where are they?

Lebed: Somewhere in Georgia, somewhere in Ukraine, somewhere in the Baltic countries. Perhaps some are even outside those countries. One person is capable of triggering this nuclear weapon—one person.

Kroft: So you are saying these weapons are no longer under the control of the Russian military?

Lebed: I'm saying that more than one hundred weapons are not under the control of the armed forces of Russia. I don't know their location. I don't know whether they have been destroyed or whether they are stored or whether they've been sold or stolen. I don't know.[21]

Miniter maintains that General Lebed contradicted himself in later statements about the missing suitcase nukes. But, to his dying day, Lebed held fast to his charges. He never professed to know the exact number of small nukes that were missing. Originally, he believed the number to be forty-eight, but later (as the above excerpt from his interview with Kroft shows) came to believe that the number was much greater.

THICK-THINKIN' VALYNKIN

General Lebed's assertions, as Miniter points out, produced a pre-dictable outcry of denials from Russian officials. Lieutenant General Igor Valynkin, chief of the Russian Defense Ministry's Twelfth Main Directorate, convened a press conference to announce that nuclear suitcases were never produced because they would have "a lifetime of only a few months" and would be "too costly to maintain."[22] Valynkin maintained that the weapons would require a lot of shielding, and a lot of shielding meant that only a small amount of fissile material could be packed in a suitcase. What's more, he said, the radioactive materials decline at certain and steady rates and would decay into harmless elements within a matter of months.[23]

Following Valynkin's news conference, a steady stream of former and current Russian officials stepped forward to utter their adamant denials of Lebed's claims. Tatyana Samolis of the Foreign Intelligence Service said that her agency possessed no information concerning "suitcase bombs."[24] Vladimir Kryuchkov, former head of the KGB, labeled Lebed's allegations "complete nonsense."[25] And Lieutenant General Vyacheslav Romanov of the National Center for the Reduction of Nuclear Danger dismissed the notion of such a small nuke as a "myth." Romanov claimed that the minimum weight for such a device would be about "200 kilograms" and said that it would be "absurd" to think that one person could carry such a bomb, let alone attempt to detonate it.

THE CACAPHONOUS CHORUS

The carefully orchestrated denials proved to be not only inconsistent and contradictory but downright ridiculous in light of the fact that more than two thousand W-54s in US arsenals stood as irrefutable, empirical proof that such weapons not only existed but were not pro-hibitively expensive to maintain and did not require complete disas-sembly every three months for their nuclear cores to be recharged or replenished. Plutonium has a half-life of 24,000 years; uranium-234 of 256,000 years; and uranium-233 of 160,000 years. Tritium, which is used to boost the explosive yields of the weapons, has a half-life of 12.5 years.[26] This element would require only periodic recharging and less frequent replenishing.

Moreover, Valynkin subsequently admitted that RA-115, the serial number of one of "the suitcases" that Lebed made public, was actually a "production index" for a type of munitions that had been "eliminated."[27] In this way, the Russian official inadvertently admitted to the existence of the suitcase nukes that he denied had ever existed. It is remarkable that a terrorist analyst, such as Miniter, would seek to debunk Lebed rather than Valynkin, who, by informed accounts, rarely, if ever, spoke the truth about anything. The attempt to debunk Lebed by a number of journalists verifies the fact that the practice of shooting the messenger remains very much in practice. Perhaps the reality is too hard to accept.

General Lebed's position, as Miniter neglects to say, received support from Vladimir Denisov, a former head of the Russian Security Council, who had been placed in charge of a special commission to account for the suitcase nukes. Denisov confirmed that his office had received word that several of the suitcase nukes were missing and that some may have fallen into the hands of the Chechen separatists. Speaking to Interfax on September 13, 1997, he said that his commission had concluded that no Russian military units had any of the "suitcases" in its arsenals and that all bombs were stored in secure facilities. But he added that "it was impossible to say the same about former Soviet military units which remained on the territory of the other states in the CIS" (including Ukraine, Georgia, the Baltic states, and Chechnya).[28]

GONE BUT NOT FORGOTTEN

Additional support came from one of Lebed's most vehement detractors: Georgi Kaurov of the Ministry of Atomic Energy, who after denouncing the general as a political hack, said that Russia's capacity to develop "very small nuclear weapons" testified to the country's "high level of technology and its ability to create multipurpose and even aesthetically attractive weapons." The nukes, in other words, were not just small and deadly but also, in Kaurov's opinion, downright good-looking.[29]

The final word on the argument came from Aleksey Yablokov, an environmental advisor to President Boris Yeltsin, who confirmed that he had met with the scientists who had designed the suitcase nukes, that the weapons were "not recorded on Defense Ministry records" since they were manufactured for the KGB, and that over seven hundred of these weapons remained unaccounted for.[30]

THE SKINNY ON THE SUITCASES

But what if these weapons are not nuclear mines shoved into a suitcase for transport to the United States? Would it have been possible for the Soviets to design a fission bomb with a big bang to fit securely in a piece of luggage for detonation by a single agent? Richard Miniter says no. But leading nuclear physicists say otherwise. Carey Sublette of the Nuclear Weapon Archive, for example, believes that the Russian suitcase nukes represent technology that was available decades ago. These nukes, he maintains, represent 155-millimeter nuclear artillery shells that have been shortened by omitting the nonessential canonical oglives and fuses so that they will fit into small suitcases, even attaché cases. To exact an explosive yield of ten kilotons from the compact device, Sublette continues, the weapons would be boosted by thin beryllium reflectors. Such devices are based on a design approach called linear implosion. Linear implosion occurs when an elongated (oval-shaped), lower-density, subcritical mass is compressed and deformed into a critical, higher-density, spherical configuration by embedding it in a cylinder of explosives, which are ignited at both ends. As the detonation progresses from both directions toward the middle, the fissile mass is squeezed into a supercritical mass until the big boom occurs.[31]

This discussion may seem academic, even pedantic. But the fact that a portable weapon (less than sixty pounds) with a kick of ten kilotons (a bomb equal to the "Little Boy" that was dropped on Hiroshima) can be constructed to fit into a compact piece of luggage should be a matter of grave concern to everyone who has the ability to read a newspaper. Moreover, testimony from intelligence sources that these weapons are now in the hands of al Qaeda should receive priority above anything else dominating the news.

THE BURIED NUKES

In 1999 Curt Weldon (R-PA), chairman of the House Armed Services Subcommittee on Military Research, displayed a mock-up of the device described by Sublette to members of Congress. The demonstration, by and large, was greeted with indifference, as was Weldon's announcement that the Soviets had planted a number of such weapons at strategic locations throughout the United States. These weapons, Weldon argued, were to be recovered when the cold war became hot and were to be used for the blowing up of dams, power stations, telecommunications centers, and landing strips for Air Force One.[32] "There is no doubt that the Soviets stored material in this country," Weldon said. "The question is what and where."[33]

Two years later, Congressman Weldon's statement about the buried nukes was verified by Col. Stanislav Lunev, the highest-ranking military spy to defect from the Soviet Union and the leading confidential source on Russia's nuclear arsenal. Lunev told a congressional committee that nuclear suitcase bombs, indeed, had been buried in the United States, although he could not pinpoint the exact locations. Such information, Lunev said, remains secret since Russian officials remain convinced that a nuclear conflict between Russia and the United States remains "inevitable" despite the collapse of communism and the spirit of perestroika. The colonel concluded his remarks by saying: "And just now what we are talking about, location of technical nuclear devices, these places we have selected extremely carefully for a long, long period of time, and to believe it is possible to find these places just like that without using extremely, extremely large resources of the country, I don't think that it would be realistic until the Russian government, which still has the keys to these locations, will disclose their locations."[34]

A BOMB IN BRAINERD?

Colonel Lunev's comments could be dismissed as less than credible, save for the fact that his testimony was upheld by Vasili Mitrokhin, who served as a chief archivist for the KGB. Mitrokhin confirmed to the same committee that secret stockpiles of suitcase nuclear devices had been buried in upstate New York, California, Texas, and Minnesota.[35]

These weapons, if unearthed by al Qaeda, might represent a threat of no great significance to national security since they may not have been properly maintained. The nukes, which exude a constant temperature of one hundred degrees Fahrenheit, would be subject to oxidation and rust. The triggers that emit large quantities of neutrons at high speeds would decay rapidly, causing the bomb to produce a pop and fizzle rather than an atomic boom.

NURTURING NUKES

But the weapons obtained by al Qaeda have received proper care and attention. By 1996 more than three thousand unpaid and disillusioned Russian scientists and technicians with expertise in nuclear weapons had left the country. Some went to North Korea, Libya, and Iran. Others found gainful employment with al Qaeda and other Muslim terrorist groups.[36] The possibility of a nuclear weapon exploding in

America suddenly rose to a red-alert level—the highest level since the Cuban missile crisis.[37] From 1996 to 2000 bin Laden spent an amount estimated to be between $60 and $100 million for the assistance of nuclear scientists from Russia, China, and Pakistan.[38] In addition, bin Laden kept a score of SPETSNAZ (Soviet Special Forces) technicians on his payroll. These technicians had been trained to open and operate the suitcase nukes to prevent any unauthorized use.[39] To simplify the process of activation, the SPETSNAZ technicians came up with a method of hot-wiring the small nukes to the bodies of suicide bombers.

For some nukes in bin Laden's possession, little decoding is necessary. The tactical nukes, including the mines and RA-155s, were designed for use by troops in battle. They were equipped with unsophisticated anti-use systems. Indeed, as Bill Keller, now editor of the *New York Times*, points out, "setting one off is as easy as hot-wiring a car."[40]

Along with recruiting scientists and technicians, bin Laden began to purchase highly classified documents for the care and assembly of nuclear weapons from Russian officials. In 1998 an employee at Russia's premier nuclear laboratory in Savov was arrested for attempting to sell weapons documents to representatives of al Qaeda and the Taliban. The regional head of the Federal Security Service said that there had been other similar situations at Savov and that the sales of such top-secret information were a result of the "very difficult financial position of the workers."[41]

MISINFORMATION AND MENDACITIES

Miniter writes that the Russians "do not keep their nuclear weapons as secure as we do" but "do well enough."[42] Apparently, he is unaware that the United States, which has an infinitely better track record in securing its nukes than the Russians, has lost not only tactical but also strategic nuclear weapons. One missing nuke from the US arsenal is a hydrogen bomb with an explosive yield of one hundred kilotons, capable of wiping out much of the southern coast. The incident occurred on February 5, 1958. The bomb remains lost at sea some-where off the coast of Savannah, Georgia.[43] Other US hydrogen bombs have been lost in such places as Palomore, Spain, and the Thule Air Base in Greenland.[44]

But no nation comes close to matching Russia in dereliction of duty concerning weapons of mass destruction. In the first three years after the collapse of the Soviet Union, Germany reported more than seven hundred attempted sales of nuclear weapons and materials—all coming from Russia.[45] In 1992 Iran reportedly bought four nuclear warheads from Kazakstan for $150 million.[46] This report was verified by Russian intelligence. One year later, two fully armed nuclear weapons were stolen by employees from Zlatoust-36, a weapons-assembly plant in Chelyabinsk.[47]

Miniter contends that "there are no documented cases of the Russian mafia or Russian officials selling nuclear weapons or mate-rial."[48] In truth, the cases are too numerous to mention within the con-fines of this book. The activities of Semion Mogilevich, a Ukrainian arms dealer and prominent member of the Russian *mafiya*, would con-sume several chapters. Suffice it to say that Mogilevich sold more than twenty kilos of uranium-236 to bin Laden. For one delivery of twelve kilos, Mogilevich received a payment of $70 million. This uranium had been enriched to 85 percent—far above the standards of enrich-ment for weapons-grade material.[49]

Regarding Russian officials selling nuclear material, Miniter need only turn to the case of Captain Alekei Tikhomirov of the Russian navy, who stole three pieces of a reactor core, each containing 3.4 kilo-grams of highly enriched uranium, from the Sevmorput shipyard near Murmansk.[50]

FINAL BONER

At the conclusion of his argument, Miniter makes the claim that the total loss of highly enriched uranium amounts to eight grams, and "even these eight grams, which have differing levels of purity, could not be productively combined."[51] Where he got this information remains anyone's guess. In actuality, the Center for International Security and Cooperation at Stanford University reported in 2002 that more than forty kilograms of highly enriched uranium (HEU) has been reported missing from Russia and that the actual amount of missing HEU is ten times that amount.[52] The study mentioned that thefts of HEU have been reported in fifty other countries, including Romania, India, Germany, and the Congo. Regarding the actual amount of missing HEU and plutonium, Bill Keller writes: "No doubt enough nuclear material to build twenty nukes was lost in the transition from the Soviet Union to Russia. Indeed, 1,000 pounds of HEU was purchased by the U.S. government; removed from an unprotected site in Almaty, Kazakstan; and stored at a nuclear facility in Oak Ridge, Tennessee."[53]

Most experts agree that suitcase nuclear devices, if not boosted by tritium and equipped with beryllium reflectors, would emit an explosive yield of one kiloton, thereby qualifying as "junk nukes." Lest anyone dismiss a "junk nuke" as a weapon of little concern, consider what impact the detonation of one of these devices by a single al Qaeda agent would have on New York City. The blast alone would gut buildings for several square blocks and kill more than 20,000 people in a matter of seconds. All exposed to the fireball that would emerge from the blast would die of radiation poisoning within twenty-four hours. This figure would probably amount to 250,000 to 300,000 victims. All inhabitants within half a mile of the explosion would die of radiation within a matter of months, if not weeks. This would come to 500,000 additional casualties. The mushroom cloud of irradiated debris would blossom two miles in the air. Forty minutes later, the deadly fallout would doom rescue workers and survivors. Add another 500,000 people to the death toll. The radiation would travel five miles into the five boroughs of New York, exposing millions more to the poison.[54] That's not all. In addition to the death toll, the financial and cultural center of the United States would cease to exist. The GNP would drop more than 3 percent in the blink of an eye.[55] Millions would lose their jobs and life savings. The unprecedented number of wounded and traumatized victims would create an enormous crisis in healthcare. Makeshift hospitals would be set up in schools, museums, libraries, and other public buildings, where patients would languish without proper medical care. Populations would desert major urban areas. The process of commerce would come to a screeching halt.[56] Within hours, America (along with every leading industrialized country in the world) would fall into a deep depression from which there would be little chance of recovery.

Unfortunately, this is a best-case scenario since it involves a low-grade, "off-the-shelf nuke." The outcome would be hellish beyond imagination if the attack took place with a "bespoke nuke"—a weapon created by scientists in Pakistan or Iran from the raw materials of highly enriched uranium or plutonium.[57] Has al Qaeda developed such weapons? If so, is there any hope for the Western world?

CHAPTER SIX
EIGHT NIGHTMARES

"Is nuclear mega-terrorism inevitable?" Harvard professors are known for being subtle or ambiguous, but I'll try to be clear. "Is the worst yet to come?" My answer: Bet on it. Yes.

Dr. Graham Allison, director of Harvard University's
Belfer Center for Science and International Affairs

It's not a matter of if; it's a matter of when.

General Eugene E. Habiger,
former executive chief of US strategic weapons

It's the most dangerous threat we face. We can find a way to deal with biological terror. But if these guys acquire enough nuclear weapons and blow up major cities, it wouldn't end civilization as we know it, but it would come pretty close.

Ambassador Thomas Graham,
Special Representative for Nonproliferation and Disarmament

We know that bin Laden made strenuous efforts to buy these weapons; we know that security at some Russian nuclear arsenals was terrible; we know that some Russian officials were corrupt. We are told of attempted thefts and of plots that were foiled, but we are never told of the plots that succeeded.

Congressman Christopher Shays (R-CT)

INCIDENT ONE

I n 1999 two British agents of Arab descent managed to infiltrate al Qaeda by becoming members of a radical mosque in the east end of London and answering the call for recruits in the great jihad. The mission had required the agents to undergo months of immersion in Arabic until they became proficient enough to speak the language without a trace of their English upbringing. They also underwent training in Islamic customs and proper protocol, memorized entire surahs (chapters) from the Koran, and labored as blue-collar workers in menial positions among Muslim émigrés. Upon receiving the approval of the imam of the mosque and meeting with agents of Egyptian Islamic Jihad, they were sent to Kandahar in southern Afghanistan for basic training. After six weeks of instruction in guerrilla warfare, they took the blood oath to Osama bin Laden and were transported northwest to Herat in western Afghanistan for advanced training in special operations.

In Herat, they came upon the proverbial mother lode—a laboratory where al Qaeda scientists and technicians labored to create weapons of mass destruction. At the time of the agents' visit, the lab workers were applying finishing touches to a radiological device.[1]

The situation was far worse than expected. Al Qaeda was not only sinister, well financed, and widely supported throughout the extremist Islamic world but also sophisticated in its weaponry and delivery system. The news was too important to hold. By the end of the week, the agents managed to smuggle from the facility several manuals on the proper way to detonate a dirty bomb for maximum effect before making their escape by heading off toward the Caspian Sea.

Upon their return, the agents reported their findings to Eliza Manningham-Butler, head of MI5, Britain's Security Service. Several years later, Butler blew her cover regarding the operation by telling an audience at the Royal United Services Institute in London: "We are faced with a realistic possibility of a form of an unconventional attack that could include chemical, biological, radiological, and nuclear [CBRN] weapons. We know renegade scientists have cooperated with al Qaeda and provided them with the knowledge they need to develop these weapons. It is only a matter of time before a crude version of a CBRN is launched on a Western city and it is only a matter of time before the crude weapon becomes more sophisticated."[2]

When the story of a laboratory in Herat finally broke on the BBC, Abdel Bari Atwan, the editor of *Al-Quds Al-Arabi*, said that the news release represented an attempt to incite fears against Muslims in Britain and the United States.[3]

The bomb that the British saw being manufactured has not been recovered to this day.

INCIDENT TWO

But this discovery paled in comparison with an incident that occurred one month after 9/11 on the Allenby Bridge between Jordan and Israel. A Pakistani operative with ties to al Qaeda attempted to cross the bridge in a Volkswagon mini-bus. In the rear of the bus, he had placed a rucksack that weighed nearly seventy pounds.

But Allah was not smiling upon his servant this day. Israeli soldiers approached the Pakistani and inquired about the contents of the rucksack. He smiled and said computer equipment. The ploy didn't work. One of the soldiers opened the sack and discovered a bomb.

The soldiers delivered the bomb to Mossad officials at Ramallah, who, after a cursory inspection, ruled it to be a radiological device. This information was conveyed to the journalists who appeared at the scene, including representatives of United Press International. The story about the "dirty nuke" broke the next day but failed to capture the attention of the major media outlets in the United States.[4]

The device was transported to Dimona, where it was examined at the Negev Nuclear Research Center by Israeli scientists, who were horrified by what they found. This was not a radiological device, as first supposed—not even a crude nuclear bomb that had been manufactured with highly enriched uranium. The bomb was the most sophisticated of all tactical nuclear weapons—a plutonium-implosion device that had been developed by the KGB.[5] Tangible proof had been uncovered so that the nuclear capacity of radical Islam no longer could be in doubt.

Confidential information regarding the finding was dispatched to the Bush administration, which prompted Congressman Christopher Shays to admit in a news conference: "I wouldn't be the least bit surprised if there [would be] a nuclear explosion in Israel or the United States."[6]

INCIDENT THREE

The CIA pressed Pakistani intelligence (ISI) to seek out and arrest all accomplices of the operative who tried to smuggle the nuke into Israel. By early November a number of suspects were taken into custody. One said that al Qaeda had managed to smuggle at least two portable nukes into the United States. "What was disconcerting about this information," one US expert analyst said, "was that he [the suspect] knew details about the activation of the weapons and their construction that are not in the public domain."[7]

The information obtained from the suspect confirmed a report that had been received by George Tenet, director of the CIA, on October 11, 2001, of suitcase nukes that had reached al Qaeda operatives in the land of the free and the home of the brave. Each suitcase, according to the initial report, weighed eight kilograms and contained two kilograms of fissionable plutonium (similar to the device confiscated on the Allenby Bridge). One suitcase bore the serial number 9999 and the Soviet manufacturing date of 1999.[8]

When briefed by Tenet about the nukes already in the country, President Bush reportedly went "through the roof" and ordered the activation of nuclear contingency plans, including the installation of underground bunkers away from major metropolitan areas so that a cadre of federal managers could proceed with the business of government after a nuclear attack occurred.[9] He also ordered the installation of new and highly sophisticated Gamma Ray Neutron Flux Detector sensors at various "choke points" around Washington and several overseas facilities to detect the presence of radiological devices.[10]

To some observers, the possibility of two nukes—as opposed to more—being readied for the next attack by al Qaeda on US soil was somewhat of a relief. After all, several highly informed sources had confirmed that a score of nuclear warheads in suitcases had made their way to the United States and that five thousand sleeper agents were in place for the American Hiroshima. One such source was Shaykh Hisham Kabbani, chairman of the Islamic Supreme Council of America, who made the claim of twenty al Qaeda nukes already in America. Kabbani presented this testimony before the US State Department on January 7, 1999, and reiterated the claim to members of the press in the wake of 9/11.[11]

To beef up security and prevent more nukes from arriving, federal authorities began investigating all suspicious cash rentals of trucks and cash leases of small aircraft, since a small nuke could be dropped by terrorists via parachutes into remote areas of the country for awaiting al Qaeda agents. Airfreight appeared vulnerable since less than 25 percent of the cargo carried by private planes was subjected to inspection.[12]

But the most nagging fear for federal officials was that the nukes had arrived or would arrive by ship, since America, even in the era of post-9/11, possessed "zip port security."[13] Bin Laden, the officials knew, owned twenty-three ships and maintained close relations with many shipping firms, including Saudi oil companies. The open seas represented the easiest way to transport deadly cargo—particularly cargo stored in oil containers—into the United States.

Regarding the possibility of nukes arriving by sea, Stephen Flynn, senior fellow for national security studies at the US Council of Foreign Relations, said: "The United States has 16,000 ships entering its ports every day. Adding in shipments by truck, train, or air freight, the total number of import shipments to the U.S. is 21.4 million tons a year. You could put a nuclear or chemical weapon aboard a ship leaving Karachi and that ship will land at Vancouver, Oakland, San Francisco, or the Gulf Coast, and we would never know the difference." Flynn said that less than 3 percent of ship containers are ever inspected— even the containers that arrive from the Middle East.[14]

On September 9, 2002, the *Palermo Senator*, a Liberian-registered 704-foot freighter, steamed into New York harbor. Dockworkers reported that strange noises were coming from the ship's cargo holds. The ship was diverted to Port Newark, New Jersey, where it was inspected for stowaways. None were found. But when an FBI agent turned on his portable Geiger counter, it registered strong traces of low-level radiation. This finding triggered alarms throughout the intelligence community since the *Palermo Senator* purportedly had made stops at Jeddah, Saudi Arabia, and Khafakkan, United Arab Emirates, before landing at the Italian hub port of Gloria Touro on August 25.[15]

Gloria Touro, located on the southern Italian coast near the Strait of Messina, had long been on the US Coast Guard's list of "high-risk" ports of call since it served as a shipping center for the international drug trade and arms dealers. Moreover, it had become a favorite transit point for the budding black market in nuclear weapons and materials.[16]

From Port Newark, the *Palermo Senator* was ordered to sail six miles off the coast of New Jersey for inspection by a team of Navy SEALs. The team could not determine the cause of the radiation but speculated that it could have been produced by fifteen containers of clay tile from Spain.[17] Others guessed that several containers may have been removed from the ship at sea and transported to some site along the Atlantic coastline. In any case, concern over the cargo was so intense that Vice President Dick Cheney purportedly was confined for several days to a secure nuclear facility in Virginia.[18]

INCIDENT FOUR

Another event occurred in October 2001 that failed to attract the attention of the nation's leading news outlets. In Kearny, New Jersey, a Pakistani was taken into custody on immigration charges in the course of an FBI investigation into the events of 9/11. The suspect was transported to the Hudson County Jail, where he began to complain of bleeding gums and acute diarrhea. An attending physician noted other symptoms—a high temperature, signs of delirium, purple fingernails, and clumps of hair around his pillow. The prisoner was treated with antibiotics, but his condition continued to worsen. Three weeks later, the Pakistani was dead. Neither the victim's identity nor the cause of his death was released to the media. But a team of medical experts, who became aware of the case, expressed their belief that the prisoner may have been a mule who served to transport nuclear material into the country for al Qaeda. This belief gained substance when an autopsy showed that the victim had contracted gingivitis as a result of radiation-induced leukemia.[19] Meanwhile, in Israel, the Pakistani agent who had been taken into custody at the Allenby Bridge began to manifest the same symptoms as the dead Pakistani in New Jersey.[20]

INCIDENT FIVE

Eddy Maloof, a satellite engineer from CNN, roamed through a house in Kabul in November 2001, one month after the launch of Operation Enduring Freedom, the US-led invasion of Afghanistan. The house had belonged to Abu Khabab, a member of the al Qaeda high command. It had been stripped of everything except a bag of garbage in the corner of a bedroom. Maloof, who is fluent in Arabic, opened the bag to take a look at the contents. He came upon a twenty-five-page, hand-written document, replete with drawings, called "Superbomb." The first pages were missing, so it was impossible to know the name of the author, the date on which it had been written, or the audience for which it was prepared. But it contained discussions of such topics as types of nuclear weapons, the physics of nuclear explosions, and the properties of nuclear materials.[21]

Maloof conveyed the document to US military officials, who sent it to David Albright, a physicist and president of the Institute for Science and International Security in Washington, DC. Albright soon realized that it was a highly sophisticated paper that included little-known shortcuts to making nuclear weapons.[22] The document further showed that al Qaeda was primarily interested in creating weapons based on a gun-type nuclear design. This design was developed at Los Alamos during World War II. It called for a bullet of highly enriched uranium (HEU) to be fired from a gun down a barrel into another piece of HEU. Slammed together, the two pieces of HEU form a supercritical mass and detonate. The Los Alamos scientists believed so strongly in the capabilities of the design that military authorities decided to drop this bomb, untested, on Hiroshima. South Africa also employed this model in making its covert nuclear arsenal without conducting a single test.[23] Now al Qaeda was doing the same.

How did bin Laden obtain this design? The answer for Albright and others wasn't long in coming. *The Los Alamos Primer* and *Atomic Energy for Military Purposes*, two declassified US government publications based on the research conducted by scientists and technicians for the Manhattan Project, were available on Amazon.com for the combined price of $40.76 plus shipping.[24]

Eventually, US military officials came upon student notebooks in other houses in Kabul, which confirmed the suspicion that "Superbomb" was an instructional manual for al Qaeda students. One notebook contained the date 2000 and replications of illustrations in the manual. This led Albright to pen the following conclusion: "The documents show that al Qaeda was creating a quasi-state nuclear weapons program with the tacit or direct approval of the Taliban government. Moreover, this effort was largely invisible to the rest of the world prior to September 11th. Although intelligence agencies were intensely scrutinizing al Qaeda's activities, they had little success in penetrating al Qaeda's secret weapons program."[25]

INCIDENT SIX

Late in November 2001, Haji Gulalai, the interim intelligence chief for the province of Kandahar, informed coalition forces of a place known as Turnak Farms, a sprawling desert complex near the Kandahar airport where al Qaeda had established laboratories to develop weapons of mass destruction. A bombing campaign got under way before tribal fighters, led by tribal chieftain Gul Agha, closed in on the complex from the south and the east.[26]

At the height of operations, eighteen hundred members of al Qaeda lived and worked at Turnak Farms. The five apartment buildings were originally built to house workers and the command headquarters served as an air traffic control center.

As soon as the bombing began, most of the inhabitants headed for safety in the mountains. A few hundred, determined to attain martyrdom, stayed behind and fought to the end. Some ambushed their Afghan foes by holding up their hands in a gesture of surrender only to pull the pins on concealed grenades, blowing themselves and their captors to kingdom come.[27]

On December 5 the battle was over and the bodies of the Arabs were left by the airport gates for collection by the Red Cross. The complex, for the most part, remained in rubble. Within the few apartments that had not been completely demolished by the explosions, tribal troops found furniture, appliances, and clothing. In command headquarters by a crumpled radar dish was a note scribbled in Arabic that said: "Victory is near."[28]

Beneath the complex was a maze of concrete tunnels leading to laboratories where nuclear supplies and materials were stored. In one laboratory the soldiers found a canister of uranium-238 and empty containers and drums with radioactive residue. Haji Gulalai later told the press about the material in the laboratory, including "small jars and big jars, sealed with metal lids and containing powders and liquids, white and yellowish in color."[29]

Uranium-238, enriched to 89 percent, is the basic ingredient for a nuclear bomb. The uranium in the canister had not been enriched but represented the perfect material to create a quantity of "dirty nukes." The finding was disconcerting. If the retreating al Qaeda fighters left behind such valuable material—worth millions on the black market—what had they taken with them? "Nuclear material used in nuclear weapons is relatively easy to hide or transport," David Albright informed US military officials. "Given that most of the al Qaeda leadership escaped capture, it would be foolish to assume that al Qaeda would have left behind any valuable, transportable radioactive material."[30]

But one canister had been left behind as if to hint at the scribbled message within command headquarters.

INCIDENT SEVEN

Despite the fall of the Taliban and the establishment of a "democratic" regime in Afghanistan under Hamid Karzai, Afghan and Pakistani smugglers were still able to move so much radiological contraband out of Russia that they had to stockpile it in at least one warehouse in Peshawar, Pakistan. Robert Puffer, a US dealer in antiquities, told authorities that he had visited the warehouse, where dozens of canisters of nuclear material were stored in the basement. "There Afghans didn't know anything about radioactivity," Puffer told a correspondent for *Time*. "They were walking around with stuff they said was 'yellowcake,' which they kept in a matchbox in their pocket."[31]

Yellowcake is the key precursor to the creation of highly enriched uranium for nuclear bombs. It is produced by drying and filtering pure uranium (uranium that has been crushed, ground, and soaked in sulfuric acid) into a coarse powder.[32] The fact that al Qaeda operatives were walking about with yellowcake in their pockets shows that they were working in cahoots with highly trained scientists to produce "bespoke nukes."

INCIDENT EIGHT

It seemed like a joke or a false arrest. An overweight, balding, disheveled Arab in a soiled T-shirt and wrinkled pants was removed in handcuffs at 3 AM from the home of Dr. Abdul Qadoos Khan in Rawalpini, Pakistan. The guy looked stunned and disoriented. He made no comment. Instead, he mumbled verses from the Koran while being led by ISI (Pakistani Inter-Services-Intelligence) to a police van and hauled off to Karachi for questioning.[33]

The slovenly figure taken into custody turned out to be Khalid Shaikh Mohammed, al Qaeda's military operations commander and a key planner of 9/11. The arrest, according to President George W. Bush, represented one of the most significant developments in the "war on terror."[34]

After several days of questioning, coupled with sleep deprivation, the caged al Qaeda chieftain began to sing like a canary. He spoke of a plot to attack nuclear power plants on US soil, of a plan to blow up the Brooklyn Bridge, and of a plot to disperse anthrax by crop dusters on towns and villages throughout "the land of the Great Satan." He mentioned names: José Padilla, Zacarias Moussaoui, Amer el-Maati, Anas al-Liby, Jaber Elbaneh, Jafar al-Tayyar ("Jafar, the Pilot"), and Mohammed Sher Mohammed Khan, whom he identified as the "commander of the next 9/11."[35]

Khalid Shaikh Mohammed spoke of other things as well, including bin Laden's plans to unleash a "nuclear hell storm" throughout the United States. Unlike other attacks that could be planned and conducted by lower-level al Qaeda leaders, the terror chief said, the chain of command for the so-called American Hiroshima answered directly to bin Laden, al-Zawahiri, and a mysterious figure called "Dr. X."[36]

Who was Dr. X? The answer to this question led to the greatest nightmare of all.

CHAPTER SEVEN

THE MAD SCIENTIST

Mahmood was one of the nuclear hawks. People say that he was a very capable scientist and a very capable engineer, but he had this totally crazy mind-set.

Rifaat Hussain, chairman of Strategic Studies
at Quaid-i-Azam University in Islamabad

UTN claims to serve the hungry and needy of Afghanistan. But it was the UTN that provided information about nuclear weapons to al Qaeda.

President George W. Bush

If a nuclear weapon destroys the U.S. Capitol in coming years, it will probably be based in part on Pakistani technology.

Nicholas D. Kristof, *New York Times*, September 27, 2004

I have a nightmare that the spread of enriched uranium and nuclear material could result in the operation of a small enrichment facility

in a place like northern Afghanistan. Who knows? It's not hard for a
non-state to hide, especially if a state is in collusion with it. Some of
these non-state groups are very sophisticated.

Mohamed el-Baradei, director-general of the
International Atomic Energy Agency (IAEA), 2004

When India conducted an underground nuclear test in 1974, Dr. Sultan Mahmood, who had gained international prominence by inventing a device to detect heavy water leaks at nuclear reactiors, broke into tears and vowed to make his native Pakistan a nuclear power.[1] He kept his vow and is widely credited with playing the central role in the development of highly enriched uranium through centrifuge technology. Sure, the notorious Dr. Abdul Qadeer Khan provided the blueprints for this technology by stealing them from Urenco, a top-secret uranium enrichment plant in the Netherlands where he had worked as a technician.[2] But Khan lacked the ability to implement the design and to actualize the enrichment. By trade and training, he was a metallurgist, not a nuclear scientist. For this reason, Khan, although his birthday has become a national holiday in Pakistan, does not deserve his hallowed title of "father of the Islamic bomb." That title belongs to Dr. Mahmood.

RECIPE FOR A MADE-FROM-SCRATCH NUKE

To enrich uranium and to produce an atomic bomb requires the expertise of a highly trained nuclear scientist. The process begins with the conversion of yellowcake (pure uranium that has been dried and filtered) into uranium hexafluoride, a highly volatile gaseous compound. This conversion is accomplished by exposing the yellowcake to fluoride gas and heating it to a temperature of 133 degrees Fahrenheit. The uranium hexafluoride must be sent through high-rotation machines called gaseous centrifuges. These sophisticated machines spin at the speed of sound and consist of nearly one hundred compounds that must be built to exact specifications or else they will explode into millions of microscopic pieces.[3]

As the tubes spin, the different weights of the uranium isotopes cause them to split, with the heavier uranium-238 being cast against the outer wall of the centrifuge and the lighter uranium-235 remaining on the inner wall. The gas created by this separation passes from centrifuge to centrifuge—each pass producing the extraction of more and more uranium-235.[4] The task of creating enough uranium-235 for a single bomb requires about fifteen hundred centrifuges working in a chain called a "cascade" for about a year.[5]

Once a sufficient amount of enriched uranium-235 gas is produced, it is converted into uranium oxide, a metal powder, by a chemical process involving hydrogen at a temperature of 1,500 degrees Fahrenheit.

The process is intricate, intense, and expensive. Indeed, it takes the resources of a state to commence the process of enriching uranium as well as a team of hundreds of highly trained scientists and technicians. There is no way a rogue organization, such as al Qaeda, even with its riches from the drug trade and its support throughout the Muslim world, could embark on such a venture. Al Qaeda has always been dependent upon gaining possession of the raw materials of highly enriched uranium and plutonium from black market sources in order to manufacture its arsenal of small nukes. On occasion, the terrorist organization also purchased ready-made weapons, such as the suitcase nukes, from Russia and from the newly created Russian republics.

THE QUICK AND EASY ALTERNATIVE

Given the essential ingredients of highly enriched uranium and plutonium, it no longer takes a Manhattan Project to produce an atomic bomb. How daunting is such a task? Graham Allison maintains that, given the requisite fissile material, the task would be relatively easy.

Designs for a gun-type devise are readily available from libraries and the Internet.

MAHMOOD: DISTINGUISHED SCIENTIST

Dr. Mahmood was solely responsible for the design of the Khushab reactor. This unsafeguarded reactor depended extensively on illicit procurements of uranium and plutonium from Russia and various Russian republics. When the key plant went critical in April 1998, it was capable of producing two to three nuclear warheads per year.

For his part in making Pakistan a member of the elite nuclear club, Mahmood became chairman of the Pakistan Atomic Energy Commission (PAEC) and received the Sitara-e-Imtiaz, the country's highest civilian award, along with a gold medal from the Pakistan Academy of Science in 1999.

MAHMOOD: MUSLIM EXTREMIST

In addition to his accomplishments as a scientist, Dr. Mahmood has been a staunch supporter of radical Islam and a central figure within Lashkar-e-Toiba (the "Army of the Pure").[6] Lashkar-e-Toiba is the officially banned terrorist arm of Markaz Dawa-Wal-Irshad, a Sunni organization of the Wahhabi sects in Pakistan. Such sects follow the radical teachings of eighteenth-century emir Abdul al-Wahhab, who led a rebellion against the Ottoman Empire. Bin Laden, al-Zawahiri, and all high-ranking al Qaeda officials are Wahhabists.

Lashkar-e-Toiba, a group that signed bin Laden's 1998 declaration of "Jihad against Jews and Crusaders," specializes in the mass murder of Hindus. It was responsible for many horrific attacks in India and Bangladesh, including the slaughter of twenty-three people in Wandhama on January 23, 1988; the cold-blooded slayings of twenty-five members of a wedding party, including small children, in Doda on

June 19, 1998; the Chattisinghpora massacre of March 20, 2000, in which twenty-five men, women, and children were hacked to pieces by machetes; and the November 24, 2002, attack on two Hindu shrines in Hammu that left thirteen Hindus dead and forty-five injured.[7]

In 2003 Lashkar-e-Toiba changed its name to Jamaat-ud-Dawa and became the coordinating agency for bin Laden's activities throughout the world.[8] On February 2, 2002, Abu Zubaydah, a member of al Qaeda's Majilis al-Shura (Central Consultation Council), was found hiding within a Lashkar-e-Toiba safe house in Faisalabad. A key strategist of 9/11, Abu Zubaydah was the terror chief who sent Richard Reid, the "shoe bomber," on a mission to blow up an American Airlines plane in December 2001.[9] Within Zubaydah's address book were the names of key al Qaeda operatives throughout Latin America.[10]

TWO MORE TERRORIST NUKES COME TO LIGHT

Throughout 2004 Hafiz Mohammed Saeed, the emir of Lashkar-e-Toiba (now Jamaat-ud-Dawa), barnstormed the provinces of Pakistan, calling upon all Muslims to join in the jihad against the United States. In several speeches, Saeed maintained that Pakistan's nuclear weapons should be used to benefit all Islamic states. In addition, he claimed that his terror organization remained in control of "two nuclear missiles." These missiles, Saeed assured readers on his Web site (www.jamat-dawa.org), were being prepared for use against the "enemies of Islam."[11] Was the terrorist group really in possession of these weapons? Or was Saeed simply speaking through his teeth? The question begs an answer since an investigation into this claim has yet to be conducted.

In the wake of 9/11, nine members of Lashkar-e-Toiba were arrested for attempting to recruit suitable candidates for the jihad (including an attack on nearby Washington, DC) by conducting paint-ball rallies for Islamic groups in northern Virginia.[12]

THE *UMMAH* UNITED BY WARHEADS

Dr. Mahmood shared Hafiz Saeed's belief that Pakistan's nuclear weapons program should be used to benefit the Islamic world. He advocated extensive production of weapons-grade plutonium and uranium at the Khushab reactor so that Muslim nations could develop their own nuclear weapons. Indeed, in speeches before Lashkar-e-Toiba and other radical groups, he insisted that Pakistan's nuclear capability was "the property of the whole *Ummah* [the international community of Muslims]."

This belief prompted Mahmood, as chairman of PAEC, to protest Pakistan's willingness to sign the Comprehensive Test Ban Treaty. He argued that signing the treaty would impose massive political and military costs on Pakistan while producing few rewards. "If we keep developing nuclear technology on the path of self reliance, and also extend cooperation to other [Muslim] countries in this field," he wrote in one of his articles, "shall we not be the gainers ultimately?"[13] He explained the gain by pointing out that such proliferation would permit developing Muslim nations to defend themselves against Western "crusaders" who are intent upon the destruction of their beliefs and their way of life.[14]

Mahmood went further. He began to speak at public gatherings in favor of the Taliban, saying that Mullah Omar's government represented an ideal model for Pakistan. Even after 9/11, Mahmood remained supportive of the Taliban, addressing a symposium of intellectuals and public officials in mid-October 2001, where he called for a three-month cease-fire to resolve the situation in Afghanistan.[15]

MAHMOOD: THE MADMAN

Mahmood was not only a distinguished scientist and an Islamic fanatic; he was also a person of questionable sanity. Evidence of his lunacy is on ample display in his writings. In *Mechanics of the*

Doomsday and Life after Death, published in 1987, he maintains that natural catastrophes occur in places where moral degradation becomes rampant. In the closing chapter, he maintains that his "scientific mind can work backward and analyze the actual mechanism of the great upheaval before the Earth's Doomsday."[16] In *Cosmology and Human Destiny*, published in 1998, he argues that sunspots control the events of human history, including the French Revolution, the Russian Revolution, and World War II. He notes that governments across the world "are already subjected to great emotional aggression under the catalytic effect of the abnormally high sunspot activity under which they are most likely to adapt aggression as the natural solution."[17] In this same work, he writes that Pakistan's energy problems could be solved by harnessing the energy emitted by the *djinns*, the fairylike spirits who inhabit the world of Islam.[18]

KABUL'S CHARITABLE FOUNDATION

Under the spell of a *djinn* or a mental flux caused by a sunspot, Dr. Mahmood left his position with PAEC in order to establish Ummah Tameer e-Nau ("Reconstruction of the Muslim Ummah" or UTN), a so-called charitable foundation, in Kabul. The stated purpose of UTN was to conduct relief work and to attract foreign investment in Afghanistan. The cofounders of the organization were Dr. Chaudry Abdul Majid, the chief engineer of the PAEC and a top official at the A. Q. Khan Research Laboratories near Islamabad, and Dr. Mirza Yusuf Baig, another PAEC engineer.

UTN managed to attract huge sums of money for its projects, including its plans to build a flour mill, a dam, and an oil refinery in Afghanistan. The organization established offices in the wealthiest section of Kabul and a staff of scientists and workers, many of whom were leading scientists and technicians from the A. Q. Khan Research Laboratories.

But UTN was not primarily involved in humanitarian efforts, and the millions that poured into the organization from the Taliban and the government of Pakistan were not used to produce flour or refine oil, although UTN did purchase 1,155 sheep and 631 cows for sacrifice on Eid-ul-Afha, a major Muslim celebration. The firm was more intent upon mining uranium and developing weapons of mass destruction for the great jihad. This became apparent when US forces entered the UTN offices and Mahmood's residence in Kabul and discovered evidence that the flour mill may have been an anthrax factory. Indeed, the walls of the UTN headquarters were covered with illustrations that showed how high-altitude bombs could spread anthrax spores, cyanide, and bubonic plague bacilli over major metropolitan areas of the United States.[19] They also found documents outlining a plan to kidnap an American attaché, mounds of data on the construction and maintenance of nuclear weapons from the A. Q. Khan facility, and correspondence linking UTN to Lashkar-e-Toiba and al Qaeda.[20] But most disturbing were the records of meetings between Dr. Mahmood, Dr. Majid, and other scientists from the A. Q. Khan Research Labotatories with bin Laden, al-Zawahiri, and other high-ranking al Qaeda officials. There was also evidence that Dr. Khan himself spent a considerable amount of time commiserating with bin Laden in Kabul. This finding was so alarming that CIA director George Tenet boarded a midnight flight to Islamabad to get to the bottom of the matter.[21]

MAHMOOD BECOMES MUNCHHAUSEN

On October 23, 2001, Dr. Mahmood and Dr. Majid were "detained for questioning" by ISI and CIA officials. Dr. Mahmood, at first, denied that he had ever met bin Laden or made contact with any al Qaeda officials. Yes, he said, he had met with Mullah Omar, the supreme leader of the Taliban, but only to discuss the matter of the flour mill and to come up with ways to provide bread to the Afghan masses. He was given a lie-detector test, which he failed.

Back on the hot seat, Mahmood continued to insist that he knew bin Laden only by reputation as a "fellow humanitarian" who "was helping in different places, renovating schools, opening orphan houses, and helping with the rehabilitation of widows."[22] He was given additional lie-detector tests and failed them all.

The polygraph results prompted him to come (somewhat) clean. Yes, he admitted, he had met with bin Laden, al-Zawahiri, and other al Qaeda officials in Kabul to discuss the benefits of a nuclear blast in an American city. He had even met with them on the fateful morning of September 11, 2001.

Bin Laden, Mahmood said, was most sincere in creating an American Hiroshima and had managed to obtain fissile material from various sources, including the Islamic Movement of Uzbekistan.[23] Yes, he could even admit that al Qaeda was actively involved in speeding up the process of producing "bespoke nukes" for the jihad.[24] But, no, he insisted, he had *never* provided nuclear materials to bin Laden and, no, he had *never* provided him with hands-on assistance in making such weapons. After making these pronouncements, the scientist yet again was subjected to another battery of lie-detector tests and, true to form, once again managed to fail them all.

When questioned about his miserable performance on the seven polygraphs, Dr. Mahmood said: "I could never stay before the machine beyond a few minutes because of my age and health, as it was very strenuous exercise that made my blood pressure go erratic and rendered my heart unstable."[25]

"TRUE CONFESSIONS" CONTINUED

The grilling of Dr. Majid, Dr. Mahmood, and Dr. Baig resulted in an admission by the scientists that, indeed, they had met with bin Laden and other al Qaeda officials on several occasions to discuss the ways to manufacture nukes from weapons-grade uranium and plutonium and how to maintain the weapons for proper detonation.[26]

After a few months of house arrest, Drs. Mahmood, Majid, and

Baig were quietly released without charges being filed. Knowing that UTN was a money-laundering front for al Qaeda, the Bush administration placed the "charity" on its "terrorist list" and labeled Dr. Mahmood "a global terrorist."[27] Despite the label, Mahmood remains a free man and a celebrated figure among the Ummah.

ESCAPE TO MYANMAR

But the problem of nuclear scientists from Pakistan working with al Qaeda went much deeper than the three PAEC scientists. The CIA discovered from records in UTN's headquarters that Dr. Mohammad Ali Mukhtar and Dr. Suleiman Asad, top-flight nuclear scientists who had worked for many years at two of Pakistan's most secret nuclear installations, had met with bin Laden and other al Qaeda leaders on a regular basis. When US officials requested the detention of Mukhtar and Asad for questioning, they were told that the two scientists were unavailable since they had been sent to Myanmar on official business.

The official business, as it turned out, was helping Myanmar develop a nuclear reactor on the slopes of the Shan hills, forty-two miles from Mandalay. Myanmar, better known as Burma, is one of the poorest countries on earth and is ruled by a military junta.[28] The two scientists from Pakistan proved to be of invaluable help in the construction of the ten-megawatt reactor, which is now up and running and producing highly enriched uranium that may be sold to rogue nations and terrorist groups throughout the world. Little has appeared in the US press about the developments in Myanmar, which remain as disconcerting for many Western observers as the nuclear developments in North Korea and Iran. Commenting on the Myanmar reactor, Ian Bremer, senior fellow at the World Policy Institute, said: "Maybe the Myanmar government believes a nuclear weapon offers the ultimate insurance against a US invasion. After all, the United States has invaded Iraq, which does not have nuclear weapons, but has not attacked North Korea, which has."[29]

As more and more information about UTN came to light, US officials became increasingly aware that a host of other nuclear scientists from the Khan laboratories had been working with al Qaeda on its Manhattan project. Unfortunately, by the time they were sought for questioning in 2002, the scientists had fled for unknown destinations. The list of such "absconders" includes the names of Muhammad Zubair, Murad Qasim, Tariq Mahmood, Saeed Akhther, Imtaz Baig, Waheed Nasir, Munawar Ismail, Shaheen Fareed, and Khalid Mahmood.[30]

NUKES IN NIGERIA?

Where did they go? Neither ISI nor CIA officials could come up with an answer. The Pakistani scientists could have found a welcome reception in every country where Dr. A. Q. Khan had sold his blueprints for centrifuge technology and his designs for nuclear weapons. The buyers included not only Libya, Iran, and North Korea but also such countries as Egypt, Saudi Arabia, Malaysia, Indonesia, Algeria, Kuwait, China (which remained in need of new enrichment techniques to replace its outdated technology), Sudan, Nigeria, and Brazil.[31]

Dr. Khan appeared to have sold his plans and designs with the blessing of the Pakistani government of Pervez Musharraf. Throughout his travels, Khan has been awarded the due honors of protocol as an official representative of the Pakistani Foreign Office, and he has always been accompanied by senior serving scientists of Pakistan's nuclear achievement.[32] What's more, his sales brochures—the glossy, four-color publications from his research facility—bear the official seal of the government of Pakistan.[33] The brochures offer a variety of hard-to-find sales items, including "starter kits" for uranium enrichment; P-1, P-2, and P-3 centrifuge designs; blueprints for nuclear weapons; and consulting services for assembly and repair. What terror chief or aspiring dictator with a few million to spare could resist the temptation of making a purchase or two?

Such publications forced US officials and weapons experts to conclude that the greatest threat to national security comes not from Iran and North Korea but rather from America's newest ally. Robert Gallucci, a former UN weapons inspector and dean of Georgetown University's School of Foreign Service, said: "Bad as it is with Iran, North Korea, and Libya having nuclear-weapons material, the worst part is that they could transfer it to a non-state group. That's the biggest concern and the scariest about all this—that Pakistan could work with the worst terrorist groups on earth to build nuclear weapons. The most dangerous country for the U.S. now is Pakistan, and the second is Iran. We haven't been this vulnerable since the British burned Washington in 1814."[34]

CHAPTER EIGHT

KING KHAN

Dr. A. Q. Khan is my hero. He always was and still is, because he made Pakistan a nuclear power. If all the nuclear powers of the world are reviewed from the start, all of them established themselves through the underworld. We have also acquired it [nuclear capability] through the underworld. India has also acquired it through the underworld.

Pervez Musharraf, president of Pakistan, 2004

The plan is going ahead, and, God willing, it is being implemented. But it is a huge task, which is beyond the will and comprehension of human beings. If God's help is with us, this will happen within a short period of time; keep in mind this prediction. . . . We are hopeful for God's help. The real matter is the extinction of America. And, God willing, it [America] will fall to the ground.

Mullah Mohammed Omar, November 14, 2001

117

Saudi Arabia certainly supplied much of the funding for Pakistan's nuclear program under Dr. Khan, as confirmed by [Pakistani] Prime Minister [Zulfiqar Ali] Bhutto's press adviser, Khalid Hasan. In 1999, the Saudi defense minister, Prince Sultan, was given a tour of Pakistan's nuclear program at which time he invited Dr. Khan to visit Saudi Arabia. After Dr. Khan's visit to the desert kingdom, a Saudi nuclear expert declared, "Saudi Arabia must take plans aimed at making a quick response to face the possibilities of nuclear warfare agents being used against the Saudi population, cities, or armed forces." Over the past decade, Riyadh has given Islamabad roughly $1.2 billion worth of oil annually, for which it has not been paid.

Graham Allison, *Nuclear Terrorism: The Ultimate Preventable Catastrophe*

N o one could quibble about Dr. Khan's price. For $100 million, a well-heeled terrorist or banana republic dictator could purchase centrifuge technology for the production of highly enriched uranium, designs for state-of-the-art nuclear bombs, and ongoing technical support and assistance from Khan and his team of highly skilled Pakistani scientists. Caches of conventional weapons were more expensive. Saudi Arabia shelled out $2 billion in 1989 for twenty Chinese CSS-s intermediate-range missiles and twenty launchers.[1] And this weaponry was outdated and relatively unreliable.

IRAN STARTS TO GLOW

Dr. Khan's first customer was Iran. The sale to the mullahs purportedly was arranged by General Aslam Beg, a former Pakistani army chief, who sought to establish an Iranian-Afghan-Pakistani alliance that would operate in "strategic defiance" of the West. Such an alliance, Beg believed, could best be forged by nuclear cooperation.[2] Negotiations began in 1989, nine years before Pakistan successfully tested five atomic bombs beneath the scorched hills of the Baluchistan desert.

By 1990 the first shipment of centrifuges began to arrive in Iran. Khan thought he had performed a coup. After all, the P-1 centrifuges, which he unloaded on Iran, were of the old design that had been built with aluminum. But Khan wanted to keep his customers pleased and happy. For this reason, he personally agreed to supervise the building of a cascade of thirty thousand centrifuges (a task that no Iranian was equipped to perform) at the Bushehr Nuclear Power Plant. What's more, he also reportedly oversaw the construction of nuclear facilities in Arak and Natanz.[3] And eventually Dr. Khan was even kind enough to replace the outdated technology by teaching the Iranians ways of using maraging steel to replace the aluminum so that the cascades could produce uranium-235 faster and more efficiently for the creation of a nuclear arsenal.

IRAQ HOLDS BACK

In 1990, to show his lack of Islamic bias, Dr. Khan offered the same deal to Iran's deadliest enemy—Iraq. At the end of his ten-year war with Iran, Saddam Hussein had managed to squeak out a victory by a massive chemical bombing of the Iranian town of Oshnavieh.[4] But Saddam was strapped for cash. His war with Iran had been one of the longest (over eight years) and costliest (over $100 billion) conflicts of the twentieth century. He was unprepared to cough up the $100 million for Dr. Khan's technology. What's more, he had just completed a successful invasion of Kuwait and was preparing for the Arab and American reaction. For this reason, Saddam viewed the nuclear offer as bait to lure him into a trap with the United States over the matter of weapons of mass destruction.[5] To waylay this suspicion, Khan assured the Iraqi dictator that he could ensure any technical requirements and stave off any investigations from America and the United Nations by shipping the parts from Gulf Technical Industries, a company he owned in Dubai. Hussein, however, still refused to bite.[6]

KHAN, KOREA, AND THE KIMS

Next, Khan traveled to North Korea to peddle his atomic wares and received a very welcome reception from Kim Il Sung (the Great Leader). By 1992 Pakistan entered into a nuclear cooperation program with the communist country. North Korean scientists began working on the development of the Ghouri missiles from their No-Dong designs at Khan's facilities in Pakistan, and Pakistani scientists began working on the development of centrifuge technology at North Korea's top-secret Building 500 in Yambyon.[7]

The relationship with North Korea continued under Kim Jong Il (the Dear Leader), Kim Il's son, with Dr. Khan making thirteen trips to Pyongyang from 1998 to 2001. During his visits, he consulted with technicians from the Yambyon Uranium Enrichment Plant and instructed them in shortcuts that could be taken in the process of producing highly enriched uranium and plutonium.[8] By 2005 North Korea had emerged as the most formidable nation within President Bush's infamous "axis of evil" with an arsenal of eight atomic bombs.[9]

NUCLEAR GOODS FOR GADHAFI

By 1996 Dr. Khan was off to Libya to sell his goods to Colonel Muammar Gadhafi. The Libyan dictator wrote a check, and within a year the centrifuge components arrived at the Tajura Nuclear Research Center outside of Tripoli.[10]

Business, by this time, was so brisk for the scientists and technicians at the A. Q. Khan Research Laboratories that Dr. Khan decided to establish Scuomi Precision Engineering (SCOPE), a manufacturing factory for centrifuge components in Malaysia.[11]

Gadhafi's attempt to join the nuclear club came to a screeching halt when Italian officials intercepted a shipment of centrifuge parts from Malaysia to Libya in April 2003. Two months later, with UN officials from the International Atomic Energy Agency (IAEA) swarming around

Tripoli, Gadhafi announced that his country would abandon its nuclear program and dismantle its weapon sites. US and British specialists shipped Libya's most sensitive materials, equipment, and documentation to the United States. The shipments included uranium hexafluoride, missile guidance devices, the components for centrifuge technology, and a box of blueprints for ten-kiloton nuclear bombs.[12] When the IAEA examined the blueprints, they were horrified. "This was the first time we had ever seen a loose copy of a bomb design that clearly worked," one IAEA official told the *New York Times*, "and the question was: Who else had it? The Iranians? The Syrians? Al Qaeda?"[13]

A SHORT LIST OF KHAN'S CUSTOMERS

The world community could no longer turn a blind eye to Dr. Khan's activities. IAEA inspectors soon discovered that the mad metallurgist had made sales not only to Iran, North Korea, and Libya but also to Saudi Arabia, Sudan, and Nigeria. And there were other customers on his list, including Algeria, Kuwait, Myanmar, and Abu Dhabi.[14] To make matters worse, investigative journalists had amassed evidence that agents of Pakistan's Inter-Service Intelligence (ISI) executed American reporter Daniel Pearl because the journalist had obtained information concerning meetings between Dr. Khan and bin Laden and evidence of the trafficking of nuclear supplies and materials from Khan's research facility near Islamabad to an al Qaeda laboratory in the North-West Frontier Province of Pakistan.[15]

MUSHARRAF'S DILEMMA

President Musharraf was up to his neck in a political quagmire. Dr. Khan was a hallowed figure in Pakistan, where his birthday was sanctified in mosques.[16] Khan was the only Pakistani to receive his country's highest civilian award—the Nishan-i-Imtiaz—on two separate occasions. "Anything said or done against this scientist," Rajesh Kumar Mishra of the South Asia Analysis Group pointed out, "would be considered anti-Pakistan, anti-Islam, and intolerable."[17]

What could Musharraf do? If he arrested the scientist, there would be political turmoil and religious upheaval throughout Pakistan that could result in the toppling of his government. How could he placate the West without offending the common populace? Musharraf attempted to walk upon eggshells by retiring Dr. Khan as head of Pakistan's nuclear programs and appointing him as a "special presidential advisor."[18]

The ploy didn't work. Dr. Khan's demotion was decried by Nawaz Sharif, the former prime minister, as a hideous conspiracy between Musharraf and the Bush administration to roll back Pakistan's nuclear program and to weaken the country's defenses.[19] Musharraf attempted to put a positive spin on his decision by saying: "Nations cannot afford to sit on their laurels. Success must be reinforced. New ideas and new blood must be injected. I always believed that transition must be effected smoothly so that there is no dislocation of objectives. Giving any other color or meaning to my decision is unfair."[20]

KHAN'S CARNIVAL ACT

On February 4, 2004, Dr. Khan appeared on Pakistani TV to issue a statement in which he confessed that he had sold his centrifuge technology to Libya, Iran, and North Korea. He expressed "the deepest sense of sorrow and anguish" that he had placed Pakistan's national security in jeopardy. "I have much to answer for it," he said.[21] In the spirit of goodwill, Pakistan's Federal Cabinet and President Musharraf, who also appeared on camera, immediately responded by granting the humbled metallurgist a full pardon for selling state secrets and promoting nuclear proliferation throughout the globe. Musharraf said that Dr. Khan, and the scientists who worked with him, had been motivated solely by "money."[22]

The public confession and presidential pardon, according to many observers, represented the Pakistani version of a "dog and pony" carnival act in which Musharraf attempted to appease both Western observers and religious mullahs by having Khan recite a confession to his crimes and granting him absolution without any act of contrition. Seymour Hersh described the event as follows:

> It was a make-believe performance in a make-believe capital. In interviews last month in Islamabad, a planned city built four decades ago, politicians, diplomats, and nuclear experts dismissed the Khan confession and the Musharraf pardon with expressions of scorn and disbelief. For two decades, journalists and American and European intelligence agencies have linked Khan and the Pakistani intelligence service, the I.S.I. (Inter-Service Intelligence), to nuclear-technology transfers, and it was hard to credit the idea that the government Khan served had been oblivious. "It is state propaganda," Samina Ahmed, the director of the Islamabad office of the International Crisis Group, a nongovernmental organization that studies conflict resolution, told me. "The deal is that Khan doesn't tell what he knows. Everybody is lying. The tragedy of this whole affair is that it doesn't serve anybody's needs." Mushahid Hussain Sayed, who is a member of the Pakistani senate, said with a laugh, "America needed an offering to the gods—blood on the floor. Musharref told A.Q., 'Bend over for a spanking.'"[23]

As of this writing, the Musharraf government has forbidden any Western reporter or foreign intelligence official the right to question Dr. Khan, Dr. Mahmood, Dr. Majid, and other members of the Pakistani nuclear community about their dealings with rogue nations and al Qaeda. Surely, this refusal is incomprehensible on the grounds of the sheer magnitude of the matter. Khan and company could provide the details of the nuclear operations in Iran, North Korea, and a host of other countries—all hostile to the West. In addition, they could disclose the plans of the American Hiroshima and the types of nuclear weapons within the al Qaeda arsenal.

KHAN AND THE CIA

Why has the Bush administration failed to press Pakistan for the right of interrogation? Khan had traveled to eighteen countries to peddle his nuclear technology. He had established a factory with hundreds of workers to manufacture centrifuge components in Malaysia and a large shipping company in Saudi Arabia. His accomplices had set up nuclear facilities in such diverse places as Burma and Sudan. If no intelligence had been gathered by the United States during Khan's twenty years of nuclear proliferation, then the intelligence level of the officials at the Central Intelligence Agency would have been dull to moronic at best. The only other explanation is that such officials knew about the wholesale nuclear proliferation and opted to turn a blind eye to Khan's activities.

This latter interpretation, seemingly bizarre, is, nevertheless, supported by investigative findings. In 1974 Dr. Khan, after receiving a PhD in metallurgical engineering from the Catholic University of Leuven in Belgium, accepted a position with the Physical Research Laboratory in the Netherlands.[24] The Physical Research Laboratory served as a subcontractor for Ultra Centrifuge Nederland (Urenco). One of Khan's tasks was to translate German documents dealing with highly classified German centrifuge technology into Dutch for Urenco. As soon as he completed this assignment, Khan shoved copies of the classified blueprints and the names of one hundred subcontractors and suppliers of Urenco into an attaché case and fled into the night to Pakistan in order to help his homeland become a nuclear power.

Before his flight, Khan had been under surveillance by Dutch intelligence. The Dutch realized that the Pakistani scientist was in the process of pilfering top-secret documents and decided to confer with CIA officials before making an arrest. The CIA, in turn, advised the Dutch authorities neither to collar Khan nor to request his extradition from Pakistan. The prevailing opinion from the United States, according to Ruud Lubbers, a former Dutch prime minister, was that a cat-and-mouse policy would serve the best interest of the NATO

nations. "I think the American intelligence agency put into practice
what is very common there; just give us all the information and do not
arrest the man; just let him go ahead. We will have him followed and
that way gain more information," Lubbers said in a recent interview
with VPRO Argos Radio.[25]

The results of this decision were disastrous. "My long stay in
Europe and intimate knowledge of various countries and their manufacturing firms was an asset," Dr. Khan would later recall. "Within two
years we had put up working prototypes of centrifuges and were going
at full speed to build the facilities at Kahuta."[26]

COVERT AID AND LOST RECORDS

The CIA position appears to have been grounded in the belief that Pakistan and Afghanistan were key allies for the West in the struggle against
the Soviet Union. For this reason, the United States, shortly after the
Khan heist, began to provide munitions and money to the *mujahadeen*,
including Osama bin Laden, to tip the scales against the Red Army. By
1988 the annual amount of US dollars flowing to the Afghan Arabs
exceeded $700 million. By this time, the CIA was even shipping Ten-
nessee mules to Afghanistan to carry all the weapons into the hills.[27]
The CIA also provided training to Pakistan's Inter-Services Intelligence on techniques for covert operations.[28] "This was part of a long-
term foolish strategy," says Anwar Iqbal, the Washington correspondent for the Pakistani newspaper *Dawn*. "The U.S. knew Pakistan was
developing nuclear weapons but couldn't care less because they were
not going to be used against them. It was a deterrent against India and
possibly the Soviets."[29]

In 1986 Dutch authorities again came close to arresting Dr. Khan
and again the CIA advised them to allow the fugitive metallurgist to
act freely, even to slip in and out of Holland on several occasions.
"The man [Khan] was followed for almost ten years and obviously he
was a serious problem," Lubbers said. "But again I was told that the

secret services could handle it more effectively. The Hague did not have a final say in the matter. Washington did."[30]

When asked about the CIA's involvement in the case of Dr. Khan, Washington officials remained elusive. "It is not something I feel we really have anything to say about because it deals with events long in the past; it deals with intelligence matters and for those reasons, I don't have anything to say about it," said Adam Ereli, a US State Department deputy.[31]

The story of Khan and the CIA took another bizarre turn on September 10, 2005, when the Amsterdam court, which had sentenced Dr. Khan in absentia to four years in prison, announced that it had lost all of the legal documents dealing with the case of "the godfather of nuclear proliferation."[32] Judge Anita Lesser, the court's vice president, voiced her suspicion that the CIA was involved in the missing files. "Something is not right, we don't lose things like them," she told Dutch news show *NOVA*. "I find it bewildering that people lose files with a political goal, especially if it is on request of the CIA. It is unheard of."[33]

PAKISTAN'S NEW DIRECTION

While Dr. Khan remained safe and secure, Pakistan completed building a thousand-megawatt reactor for producing plutonium, a move that signaled a major expansion of the country's nuclear program and a dramatic escalation in the region's arms race. Prior to the construction of the new reactor, Pakistan relied on a simpler, uranium-based warhead design. With the new facility, which was constructed in the heart of the Khushab district, Pakistan will be able to produce forty to fifty additional nuclear weapons a year.[34] The good doctor is a frequent visitor at the new facility.

KHAN'S BRAZILIAN CONNECTION

Other aspects of Khan's nuclear legacy continue to come to light. By 2003 IAEA inspectors from the United Nations reportedly discovered that the revered metallurgist had sold his centrifuge technology and designs for nuclear weapons to the Brazilian government of President Luiz Inácio Lula da Silva, affectionately known by his supporters as "Lula."

A lifetime Marxist and ally of Fidel Castro of Cuba and Hugo Chavez of Venezuela, Lula is the cofounder of the Forum of São Paulo, an organization that supports anti-US policies throughout the world.[35] He is also one of the sharpest critics of Operation Enduring Freedom (the US-led invasion of Afghanistan) and the war in Iraq.[36] "The United States," he said, "showed a total disrespect for Iraq and the rest of the world. It does not have the right to decide for itself what is good and what is bad for the world."[37]

While campaigning for the presidency, Lula criticized Brazil's compliance with the 1970 Nuclear Nonproliferation Treaty by saying: "I imagine this would make sense only if all the countries that already have nuclear weapons also gave them up. It is not fair that developed countries, which have nuclear weapons technology, demand that others not have them or deactivate what they have. All of us developing countries are left holding a slingshot while they have atomic bombs."[38]

As soon as he won the election, Lula launched a massive program to transform Brazil into a technological and military superpower. By 2004 his government announced that the Resende nuclear facility had achieved the ability to enrich uranium by means of ultracentrifugation.[39]

The news sent shock waves through the Western world, which remained transfixed on nuclear developments in Iran and North Korea. The then secretary of state Colin Powell made a visit to Brazil to meet with officials from Lula's government and expressed his confidence that Brazil possessed no plans to develop nuclear weapons. Powell's proclamation rang hollow and did little to allay fears that Brazil was one of Dr. Khan's leading clients and that the Latin American country was well on its way to producing an arsenal of nuclear weapons.

Indeed, *Science* magazine predicted that Brazil by 2007 might be capable of producing five to six warheads a year.[40]

Such suspicions were intensified by Lula's refusal to grant IAEA inspectors from the UN the right to conduct a full inspection of the Resende facility.[41] The inspectors were merely permitted to view parts of the centrifuge process, while other parts were kept under wraps.[42] "They [the IAEA inspectors] are specifically worried about the Khan network being one of the sources of the program," said Henry Sokolski, former Pentagon official and head of the Nonproliferation Policy Education Center in Washington, DC. "I can't tell you how I know, but I know."[43]

How did Lula become one of Dr. Khan's nuclear customers? The question baffled White House officials since there appeared to be no traceable link between Brazil and Pakistan. The answer came in the person of Khalil bin Laden, Osama's younger brother.

OSAMA'S BAD BABY BROTHER

Khalil bin Laden owns a twenty-acre estate in Winter Garden, Florida, where he lived with his Brazilian wife until September 20, 2001, when he boarded a chartered jet plane, along with fourteen other members of the bin Laden family, and departed for Saudi Arabia. The flight was approved by the Bush administration and represented an effort to safeguard "innocent" Arabs from the backlash of 9/11.[44] However, Khalil, like several of the others involved in Operation Arab Airlift, was not an innocent Saudi. Several weeks after the US State Department waved good-bye to him at the airport, Bosnian police seized documents from the Muslim Benevolence International Foundation, a terrorist front in Sarajevo. One document contained a list of the top twenty financial supporters of al Qaeda throughout the world. Near the top of the list was the name of Khalil bin Laden.[45]

Investigators soon discovered that Khalil made frequent trips to the notorious Triangle of South America. The central city within the

Triangle is Ciudad Del Este, Paraguay, a smuggler's paradise and a major base for the shipment of Bolivian cocaine via hidden landing strips in the rain forest.[46] The second city is Foz do Iguaçu, Brazil, a haven for "hot" goods, including sophisticated weaponry, and radical Islam.[47] Puerto Iguaçu, Argentina, the third city, remains an ideal place for fugitives and international terrorists to acquire counterfeit documents, including Argentine passports.[48]

Khalil met on numerous occasions with representatives of al-Said Ali Hassan Mokhles and Mohamed Ali Aboul-Ezz al-Mahdi Ibrahim Soliman, the commanders of the South American al Qaeda cells. He also went on outings to Minas Gerias, the site of an al Qaeda training camp within the lush rain forests of Brazil, where he engaged in what Argentine and Brazilian officials call "suspicious business activities."[49]

The younger bin Laden came to develop close relationships with Brazilian officials and, in 1998, became Brazil's honorary consul to the Saudi Arabian city of Jeddah.[50] As an honorary consul, Khalil could offer wealthy Arabs choice Brazilian coffee and cannabis and the opportunity to invest in Brazilian beef and bauxite. He could offer Brazilian officials an invitation to confer with Dr. Khan and a chance to make their country a power to be reckoned with on the world stage.

While America remained transfixed by Iraq, Iran, and the deteriorating situation in the Middle East, the direst developments in the war on terror were occurring beneath the radar south of the border.

And nobody was paying attention.

CHAPTER NINE

HEZBOLLAH AND AL QAEDA MARRY IN SOUTH AMERICA

The period between 1991 and 1993—Osama bin Laden's formative years in Sudan—was critical for the Sunni Islamist movement. The Muslim world was slowly recovering from the shock of what is known in the West as the Gulf War. For the Muslim world, it was a traumatic experience in which the sacred all-Muslim unity was so shattered that Arab-Muslim states joined ranks with the hated West to fight and defeat another Arab-Muslim state.

Yossef Bodansky,
Bin Laden: The Man Who Declared War on America, 1999

The tri-border region of South America is the Hilton of Islamic extremism. It's been on the radar screen since the early '90s but no one's ever done anything about it.

Magnus Ranstorp, director of the
Centre for the Study of Terrorism,
University of St. Andrew, Fife, Scotland, 2003

I certainly wouldn't put it past al Qaeda to use Latin America as a route to place its assets in the United States.
                Former CIA director James Woolsey, November 2, 2001

I t is an event known as al-Azma or "the crisis" among Muslims. It represents one of the cataclysmic events in the history of Islam. This event, the so-called Persian Gulf War under the administration of President George H. W. Bush, is superceded in importance only by al-Naqbi or "the calamity," that is, the creation of the state of Israel in 1949.

Al-Azma was precipitated by Saddam Hussein's invasion of Kuwait. The Iraqi dictator believed that the invasion was justified. Indeed, he had a long list of grievances against the Kuwaiti emir, Amir Jaber al-Ahmad al-Jaber al-Sabah. The emir had pilfered $2.4 billion in oil from the Rumdia oil field—an Iraqi oil field—and had refused to forgive Iraq's sizable debt to his country, even though he had called upon Hussein as the "sword of Islam" to protect his oil reserves from a Shiite rebellion. Saddam had protected Kuwait. He had defeated Iran at an incredible cost to Iraqi resources and Kuwait had responded with niggardly ingratitude.[1]

What's more, Hussein, although far from a Muslim saint, believed that the grossly overweight emir was utterly decadent. Iraqi newspapers throughout 1990 carried front-page stories about al-Sabah's sex life. The stories, although lacking objective verification, held that the emir was syphilitic, kept seventy wives in his harem, and married a virgin every Thursday.[2]

On August 2, 1990, a half million Iraqi troops marched across the border and occupied Kuwait. It had been a cakewalk. The Iraqis had met with no resistance. Emir al-Sabah and members of his government fled to Saudi Arabia for protection. Five days later the Iraqi army moved toward the Saudi border.[3]

AL-AZMA: THE CAUSE OF IT ALL

This development almost caused President George H. W. Bush to cough up his spoonful of Wheaties. He feared that Hussein, who manifested signs of paranoid schizophrenia, would invade Saudi Arabia, roll south to absorb all the oil fields in the Persian Gulf, and, thereby, realize his dream of creating a new Babylonian Empire.[4] Within a matter of hours, Bush managed to obtain a UN resolution that condemned the invasion and called for an immediate withdrawal of Iraqi forces. Hussein, quite naturally, ignored it.[5]

Within a week of the invasion, Saudi king Fahd accepted a proposal from President Bush, presented to him by Secretary of Defense Dick Cheney, to defend the kingdom with a coalition of military forces. The Saudis had always depended upon military aid from *kafir* (unbeliever) nations. They were first protected by the British, then the Americans, who maintained an air base at Dhahran from 1946 to 1962, and finally by the French, who were called upon to suppress the seizure of the Great Mosque in Mecca from a group of fanatics in 1979.[6]

But this intervention called not for the maintenance of a peacetime air base or the use of foreign troops to crush a rebellion. President Bush's plan, which became known as Operation Desert Shield, involved the establishment of permanent military bases in the desert kingdom. One base was constructed within the nearly deserted eighty-square-mile Prince Sultan air base. The Americans set up temper tents equipped with air conditioners and environmental liners to hold in the cool or to contain the heat, along with lights and plugs. They also built mess quarters, showers, and toilet facilities. The base became known as "Al's Garage."[7] A second base was erected sixty miles south of Riyadh. It came to include a tent city, four kitchens, an air transportation hospital, six K-span structures (clamshell buildings for aviation maintenance), munitions storage units, bladder berms for fuel containment, and utility distribution centers.[8] Throughout the summer and fall of 1990, giant US C-130 transporters landed at airstrips throughout Saudi Arabia to discharge hundreds of tanks, trucks, artillery transport vehicles, and jeeps.[9] Long lines of US troops, including uniformed women in combat fatigues, walked the highway between the two holy cities of Mecca and Medina.

A BONEHEADED BOO-BOO

In 1990 the US intelligence budget exceeded fifty billion dollars, with six billion going to the CIA. But not one intelligence official bothered to ask an expert on the Middle East (such as Bernard Lewis) if the establishment of bases in the Saudi kingdom was a good idea. Such an expert, no doubt, would have told the official: "That's the stupidest idea I've ever heard! If you aren't a Muslim, you can't take up residence in Saudi Arabia, even if you are a movie star, a retired diplomat, a close friend of King Fahd, or a reclusive billionaire. Only Muslims, by law, can live in the land of the holy prophet. If you happen to die in Saudi Arabia, the Arabs won't allow your body to be buried within their sacred soil. Your rotting carcass will be shipped back to the States. But you're talking about deploying thousands of troops to permanent military installations. Anyone who knows anything about Islam will tell you that such a measure will result in serious trouble. And by trouble, I mean a jihad that could go on for centuries."[10]

Sure enough, the *ummah*, the pious community of Muslim believers, was outraged, and the *mujahadeen* seethed with righteous indignation. Bin Laden wrote: "The Arabian Peninsula has never—since Allah made it flat, created its desert, and encircled it with seas—been stormed by any forces like the Crusader armies now spreading in it like locusts, consuming and destroying its plantations. All of this is happening at a time when nations are attacking Muslims like people fighting over a plate of food."[11]

BIN LADEN GETS THE BOOT

Bin Laden began circulating pamphlets and making speeches to decry the "American invasion." Sheikh Safar ibn Abd al-Rahman al-Hawali, Sheikh Salman bin Fahd al-Awda, and other clerics and scholars who joined in the protest were rounded up and cast into Saudi prisons.[12]

In the fall of 1991, Saudi security police discovered evidence that bin Laden was engaged in an attempt to mount an armed rebellion against the royal family because of the American occupation.[13] King Fahd and the royal princes had had enough of the fanatical hothead and, despite pleas from bin Laden's influential friends and family members, they froze his financial assets and ordered his exile.

Bin Laden departed for Sudan, which proved to be a perfect place to establish his terrorist organization. Sudan had abandoned visa requirements for Arabs and had encouraged Muslim militants from around the world to settle within its borders. By the end of 1991, approximately two thousand al Qaeda operatives had moved to Sudan and set up scores of training camps for new recruits, the main one being a twenty-acre site near Soba, seven miles south of Khartoum.[14]

AL-TURABI'S VISION

In Sudan, Bin Laden formed a fast friendship with Hassan Abdallah al-Turabi, one of the world's leading Islamic writers. A Sorbonne educated scholar, al-Turabi had transformed the Muslim Brotherhood of Sudan into the National Islamic Front, a political party that came to power in 1989 under strongman Brigadier General Omar Bashir. As the speaker of Sudan's parliament and Bashir's puppeteer, al-Turabi sought to transform the North African country into a shining example of an Islamic state, where *shariah* (Islamic law) prevailed and where Sunnis could unite with Shiites in the holy war against Western civilization.[15]

The division between Sunnis, who constitute 80 percent of the world's Muslims, and Shiites, who make up 15 percent, was created by the assassination of Ali, the Prophet Muhammad's son-in-law in 661. For thirteen centuries, the two factions remained antagonistic to one another. Wars between them broke out at regular intervals, most notably in the struggle between the Sunni Abbasids and the Shiite Fatimas for control of Arabia, Egypt, and Syria. The bloody conflict persisted throughout the twentieth century. Indeed, the situation between the two groups became so open and uncontained that violence erupted within the holy city of Mecca on July 31, 1987, during the annual *hajj*, in an incident that left 480 pilgrims dead.[16]

The first step toward a real reconciliation appears to have been made by the magnanimous Dr. Khan, a Sunni, who had sold his centrifuge technology to representatives of Ayatollah Khomeini, the Shiite grand cleric, making it possible for Iran to emerge as a nuclear power at the dawn of the twenty-first century.

In 1991 al-Turabi took the second step by forming the Popular International Organization (PIO). Its purpose was "to challenge and defy the tyrannical West, because Allah can no longer remain in our world in the face of the absolute materialistic power."[17] As the permanent head of the PIO, he believed he could forge a theological compromise between the teachings of Sunni Egyptian Sayyid Mohammad Qutb (1906–1966) and Ayatollah Khomeini (1902–1989). The possibility of this compromise resulted in ongoing meetings between Sunni and Shiite religious leaders in Khartoum and Tehran.[18] At several gatherings, al-Turabi's new friend, Osama bin Laden, was in attendance.

A monumental development was taking place in the Muslim world, but few in the West were taking heed. The new spirit of rapprochement and reconciliation resulted in bin Laden making a series of calls from his Compact-M satellite phone to the Iranian Ministry of Intelligence and Security (MOIS) in which he offered to join forces with Shiite terrorist groups, including Hezbollah, for attacks on the United States and Israel.[19] Records of these calls were later discovered by the CIA and US military officials during their investigation of al Qaeda's 1998 bombings of the American embassies in Kenya and Tanzania. The stage was now set for the fateful encounter between bin

Laden and Imad Fayez Mugniyah, the founder and senior officer of Hezbollah.

MUGNIYAH: INVISIBLE MAN

Other than the place and date of Mugniyah's birth (Tayr Dibbuh, near Tyre, on July 12, 1962), little is known about him, save that his father, Sheikh Muhammad Jawah Mugniyah, gained esteem in Lebanon as a leading Shiite scholar. Only two photographs of Imad Mugniyah are known to exist, and both have been called into question. What's more, the elusive Shiite leader undergoes regular plastic surgical procedures to alter his appearance.[20] US intelligence sources believe that he is of medium height (approximately five feet seven) and weighs between 145 and 150 pounds. Such sources, however, are even uncertain about the color of Mugniyah's eyes.

According to Robert Baer, the ex–CIA officer who spent many years tracking Mugniyah, even the most basic details of his childhood and education remain a mystery. "Mugniyah systematically had all traces of himself removed," Baer told the *New Yorker*. "He erased himself. He had his records removed from his high school and his passport application was stolen. There are no civil records in Lebanon with his name on them."[21]

In 1985 Mugniyah set forth the political platform of Hezbollah as follows:

1. The solution to Lebanon's problems is the establishment of an Islamic regime as the only government that can secure justice and equality for all of Lebanon's citizens.
2. The Hezbollah organization views as an important goal the fight against Western Imperialism and its eradication from Lebanon. The group strives for complete American and French withdrawal from Lebanon, including all their institutions.
3. The conflict with Israel is viewed as a central concern. This is not

limited to the IDF [Israeli Defense Force] presence in Lebanon. Rather, the complete destruction of the State of Israel and the establishment of Islamic law over Jews is the expressed goal.[22]

ARM AND ARMY OF IRAN

The platform reflected the ideology of Ayatollah Khomeini, the revered Shiite leader of the Islamic Revolution in Iran, who upheld a vision of a pan-Islamic theocracy to be headed by Islamic clerics. Hezbollah (the "Party of God") was one of the ayatollah's creations— a terrorist organization that could serve as a vanguard for the opposition against the invading Israeli army in Lebanon, where, Khomeini believed, the second phase of his glorious revolution was destined to take place. From the time of its inception in 1982, Hezbollah has been armed and trained by the Islamic Republic of Iran through its Revolutionary Guard. It has been well oiled and equipped by financial aid in excess of $100 million a year from the Iranian government.[23] Such support for Hezbollah continued after the 1997 election of President Muhammed Khatami, who campaigned on a platform of tolerance and social reform, and through the 2005 election of President Mahmoud Ahmadinejad, who campaigned on a platform of intolerance and a return to the teachings of Imam Ali.[24] Because of its hefty funding, Hezbollah represents not only a paramilitary group of religious fanatics but also an organization that runs schools, sports clubs, hospitals, agricultural co-ops, and veterans' homes. Hezbollah has its own green and gold flag that has flown in more homes and business establishments throughout Lebanon than the Lebanese flags, along with its own award-winning radio station (Al-Nour), a highly successful daily newspaper (*Al-Ahed*), and a slickly operated and highly popular television channel (Al-Manar).[25]

HEZBOLLAH'S GIFT TO GLOBAL WARFARE

But terror remains the Shiite group's claim to fame. On April 18, 1984, Imad Mugniyah made his first appearance on the FBI's "Most Wanted List" by masterminding the bombing of the US embassy in Lebanon. The bombing was remarkable in its economy and efficiency. It had been performed by a single operative, who smashed into the embassy with a truck packed with explosives. The blast killed sixty-three people, including seventeen Americans.[26] It represented the advent of Mugniyah's contribution to the art of guerrilla warfare: the suicide bomber.

Six months later, on October 23, another suicide bomber in another truck packed with explosives ploughed into the US Marine barracks outside the Beirut International Airport. The bomb produced the largest nonnuclear explosion in history with a yield equivalent to twenty thousand pounds of TNT. It killed 220 Marines and 21 other American servicemen.[27] Several hours later, a third suicide bomber struck at the headquarters of the French paratroopers in Beirut, leaving fifty-eight dead in a mound of rubble.[28]

As a complement to the bombings, Mugniyah initiated a host of other innovative acts of terrorism, including the kidnapping of eighteen American officials. Three were tortured and killed, including William Buckley, the head of the CIA in Beirut.[29]

By 1985, three short years after the formation of Hezbollah, Mugniyah could relish the incredible results of his organization: the withdrawal of American forces from Beirut, the resignation of Israeli prime minister Menachem Begin, and the retreat of Israeli troops from southern Lebanon. As a Shiite warrior, he had proven himself a worthy successor to Hassan-i-Sabah, the fabled "Old Man of the Mountains," who had organized the "assassins" during the twelfth century. Mugniyah had accomplished more than such mighty Muslim rulers as President Gamal Abdel Nasser of Egypt, King Hussein of Jordan, and President Hafez Assad of Syria. He and his "Party of God" had defeated the mightiest military force the Middle East had ever seen.

TERRORISM UNITED IN IRAN

The first meeting between Mugniyah and bin Laden took place in 1995 at the headquarters of Ali Numeini, a Sudanese sheikh, in Khartoum.[30] Other meetings followed, leading to a financial agreement concerning the flow of heroin from Afghanistan to Turkey through the northern region of Iran.

From June 21 to 23, 1996, Iran's Supreme Council for Intelligence Affairs sponsored a terror summit in Tehran in order to transform Hezbollah into "Hezbollah International," the new vanguard of Ayatollah Khomeini's Islamic Revolution that would coordinate the activities of Sunni and Shiite organizations involved in the great struggle against the West. It attracted terror leaders from various places throughout the world, including Ramadan Shallah (the Palestinian Islamic Jihad), Ahmad Salah (Egyptian Islamic Jihad), Imad al-Alami and Mustafa al-Liddawi (Hamas), Ahmad Jibril (Popular Front for the Liberation of Palestine), Abdallah Ocalan (the Kurdish People Party), Muhammad Ali Ahmad (al Qaeda), and Imad Mugniyah.[31] The summit resulted in the creation of the "Committee of Three" that would meet on a regular basis for the "coordination, planning and execution of attacks" against the United States and Israel. The committee members were Ahmad Salah, Imad Mugniyah, and bin Laden. The first meeting of the committee rubber-stamped three terror operations that were already in the works: the bombing of the US barracks in al-Khobar, Dhahran (for bin Laden); the stabbing of a US female diplomat (for Salah); and the downing of TWA Flight 800 (for Mugniyah)—which according to the NTSB was due to a mechanical error.[32] The new spirit of cooperation among the terrorist groups would result in bin Laden's "Declaration of War against the Americans Occupying the Land of the Two Holy Places" on August 23, 1996.

RADICAL ISLAM INVADES LATIN AMERICA

In 1995, as a result of the coming together of Sunni and Shiite jihadists, al Qaeda arrived in America. It was an event that would not have occurred without the meeting of bin Laden and Mugniyah and the grandiose vision of al-Turabi. Hezbollah had been the first terrorist group to venture forth to the New World by establishing a base within Foz do Iguaçu, Brazil, in 1983. It represented an ideal place to train raw recruits and to raise money for the struggle in Lebanon. Not only was the jungle city remote from scrutiny by American and Israeli intelligence but it also benefited from the Brazilian government's recognition of Hezbollah as a legitimate political party—thus making all contributions to the agency totally legitimate.[33]

The new Hezbollah arrivals wasted no time in establishing contact with the drug cartels from Colombia, Paraguay, Uruguay, and Ecuador, along with paramilitary groups, including the Revolutionary Armed Forces of Colombia (FARC) and Peru's Sendero Luminosos ("Shining Star").[34] As money, munitions, and recruits flowed into its South American cell, Hezbollah began to launch major attacks on Jewish enclaves in Buenos Aires. An attack of March 17, 1977, on the Israeli embassy left 29 dead and 242 wounded; another against the AMIA Jewish Center on July 18, 1994, killed 86 and left 250 burned and maimed.[35]

OSAMA VISITS AMERICA

Osama bin Laden became the first member of his terrorist organization to venture forth to South America. He spent several days in the Triangle, worshiping at the mosques, visiting the Islamic centers, meeting with the local Hezbollah officials, and attending meetings with representatives from the drug cartels. News of his visit was first reported by CNN.[36] In the photographs that remain from the trip, bin Laden appears in his traditional *shalwat kameez* (the long loose-fitting shirt and baggy pants of the Afghan-Arab *mujahadeen*) with a well-trimmed goatee rather than the full beard he came to sport upon his return to Afghanistan.[37]

In the wake of bin Laden's visit, other leading al Qaeda figures made the trek to the Triangle, including Khalid Shaikh Mohammed. Proof of Khalid Mohammed's visit came with the confiscation of his passport at the time of his arrest in Karachi. The passport bears a Brazilian tourist visa, which shows that the al Qaeda military operations chief entered Brazil from Pakistan on December 4, 1995, and departed from Brazil for the Netherlands on Christmas Eve.[38]

During his three-week stay, Khalid Mohammed met with the local leaders of Hezbollah to make plans for attacks on the United States and Canada. One plan called for a series of terrorist attacks on synagogues, Jewish community centers, and landmark buildings in Ottawa in order "to undermine the Middle East peace process."[39] A second plan called for blowing up the Los Angeles International Airport on New Year's Eve 1999. Neither plan came to fruition, thanks largely to the arrest of Ahmed Ressam of Montreal, who was caught entering the United States from British Columbia with massive amounts of explosives.[40]

THE PLANTING OF THE CELLS

By 1996 al Qaeda, with Hezbollah's permission, established two cells within the Triangle. The first was placed under the command of al-Said Ali Hassan Mokhles, an operative who had been trained in special operations for fifteen months in Afghanistan. The commander of the second was Mohamed Ali Aboul-Ezz al-Mahdi Ibrahim Soliman, an Egyptian national and close friend of Ayman al-Zawahiri. From 1995 to 2002 Mokhles and Soliman kept in close contact with Khalid Mohammed and other members of the al Qaeda *Shura* (Planning Council). Copies of their communiqués were discovered by US officials within Khalid Mohammed's headquarters in Karachi.[41]

In 1997 the CIA had asked its counterparts in SIDE, Argentina's

Secretaria de Inteligencia del Estado (Secretariat for State Intelligence), to infiltrate the Triangle in order to obtain information on the workings of the Islamist extremist groups. During the course of the operation, which became known by the codename "Centauro," SIDE conducted comprehensive surveillance of the Sunni and Shiite terrorist cells by phone taps, mail interception, covert filming, and interrogation of hundreds of suspects. The evidence showed that al Qaeda was booming in Foz do Iguaçu. Within a year of their establishment, the two cells had raised millions for the jihad; manufactured thousands of counterfeit documents, including Argentine passports; and established a facility in the Brazilian province of Minas Gerias, hundreds of miles from the Triangle, for training new recruits.[42]

The relationship between the CIA and SIDE suffered a complete breakdown when US intelligence officials accused SIDE of leaking a photograph of Ross Newland, the CIA bureau chief in Buenos Aires, to a local newspaper.[43] Newland was recalled to the United States, the CIA's ties to SIDE were severed, and the evidence uncovered by Operation Centauro remained filed and forgotten.

Concerns about what was taking place south of the border were not even raised among US intelligence officials on September 3, 2001, when Abdel Fatta, a young Moroccan living in Foz do Iguaçu, gave a letter to his lawyer with instructions that it be delivered to the US embassy. The letter contained a warning about a series of attacks that were to take place in Washington, DC, and New York City the following week—on September 11, 2001.[44] Fatta, as it turned out, was an al Qaeda member who experienced a change of heart concerning the murder of innocent civilians. He remains, at this writing, within a Brazilian prison cell.

Known members of al Qaeda

(More information on these individuals is available at
http://www.fbi.gov/mostwant/terrorists/fugitives.htm.)

Osama bin Laden

Ayman al-Zawahiri

Anas al-Liby

Adnan G. el-Shukrijumah

Amer el-Maati

Abderraouf Jdey

Jaber A. Elbaneh

Faker Ben Abdelazziz

Jamal Ahmed al-Fadl

Mamdouh Salim

Islamberg in Hancock, New York
Photo courtesy of Douglas J. Hagman

Farouq Mosque in Brooklyn, New York
Photo courtesy of the FBI

A portable tactical nuclear device
Photo courtesy of the FBI

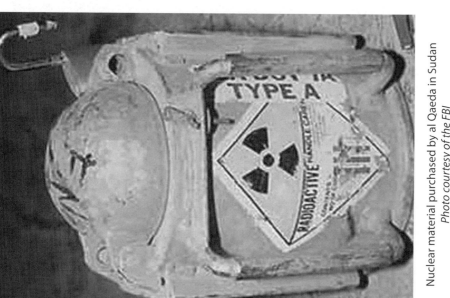

Nuclear material purchased by al Qaeda in Sudan
Photo courtesy of the FBI

CHAPTER TEN

THE CANCER SPREADS

*While the vast majority of illegals from the Middle East are not ter-
rorists, the fact that tens of thousands of people from that region—
and millions more from the rest of the world—can settle in the U.S.
illegally means that terrorists who wish to do the same face few
obstacles. We cannot protect ourselves from terrorism without
dealing with illegal immigration.*

Stephen A. Camarota, director of research,
Center for Immigration Studies, November 2001

*As a result of intermarriage and religious conversion, Islam has
become one of the fastest-growing faiths in Colombia and Latin
America. Growing disenchantment with the Roman Catholic Church
establishment in Colombia and elsewhere in the region has also led
many to seek spiritual guidance elsewhere. Many former Roman
Catholics that have strayed from the Church have come to see
Catholicism as a European colonial tradition that was imposed on
the peoples of the Americas. Therefore, conversion to Islam repre-*

sents an assertion of ethno-national, as well as spiritual, identity. Protestant missionaries have been making inroads into Latin America for many of the same reasons for decades, especially among underserved communities and indigenous populations
                                    Chris Zambelis, Jamestown Foundation, 2006

The two cells that had been implanted by al Qaeda in the belly of South America quickly metastasized so that the cancer of radical Islam spread throughout South America. One of the first locations to experience the malignancy was Pedro Juan Caballero on the northern border between Brazil and Paraguay—a jungle town known for its potent marijuana and absence of law enforcement.[1] A second was the Brazilian village of Chui, near the Uruguayan border, with a population of fifteen hundred Muslims and a mayor who allegedly served as an agent for bin Laden.[2] A third was the once sleepy town of Iquique in Chile, which almost overnight was transformed into a center of money-laundering activities by al Qaeda and other Muslim terrorist groups.[3]

THE PLAGUE HITS PARAGUAY AND PERU

Within Paraguay, immigration officials of the Silvio Petririosi International Airport in Asunción reported regular arrivals of hundreds of individuals from the Middle East with European passports. When questioned by the officials, the new arrivals were unable to communicate in the languages of the countries listed on their passports but could speak fluent Arabic.[4] Despite this discrepancy, they were allowed to enter the country. Most generally gravitate toward the Triangle or settle in Asunción. In order to escape from surveillance by Mossad and other intelligence agencies, leaders of al Qaeda cells in Asunción purportedly meet with leaders of other radical Islamic groups in churches and cathedrals where they present themselves not as pious Muslims but as part of the Roman Catholic community.[5]

But bin Laden came to favor Peru over Brazil and Paraguay. By 1998 he had purchased a host of homes, offices, and apartment buildings in cities throughout the country to serve as safe havens and bases of operation for his terrorist network. He made these purchases with the help and assistance of Vladmiro Montesinos, the former head of Peruvian intelligence. In one of the secretly recorded conversations that led to the intelligence chief's arrest on charges of money laundering, bribery, and terrorism, Montesinos told the mayor of the port city of Callao that "bin Laden's center of importance is here in Lima."[6] He went on to explain that the al Qaeda base in Lima had been established "to act against Americans in Argentina, Brazil, Chile, and the rest of South America."[7] By the close of 2001, Peruvian authorities realized that the corrupt spy chief had received millions for his assistance from the al Qaeda cells throughout his country.[8]

Bin Laden's investment in Peru was well spent. In 2002 Peruvian and US officials intercepted a criminal network with ties to al Qaeda that smuggled radical Islamists into the United States after giving them fake identification papers in Lima. Three Iraqis with the phony papers were arrested in Detroit, where they already had become naturalized US citizens, and four Jordanians with similar counterfeit documents were collared in Peru.[9] Linda Sesi, an assistant ombudsman for the city of Detroit, was collared on charges of smuggling more than two hundred migrants from Iraq, Jordan, and other Middle Eastern countries between 2001 and 2005. She and others in the network allegedly charged clients more than six thousand dollars for tourist visas to Peru, where they obtained fake papers and then flew them to Dulles Airport outside Washington, DC.[10]

TUMORS SPROUT IN BOLIVIA AND ECUADOR

From Peru, the malignancy spread to Bolivia and Ecuador. In 2002 Bolivian officials arrested nine Bangladeshis who were involved in an attempt to hijack a jumbo jet for an attack on a US target in Argentina.

The Bangladeshis were members of a virulent al Qaeda cell in La Paz with tentacles throughout the country and ties to Bolivia's drug cartels.[11] The cancer in Ecuador was evidenced by the case of Lago Agrio, a once-picturesque village in a tropical rain forest that became transformed into a fetid dump in the wake of years of oil drilling and exploration, purportedly by American oil interests. From 1964 to 1992 these oilmen reportedly spilled eighteen billion gallons of toxic waste throughout the flora, fauna, and waterways.[12] The polluted village, with its rotting infrastructures and lack of law enforcement, no longer could attract oil speculators, international entrepreneurs, or wealthy American tourists. But it represented an ideal breeding ground for al Qaeda. Environmental pollution gave way to Islamic terrorism as Lago Agrio, with its population of twenty-eight thousand, experienced an influx of thousands of holy warriors from the Triangle and the Middle East. By 2001 the village had transmogrified into a center for drug trafficking, arms dealing, smuggling, and money laundering—and with a murder rate of one to two hundred a year, it was one of the most dangerous places on planet earth.[13]

THE CANCER INFECTS COLOMBIA

Hundreds of al Qaeda operatives moved north from Peru and the Triangle to Colombia, where they took up residence with false identification papers. According to General Russo José Cerraro, Colombia's former chief of police, they came to oversee the planting, cultivation, and harvesting of poppy fields and to set up laboratories for the processing of raw opium paste into choice Number Four heroin. The poppy fields throughout the Colombian mountains came to bear an exact resemblance to the fields in Afghanistan, reflecting the symbiotic relationship between radical Islam and organized crime.[14]

Throughout Colombia, authorities witnessed massive conversions of Catholics to Islam. The conversions were precipitated by unemployment, galloping inflation, and an increase in political corruption and organized crime—all of which served to engulf Colombia in a dangerous cauldron. Chris Zambelis of the Jamestown Foundation explained this development as follows:

> *Colombian Christians who become Muslims find solace in Islam's reverence of Jesus Christ and Mary. Other Muslim converts see Islam as a native tradition untainted by the region's colonial experience. Many Muslims in Colombia also emphasize what they believe are their natural cultural and even ethnic links with Arabs and Muslims, stemming from Spain's Moorish heritage. In this regard, conversion to Islam symbolizes a reversion to their original state, which they see as having been suppressed by colonialism. There is also evidence suggesting that Colombian Muslims are becoming more open about asserting their identity, especially since Bogota abolished Catholicism as the official state religion in an effort to promote a broader definition of Colombian identity.*[15]

THE METASTASIS UNCHECKED

Radical Islam also reared its hoary head in other places throughout Latin America, including French Guiana, Guyana, Tobago, and Trinidad. The case of Surinam, a country the size of the state of Georgia with a population of 437,000, is particularly telling. By 2005 more than 40 percent of the population had become Muslim. Cells of Shiite and Sunni terrorists, including Hezbollah and Jemaah Islamiyah (the group responsible for the 2002 Bali bombing), popped up throughout the countryside along with the mosques and minarets. Thanks to an invitation from bin Laden, the Chechen Mafia also set up shops in Surinam, where the price of an AK-47 became a kilo of cocaine.[16]

VENEZUELA FALLS VICTIM

But no place in the Western Hemisphere represented a greater threat to the United States and the Western world than Venezuela. On January

5, 2003, Venezuelan air force major Juan Diaz Castillo, the personal pilot of Venezuelan president Hugo Chavez, admitted that Chavez had awarded al Qaeda a gift of one million dollars from the national treasury for the attacks of 9/11. The gift was reportedly bestowed to bin Laden through Walter Marquez, the Venezuelan ambassador to India.[17] This news was not surprising to observers of political developments in South America. On September 12, 2001, Chavez and thousands of his supporters celebrated the attacks on New York and Washington, DC, by burning the Stars and Stripes within Caracas's Plaza Bolivar.[18] When US-led forces invaded Afghanistan on October 7, 2001, Chavez condemned them as "imperialists" and "terrorists." To demonstrate his solidarity with radical Islam, Chavez, with his good friend Cuban president Fidel Castro, toured Iran, Iraq, and Libya, where Castro assured the cheering throngs: "Together we will bring America to its knees."[19]

Reports about Venezuela gradually became even more alarming. On February 13, 2004, a Muslim extremist was taken into custody at London's Gatwick Airport after a grenade was found in his luggage. His ticket showed that he had flown to London from Colombia. British officials later discovered that he was a Venezuelan who had been trained as part of an al Qaeda cell on Venezuela's Margarita Island, a place that had served as a favorite site for American tourists.[20] Bin Laden's agents were alive and well and operating less than a three-hour flight from Miami.

AN UNHOLY TRINITY

In the wake of the arrest, a covert team of British MI5 agents arrived in Venezuela to prevent the al Qaeda cell from running guns and cocaine into the United Kingdom. The agents discovered that shipments of highly sophisticated weapons were arriving on fishing boats for the Muslim terrorists and members of FARC off the virtually unguarded Venezuelan coastline. What's more, they discovered that the weapons, including surface-to-air missiles, were coming from North Korea.[21]

Chavez, as British and US intelligence officials later learned, was involved in establishing a "strategic alliance" with North Korea. The alliance called for Venezuela, the world's fifth-largest oil-producing country, to provide its energy resources to North Korea in exchange for conventional weapons, ballistic missiles, and, according to several intelligence reports, a supply of tactical nukes. Such shipments, Chavez believed, were essential in order to prepare for "asymmetrical war"—his reference to a plot by the US "empire" to overthrow his government.[22]

The possibility of a nuclear threat from Venezuela was intensified by Chavez's close relations with Iran, where he had received the country's highest state medal for supporting Tehran in its nuclear standoff with the United States. In 2005 Iranian geologists and scientists reportedly arrived in Venezuela to initiate plans for the extraction of large uranium deposits at various locations throughout the country.[23] Once this task is achieved, Venezuela will have taken its first step toward becoming a nuclear superpower. Some expect Chavez and his government will take the final step in this process before 2010.[24]

RADICAL ISLAM SPREADS TO MEXICO

Throughout these developments, radical Islam has been pressing closer and closer to the US border. In December 2003 Canadian intelligence officials and Interpol informed Mexican president Vicente Fox that al Qaeda had established a number of cells within his country to mount the next 9/11. "The alert has been sounded," José Luis Santiago Vasconcelos, Mexico's top anticrime prosecutor, told the Associated Press.[25]

But the alert did little to address the problem. In southern Mexico, hundreds of indigenous Tzozil Indians converted to Islam and reportedly became involved in subversive activities, including gun running and drug trafficking. President Fox said that he feared the Mayan unrest was a result of the growing influence of al Qaeda. Another

Mexican official spoke of the possibility of an impending culture clash and outbursts of violence.[26]

AL QAEDA AT THE BORDER

By 2004 cells of radical Islam sprouted throughout Mexico, including virulent cells of al Qaeda in the Rio Grande valley and the northern province of Sonora and a large cell of Hezbollah in Tijuana.[27] The Muslim radicals began to use Latino gangs, including Mara Salvatrucha, to shepherd them across the border into the United States. The going rate for such service ranged from $30,000 to $50,000 per client. The rate included safe passage over the border, shelter within the states, and, as a bonus, a bogus *matricular consular*.[28]

Matricular consulars are official identification cards that are issued by the Mexican government through its many consular offices. The cards verify that the holders are Mexican citizens who are living outside of Mexico with the government's permission. They may be used by Mexican nationals to open bank accounts, secure employment, and obtain driver's licenses and welfare benefits in the United States.[29] According to many US officials, the cards pose a serious threat to national security. Steve McCraw, assistant director of the FBI's Office of Intelligence, provided the following testimony to a House Judiciary Subcommittee in Washington on June 26, 2003: "The ability of foreign nationals to use the *matricular consular* provides an opportunity for terrorists to move freely within the United States without triggering name-based watch lists that are disseminated to local police officials."[30]

THE NEW BARBARIAN INVASION

Every day that President George W. Bush has occupied the White House, four thousand illegal aliens have entered the United States through the back door at the Mexican border—enough to fill sixty jumbo jetliners. This has amounted to a total of more than three million a year.[31] This invasion represents part of the Bush legacy—a legacy that will forever change, for better or worse, the ethnic makeup of the American people and the course of American history.

Of the three million who enter each year, almost two hundred thousand are dubbed OTMs or "other than Mexicans" by immigration officials. Most OTMs are from countries throughout Central and South America such as Honduras, El Salvador, Guatemala, and Brazil. In 1997 a scant 1.1 percent of the illegals apprehended at the border were OTMs. By 2005 the percentage had climbed to 13.4.[32]

SPECIAL–INTEREST ALIENS

There is another class of illegal immigrants known as SIAs or "special-interest aliens." They come from terror-sponsoring countries that pose high security concerns: Saudi Arabia, Syria, Iran, Iraq, Pakistan, Afghanistan, Egypt, Somalia, Yemen, Jordan, Bangladesh, and Lebanon.[33] By 2006 the illegal passageways into the United States—including a well-known route dubbed "cocaine alley" that leads from the Sierra Madre into Cochise County, Arizona—became strewn with discarded Muslim prayer rugs, pages from the Koran, instructions in Arabic on how to cross the Rio Grande, and beverage boxes with Farsi and Arabic letters. Among the litter, a border guard in Texas discovered a jacket with an Arabic military badge that depicted a jet headed toward a skyscraper with the words "Midnight Mission."[34]

Between October 1, 2002, and June 30, 2003, the Department of Homeland Security announced that 4,226 SIAs had been collared at the Mexican and Canadian borders. Within a year, that number climbed to 6,025, an increase of 42 percent.[35] In June 2004 border patrol guards from Willicox, Arizona, arrested seventy-seven individuals "of Middle Eastern descent" who were trekking through the Chiricahua Mountains with a caravan of hundreds of Mexican migrant workers. "These guys didn't speak English," a field agent told reporters, "and they were speaking to each other in Arabic. It's ridiculous we don't take this more seriously. We're told not to say a thing to the media." Another agent added: "All the men had brand-new clothing and the exact same cut of mustache."[36]

Commenting on this development, Colorado congressman Tom Tancredo said: "One must take into account that, even by the most conservative estimates, the number of folks not getting caught by the Border Patrol are two or three times the number caught. If so, at least 18,000 SIAs have entered America just in the first nine months of 2004."[37] Tancredo's fears were well founded. By December 2005 Homeland Security confirmed that fifty-one terror suspects had been apprehended on the border on a wide variety of charges, including arms smuggling and illegally wiring large sums of money into the country.[38]

CATCH AND CUT

With thousands of illegal aliens pouring over the two-thousand-mile Mexican border day after day, space at detention centers soon became reserved for only the most violent arrivals and hardened criminals on the lam from a foreign government. The others, including OTMs and SIAs, were released from custody as soon as they received hearing dates from immigration judges. They were granted (compliments of Uncle Sam) stipends for food and housing, an arrangement that proved to be a great boon for many owners of fleabag motels. The guests, however, rarely stayed long. Within a matter of a day or two, most vanished into the vast American landscape, and fewer than 5 percent made an appearance before an immigration judge at their scheduled hearings.[39]

The bizarre practice of "catch and cut" continued as Homeland Security raised the terror alert from code yellow to code orange, where it remained throughout 2005 and 2006. Cries of alarm were raised. Texas congressman Solomon P. Ortiz, the highest-ranking Democrat on the House Armed Services Subcommittee on Readiness, confirmed that Middle Easterners with possible ties to al Qaeda were being arrested on a regular basis and released because of lack of jail space. "It's true," Ortiz said. "It is very reliable information from the horse's mouth, and it's happening all over the place. It's very, very scary and members of Congress know about this."[40] Similarly, Sheriff D'Wayne Jernigan of Del Rio, Texas, expressed his outrage and frustration at this practice by saying: "Are they criminals? Are they terrorists? We don't know who they are. The agency at this level—here, locally, I truly believe—are just as much against these releases as I am. They feel betrayed. . . . Why are we apprehending them in the first place? They turn these people loose with a piece of paper that tells them to report to an immigration hearing at an unknown time and place, and there's no way for an agency to get in touch with them again. Are they going to show up at those hearings? Will the agency ever be able to find them? Let's be realistic. It's ridiculous! A war on terrorism? Homeland security? Ha!"[41]

Homeland Security officials responded to such criticism by saying that SIAs must be treated in the same way as illegal aliens from other countries. Asa Hutchinson, the undersecretary of the department, said that any attempt to isolate, arrest, and incarcerate the illegals who come from terror-sponsoring countries would smack of egregious insensitivity and betray an odious attitude of racial profiling.[42]

THE TALKING MULE

The absurdity of the situation became best exemplified in the curious case of Farida Goolam Mohamed Ahmed. She was arrested at the airport in McAllen, Texas, on July 28, 2004, when customs officials noticed that her South African passport was missing pages and lacked a stamp of official entry into the United States. When questioned, Ahmed, a Muslim woman, confessed: "I did not come legally. I came through the bush."[43]

Ahmed, as it turned out, was purportedly a terrorist courier who provided information from the *mujahadeen* in the Middle East to an al Qaeda cell in New York. Several of her communiqués concerned plans for a major bombing operation in midtown Manhattan. What's more, Ahmed had managed to sneak into the United States not simply once or twice but over 270 times before she was finally taken into custody.[44]

Fortunately, Ahmed was not only a faithful mule but a talking mule. Her interrogations led to the arrests of several al Qaeda agents in Mexico. These agents, along with Ahmed, were skirted off to one of the CIA's clandestine terrorist detention facilities in Eastern Europe.

OTHER ILLEGAL IMPORTS

In addition to the millions of illegal aliens, illegal contraband was flowing into the United States from Mexico as well. The three major Mexican drug cartels discovered a booming business for their products in the wake of 9/11. By 2006, despite the cries of alarm about the porous border, the Tijuana, Juarez, and Gulf cartels provided 80 percent of the marijuana, 75 percent of the cocaine, 40 percent of the heroin, and an unspecified amount of methamphetamines to its good neighbors in the land of the free and the home of the brave.[45] The Tijuana cartel under the Feliz brothers specializes in heroin and marijuana. The Gulf cartel under Oscar Malherbe de Leon represents the coca express that flows from El Paso to Brownsville.[46] And the Juarez cartel under the Fuentes group operates a drug route that extends to Michigan and New York.[47] Business is so brisk that the coke and weed are packed into massive bundles and shipped to the United States in multiengine cargo jets and cargo ships. The Mexican "black-tar" heroin comes across the border—thanks to corrupt customs officials—in commercial trucks.[48] Mexico's economy presently is deeply dependant on the $30 billion drug trade with its good neighbor to the north. The illegal trafficking fuels industries, employs thousands of workers, and distorts competition for manufactured and agricultural goods.[49]

But the drugs pale in comparison with other illegal imports, including nuclear arms and supplies from al Qaeda. In April 2004 FBI officials arrested Mohammed Junaid Babar, a leading al Qaeda operative, upon his return to Queens, New York, from a terrorist summit in the wilds of the Waziristan Province of Pakistan. Babar, who was born and raised in Queens, had been commissioned by the *mujahadeen* to launch a bombing in London on the model of the 1995 attack on the Murrah Federal Building in Oklahoma City. Faced with seventy years in a federal slammer, Babar opted to spill his guts in exchange for admission in a witness protection program. He told interrogators that al Qaeda was planning a spectacular attack on American soil—a nuclear 9/11 that will occur simultaneously in major metropolitan areas throughout the country. He further said that al Qaeda terrorists were relying on Latino gangs, most notably Mara Salvatrucha members, to transport not only operatives but also nuclear supplies and weapons across the border.[50] This testimony was later confirmed by Sharif al-Masri, another terrorist who had been in attendance at the Waziristan gathering. Both Babar and al-Masri said that the man commissioned to command the next 9/11 was Adnan el-Shukrijumah.

Adnan Gulshair el-Shukrijumah is a naturalized American citizen who speaks flawless English, Spanish, and Arabic. He is an experienced pilot and skilled nuclear technician. And, according to FBI officials, he is the most dangerous person in the Western world.

CHAPTER ELEVEN

THE SEARCH FOR ADNAN EL-SHUKRIJUMAH

If Shukrijumah has indeed succeeded in linking up with a criminal syndicate such as the Mara Salvatrucha gang, it is a sobering thought. The gang has some form of presence in virtually every Hispanic community across the United States, and can offer al Qaeda unparalleled infiltration into any city in the country.

Jamestown Foundation, October 2004

The Salvatrucha gangs are very serious, very vicious, and we have confirmed that they have contact with al Qaeda.

Congressman Solomon Ortiz (D-TX), September 2004

There's a whole pool of available young radicals and would-be radicals for whom these (al Qaeda) guys are the big heroes. All that's needed is for someone to put them in contact with the web of real al Qaeda people. The big question now is, where's that web?

Walid Phares, political science professor,
Florida Atlantic University in Boca Raton, Florida, April 2003

Adnan el-Shukrijumah possesses the uncanny ability to blend into a crowd, to alter his looks, and to assume a multitude of identities. He is the proverbial Mr. Cellophane. Few things about el-Shukrijumah indicate his radical Islamic orientation. He is often clean shaven and never wears a long shirt or chews a toothpick. He has been known to have a beer on occasion (like an average American Joe), to smoke an occasional Camel, and to carry rosary beads in his pocket. He has posed as an Italian American, a Mexican American, a Canadian, a Saudi, a Jamaican, and a Latino from Trinidad. He stands somewhere between five feet four and five feet six and weighs 140 pounds. He has black hair, black eyes, an olive complexion, and a pronounced nose. This guy's face does not appear on the nightly news, even though a BOLO (be-on-the-lookout) was issued March 21, 2004, by FBI director Robert Mueller and former attorney general John Ashcroft. He hasn't even made the spotlight of *America's Most Wanted* with John Walsh. But no one on planet earth is more of a threat to the lives and well-being of every man, woman, and child within the United States than ferret-faced Adnan.

ANOTHER PRODUCT OF BROOKLYN'S FAROUQ MOSQUE

Adnan el-Shukrijumah was born in Guyana on August 4, 1975—the first born of Gulshair el-Shukrijumah, a forty-four-year-old radical Muslim cleric, and his sixteen-year-old wife. In 1985 Gulshair migrated to the United States, where he assumed duties as the imam of the Farouq Mosque at 554 Atlantic Avenue in Brooklyn. The mosque, as noted earlier, has served for many years as a center for terrorist activities and a recruiting station for al Qaeda.[1]

In 1995 the el-Shukrijumah family relocated to Miramar, Florida, where Gulshair became the spiritual leader of the radical Masjid al-Hijah Mosque and imam of the Boca Raton Islamic Center. Adnan became friends there with such wannabe terrorists as José Padilla, who planned to detonate a radiological bomb in midtown Manhattan; Imran Mandhai, who was convicted of attempting to blow up nuclear power plants in southern Florida; Moessa Shuyeb Jokhan, who was arrested for plotting to blow up Jewish community centers and businesses; and a group of other homegrown terrorists.[2] Questioned about the aspiring jihadists, Sofian Abdelaziz Zakout, director of the American Muslim Association and a friend of the el-Shukrijumah family, said: "I saw [Adnan el-Shukrijumah, Padilla, and Mandhai] at different times in different mosques, and I always said hello. Does that make me a terrorist?"[3]

TRAINED FOR TERROR

Adnan attended flight schools in Florida and Norman, Oklahoma, along with Mohammad Atta and the other 9/11 operatives, and he became a highly skilled commercial jet pilot, although he, like Atta and the other terrorists, never applied for a license with the Federal Aviation Commission.[4]

In April 2001 Adnan spent ten days in Panama, where he reportedly met with al Qaeda officials to assist in the planning of 9/11. The following month, he obtained an associate's degree in computer engineering from Broward Community College, where Mandhai and Jokhan had been enrolled as full-time students.[5]

SLICK AS AN EEL

El-Shukrijumah came to appear as a blip on the FBI's radar screen in March 2001, after special agents in Miami launched an investigation of the Darul Uloom Institute and Islamic Training Center, which operates out of a large storefront on the Hollywood/Pines Boulevard in Pembroke Pines. The agents were interested in the activities of Imran

Mandhai, who frequented the mosque and stated his intention to create a jihad cell that would consist of twenty-five or thirty men, including his pal Adnan el-Shukrijumah. The cell, Mandhai maintained, would target electric substations, Jewish institutions, a National Guard armory, even Mount Rushmore. "It was no secret that [Adnan] was pretty radical," says a federal law enforcement source, "and that Mandhai thought he would be interested in what they were doing."[6]

But el-Shukrijumah was too slick and smart to become involved in the creation of a cell with a loudmouth like Mandhai. He declined to join their plans for jihad, correctly surmising that Mandhai already had attracted too much attention. But his name had been mentioned, and the federal investigators discovered that el-Shukrijumah had lied on his green-card application regarding a prior arrest. For this reason, a confidential report with cursory information in his name was opened at FBI headquarters. The record was filed and quickly forgotten.[7]

ADNAN'S ADVENTURES

Between 1996 and 2000 Adnan became a jet-setter. He traveled to Saudi Arabia and Pakistan, where he met with Ramzi Binalshibh, Khalid Shaikh Mohammed, and other members of the al Qaeda high command. He also spent considerable time within al Qaeda camps in Afghanistan, where he received training in explosives and special operations.[8]

In May 2001 he headed off to Trinidad, where his father, Gulshair, had worked as an official for the Saudi Arabian government. From Trinidad, he trekked to Tobago and Guyana. He managed to amass passports from Guyana, Trinidad, Saudi Arabia, Canada, and the United States and began to adopt a number of aliases, including Abu Arifi, Jafar al-Tayyar, Jaafar at-Yayyar, Ja'far al-Tayar, and Mohammed Sher Mohammed Khan (the name that appeared on his official FBI file).[9] Adnan also found time, according to Khalid Shaikh Mohammed, to take part in the 9/11 attacks as a "fixer," that is, a behind-the-scenes operative who helped with the plans for hijacking the aircraft.

A NUCLEAR MISSION IN CANADA

Following the success of 9/11, el-Shukrijumah became singled out by bin Laden and al-Zawahiri to spearhead the next great attack on America—a nuclear attack that would take place simultaneously in seven US cities (New York, Boston, Miami, Houston, Los Angeles, Las Vegas, and Washington, DC), leaving millions dead and the richest and most powerful nation on earth in ashes.[10]

To prepare for this mission, el-Shukrijumah and fellow al Qaeda agents Anas al-Liby, Jaber A. Elbaneh, and Amer el-Matti purportedly were sent to McMaster University in Hamilton, Ontario, a facility that boasted a five-megawatt nuclear research reactor, the largest reactor of any educational facility in Canada. At McMaster, el-Shukrijumah reportedly kept to himself, made few new friends or acquaintances, kept strictly to his studies, and left the facility at the same time as his colleagues.[11] He also managed to obtain employment at the reactor—allegedly as a guide.[12] Adnan's "normal' behavior on the Hamilton campus, a source said, gave him entry to places where dangerous materials were stored without raising undue suspicion. Bit by bit, the al Qaeda operative allegedly managed to pilfer approximately 180 pounds of nuclear material from the university—enough to build several radiological bombs.[13]

According to Debka, an Internet outlet for Israeli intelligence, el-Shukrijumah was under surveillance by Canadian officials in early October 2003, when he suddenly stopped attending classes and failed to show up for work. His disappearance aroused no concern, the sources say, until a few days later when the nuclear material was reported missing.[14]

Jayne Johnson, a spokesperson for McMaster University, declined to comment on the reports of el-Shukrijumah and the other al Qaeda agents at the school. Other McMaster officials denied that any al Qaeda agents were on campus and that any nuclear or radiological material was missing from the campus. But witnesses have verified el-Shukrijumah's presence in Hamilton, and the school, according to several sources, has experienced radiological "leakage."[15]

THE UNANSWERED QUESTIONS

Upon investigating the matter, Debka raised the following questions concerning el-Shukrijumah at McMaster and his mind-boggling vanishing act:

> Why were there no agents observing the subject inside the reactor? These sources did not disclose which security agencies were responsible for the surveillance.
>
> Who gave Shukrijumah, a Saudi Arabian under suspicion, access to the reactor? And how is it that no one noticed increasing amounts of nuclear or radiological materials were disappearing over a period of months?
>
> How was Shukrijumah able to give his watchers the slip?
>
> Was the subject tipped off by an inside source in the US or Canadian security services?[16]

Upon their departure from Canada, Adnan and his terrorist friends made their way to Buffalo, New York, where they may have been harbored by some members of the Lackawanna (LA) Mosque, where Jaber A. Elbaneh had been a prominent member. It is also possible that they may have received monetary and logistical support from Mohammed Albanna, who managed to escape under the radar of the bust of the LA Six (members of the Lackawanna mosque who were taken into custody for serving al Qaeda and other terrorist organizations) in 2002.

THE POCKET LITTER

In the wake of Operation Enduring Freedom (the US-led invasion of Afghanistan), CIA and military intelligence officials discovered the reoccurrence of the names of Jaffar al-Tayyar ("Jafer the Pilot") and Mohammed Sher Mohammed Khan in "pocket litter"—documents and scraps taken from prisoners and dead al Qaeda soldiers.[17] In May 2002 US intelligence and military officials started asking a pressing question to al Qaeda detainees who were being interrogated at foreign prisons and secret CIA and military facilities abroad. "Whom," the officials asked, "would al Qaeda pick to lead the next big attack against US targets?" Intelligence sources told *U.S. News & World Report* that several of the detainees coughed up the same answer: "Jaffar al-Tayyar."[18] The detainees said they had encountered "the Pilot" during al Qaeda training exercises in Afghanistan. Intelligence officers presented photos of hundreds of suspected al Qaeda operatives to the detainees. Several identified an individual who bore a resemblance to Adnan el-Shukrijumah. But the resemblance was not reality, and it would take months before FBI and CIA teams, with their sophisticated equipment and state-of-the-art search engines, would realize it. "We were pursuing a lead," said one official, "that in the end turned out to be a dead end. We found out we were after the wrong person."[19] Indeed, the teams might still be searching for the wrong suspects and hitting dead ends, if not for Khalid Shaikh Mohammed, al Qaeda's military operations chief, who was captured, quite by accident, in Karachi, Pakistan, March 1, 2003.

THE PLOT REVEALED

After days of interrogation, coupled with severe sleep deprivation, Mohammed told US officials that bin Laden was planning to create a "nuclear hell storm" in America.[20] Unlike other attacks, the terrorist chief said, the chain of command for the nuclear attack answered directly to bin Laden, al-Zawahiri, and a mysterious scientist called "Dr. X." Mohammed later admitted that "Dr. X" was Dr. Abdul Qadeer Khan, the Pakistani father of the Islamic bomb and the godfather of modern nuclear proliferation. He further confessed that the field commander for this operation was a naturalized American citizen whom he also referred to as Mohammed Sher Mohammed Khan and "Jafer al-Tayyar" ("Jafer the Pilot").[21] Both names are aliases of Adnan el-Shukrijumah.

Khalid Shaikh Mohammed went on to say that Adnan represents a "single-cell"—a lone agent capable of launching a solo nuclear or radiological attack on a major American city. The news of such a cell reportedly startled US officials, who assumed that al Qaeda cells contained several members who were supported by broad logistical backup crews.[22]

"DEMANDING, RUDE, AND OBNOXIOUS"

On March 21, 2004, Attorney General John Ashcroft and FBI director Robert Mueller issued a BOLO (be-on-the-lookout) alert for Adnan el-Shukrijumah and Amer el-Maati, along with Aafia Siddiqui, a Pakistani woman who received a biology degree from Massachusetts Institute of Technology and penned a doctoral thesis on neurological science at Brandeis University; Ahmed Khalfan Ghailani (aka "Foopie"), who took part in the 1998 embassy bombings in Kenya and Tanzania; Adam Yahiye Gadahn (aka Adam Pearlman), a convert to Islam who grew up on a goat ranch in Riverside County, California; and Abderraouf Jdey, the leader of the al Qaeda cell in Toronto.[23]

Several days after the BOLO was issued, Adnan and Jdey were spotted at a Denny's restaurant in Avon, Colorado, where one ordered a chicken sandwich and a salad. Samuel Mac, the restaurant manager, described them as "demanding, rude, and obnoxious."[24] They told Mac they were from Iran and were driving from New York to the West Coast. Upon calling the FBI headquarters in Washington, DC, Mac said the agent who answered the telephone said he had to call the bureau's Denver office and declined to take down any information. When Mac called the Denver office of the FBI, he said he was shuttled to voice mail because "all the agents were busy."[25] It was five hours before a seemingly uninterested agent called the restaurant manager. This agent, according to Mac, took a few notes and said she would pass the information along to the field agents who were handling the case.[26]

This promise represented the full extent of the government's interest in the sighting, even though el-Shukrijumah had been labeled by FBI director Robert Mueller as "the next Mohammad Atta" and even though the FBI had posted a $5 million reward for any information leading to his capture. The federal and state law enforcement officials failed to interview the restaurant workers and the patrons, purportedly even those who were willing to verify the presence of the terrorists in the restaurant. No forensic evidence was obtained from the scene by any law enforcement official—not even the utensils that had been used by the suspects. When contacted by the *Denver Post*, Monique Kelso, spokeswoman for the Denver bureau, said the office had received at least a dozen calls as a result of the BOLO. The calls, Kelo said, were all taken seriously. She added, "We follow up on every lead."[27]

THE WAZIRISTAN SUMMIT

Following the incident in Colorado, the diminutive el-Shukrijumah resurfaced at a terrorist summit in the lawless Waziristan Province of Pakistan in April 2004. The summit has been described by the FBI as a "pivotal planning session" in much the same manner as a 2000 meeting held in Kuala Lumpur for the 9/11 attacks. Attending the summit were Abu Issa al-Hindi, a Pakistani technician whose company contained plans for staging attacks at financial institutions in New York, New Jersey, and Washington, DC, and Mohammed Babar, who has been charged with buying materials to build bombs for attacks in Great Britain.[28] Babar is an American citizen and a resident of Queens, New York, where he was a leading member of the Islamic Thinkers Society, a group that burned the American flag during a demonstration before the Israeli consulate in 2006 and held up placards stating "The mushroom cloud is on its way."[29]

EL-SHUKRIJUMAH SOUTH OF THE BORDER

On May 27, 2004, Adnan el-Shukrijumah was spotted at an Internet café in Tegucigalpa, the hilly capital of Honduras, where he made calls to France, Canada, and the United States. He was described as badly dressed and bearded. At his table were Mara Salvatrucha leaders (*jefes*) from Panama, Mexico, Honduras, and El Salvador.[30] According to the café owner, who recognized Adnan from photos in the newspaper, he spoke to the *jefes* in English and Spanish. El-Shukrijumah's presence at the café was later verified by the Honduran security ministry, who confirmed that the elusive terrorist had made telephone calls from there to France, the United States, and Canada.[31]

On June 12 Gulshair el-Shukrijumah, Adnan's radical father, died in Miramar as a result of a stroke. Some sources attributed his demise to "the will of Allah." His funeral was attended by around a thousand people, who "prayed for Allah to accept their departed Sheik into his arms." Ibrahim Dremali, the imam of the Boca Raton Islamic Center, said that Gulshair had "a positive effect on people."[32]

From Tegucigalpa, Adnan made his way north to Belize in British Honduras, and from Belize to Mexico's Quintana Roo State, south of Cancun.[33] He remained in Mexico for much of the summer of 2004. In late August he was spotted in the northern Mexican province of Sonora near "terrorist alley," the main passageway for illegal aliens, including OTMs (other than Mexicans) and "Special Interest Aliens"—to the land of Mickey Mouse, MTV, and George W. Bush.[34]

NUKES ARRIVE IN MEXICO

Concern about el-Shukrijumah's extended stay in Mexico was heightened in November 2004 with the arrest in Pakistan of Sharif al-Masri, a key al Qaeda operative. Al-Masri, an Egyptian national jihadist with close ties to al-Zawahiri, bin Laden's number two man, informed interrogators that al Qaeda had made arrangements to smuggle nuclear supplies and tactical nuclear weapons into Mexico. From Mexico the weapons were to be transported across the border with the help of a Latino street gang. The gang was later identified as Mara Salvatrucha, the gang that Adnan had trekked across the North American continent to meet in a Honduran café, and the plans that he discussed with the gang leaders were the plans that had been purportedly finalized at the terrorist summit in Waziristan.[35]

In response to this information, US officials began monitoring all heavy trucks crossing the border, while Mexican officials pledged to keep close watch over flight schools and aviation facilities. Such precautions may have been adopted too late. A Piper PA Pawnee crop duster was stolen from Ejido Queretaro near Mexicali on November 1, 2004. The plane's tail number was XBCYP. The thieves, Mexican officials surmised, were either drug dealers or al Qaeda operatives, and clearly one was a highly trained pilot who met the description of Adnan el-Shukrijumah.[36]

CHAPTER TWELVE

O CANADA!
HAVEN OF
ISLAMIC TERROR!

Montreal is the leading center for Islamist and Jihadists groups in North America, many inspired by or with ties to al Qaeda. In total, with dozens of cells, Montreal has the largest number of such groups in any city in North America, not on a per capita basis but in gross numbers. Radical Muslims go to ground in Montreal.

Beryl Wajsman, president of the Institute for Public Affairs in Montreal, July 2006

You know, you cannot exercise your powers to the point of humiliation for others. That is what the Western world—not only the Americans, the Western world—has to realize. Because they (the have-nots) are human beings too. There are long-term consequences if you don't look hard at the reality in 10 or 20 (or) 30 years from now. And I do think the Western world is getting too rich in relation to the poor world and necessarily, you know, we're looked upon as being arrogant, self-satisfied, greedy, and with no limits. And September 11 is an occasion for me to realize it even more.

Canadian prime minister Jean Chrétien, September 11, 2002

171

GAO [Government Accounting Office] *actually shipped here to Washington* [in a special undercover operation] *enough nuclear materials to build two dirty bombs through our northern border and, again, through our southern border. Clearly, there is more that must be done, and clearly, we still have problems on both our northern and southern borders. We've got to put in place an integrated system that provides our citizens with maximum protection against nuclear smuggling, and do it in a way that is both efficient and cost-effective.*

Senator Diane Feinstein (D-CA), 2006

Between Mexico and Canada, the United States is caught in a geographical vise from which there exists no easy release. Indeed, the terrorist cells in Canada appear to represent a greater threat to the lives and well-being of US residents than the spread of al Qaeda and Hezbollah south of the border.

More than any other country in the world, Canada is responsible for the nuclear nightmare than now faces the Western world. Pakistan, despite the efforts of Dr. A. Q. Khan, would have remained without nuclear weapons if it had not been for Uncle Sam's neighbor to the north. Pakistan's CANDU (Canada Deuterium Uranium) nuclear reactor was acquired in a deal subsidized by the Canadian government with low-interest loans. Dubbed the KANUPP (Karachi Nuclear Power Plant), it remained Pakistan's only nuclear facility until 2004, when a second Chinese-built reactor came on line.[1]

Along with the 137-megawatt reactor, the Canadian government agreed in 1972 to train fifty Pakistani scientists and engineers to run it. One of the scientists to receive the training was Dr. Sultan Bashiruddin Mahmood, who served as a nuclear consultant to bin Laden and al Qaeda. "Canadian expertise was vital for developing nuclear weapons," claims Pervez Hoodbhoy, a physicist at the Quaid-e-Azim University in Islamabad. "There [in Canada] is no clear line that separates [civilian from weapons] programs."[2] Experts now say that Canada was willing to provide training, including training in the development of nuclear arms, because it was anxious to reap CANDU sales profits and to open new markets for its technology.[3] As early as 1993, the Center for Nonproliferation Studies reported that Pakistan was diverting plutonium from KANUPP to the A. Q. Khan Research Laboratories for the creation of the nuclear bomb of Islam.[4] Canada, Hoodbhoy says, opted not to notice for the sake of "expedience" and a good measure of greed.[5]

Canada's cooperation continued even after Pakistan was slapped with international sanctions because of a series of nuclear tests. This relationship persists to this day through Pakistan's membership in the Candu Owners Group (COG), a consortium of Atomic Energy of Canada, Ltd., and three Canadian power utilities. Asked if his group played a leading role in developing the nuclear bomb of Islam, COG president John Sommerville said: "People did get trained. How much that contributed to the program I really don't know."[6]

NUTCASE ASYLUM

The more immediate threat to the United States comes from Canada's incredibly lax immigration laws. Anyone who claims political asylum is granted immediate entry into the country with no questions asked by the customs agents and no documents required by law enforcement officials. Thirty thousand to forty thousand "refugees"—many from terror-sponsoring countries—enter the land to the north in this manner.[7] Even those with bogus passports are granted political sanctuary in Canada. None are screened for criminality, security, or even health problems. They are simply granted dates for a hearing that may not take place for eighteen months.[8] Fewer than 30 percent show up for their hearings.

To make matters worse, the political refugees, including those who fail to show up for their hearings, can obtain permanent residence under the sheltering flag of the maple leaf in three years. With such residency status comes the eligibility for genuine Canadian passports—passports that enable them to travel unrestricted throughout the

Western Hemisphere. Small wonder, therefore, that the land to the north represents a perfect place for members of al Qaeda, Hezbollah, and other terrorist groups to unlock the doors to the New World, including the United States.

TOLERANCE OF TERRORISM

The problem is compounded by Canada's outlandishly tolerant attitude concerning terrorist groups. Take Hezbollah, for instance. This Shiite terrorist group bombed the US embassy in Lebanon, killing 63 people, including 17 Americans and 6 CIA agents; it launched an attack on the US Marine barracks in Beirut, killing 220 Marines and 21 other American servicemen; and it was likely responsible for the downing of TWA Flight 800, one of the most horrific acts of the past century. Yet Canada blithely refused to label Hezbollah, along with Hamas, the Al-Aqsa Martyrs Brigade, and the Armed Islamic Front, as a terrorist group until December 2002, when government officials felt the heat from concerned citizens, and Jewish organizations.[9] Even today, the Liberation Tigers of Tamil Eelam (LTTE)—by all counts, one of the most deadly terrorist organizations—has not been placed on Canada's terrorist list. The reason? There are more than 250,000 ethnic Tamils living in Toronto and many of them are openly supportive of LTTE.[10]

THE OPEN ROADS

The situation is compounded by other mind-boggling policies. Canadian border guards are not armed and must rely on the Royal Canadian Mounted Police (RCMP) for backup when faced with a serious problem. In 2005 the RCMP withdrew their services in the province of Quebec. This resulted in more than one hundred incidents of vehicles smashing through border posts in order to escape inspection.[11] But, at least, there are guards at these posts. The same cannot be said of other places in Canada. At this writing, 225 cross-border roads leading to and from the United States remain completely unguarded.[12]

A SHORT LIST OF CANADIAN TERRORISTS

This might be all well and good, save for the fact that there are tens of thousands of terrorists and wannabe jihadists in Canada. Some of the most troubling are as follows:

Almrei, Hassan. Born in Syria, this Toronto resident served as the member of a forgery ring that provided false documents, including Canadian passports, to members of al Qaeda. At the time of his arrest in Mississauga, Ontario, agents of the Canadian Security Intelligence Service (CSIS) discovered photos of bin Laden, an assortment of guns, a security badge, and diagrams of the cockpits of commercial jetliners. His order of deportation was overturned by Judge Edmond Blanchard, who, on November 27, 2003, ruled that any attempt to remove Almrei from the country would cause the al Qaeda operative "irreparable harm."[13]

Amhaz, Ali. A Hezbollah operative, Amhaz immigrated to Canada and, according to the Mackenzie Institute, helped to launder hundreds of thousands of dollars through Canadian banks for the terrorist group and used some of the proceeds to purchase demolitions material, night-vision goggles, new computers, and camera equipment for the group. His home is in Burnaby, British Columbia.[14]

Atmani, Karim Said. A Moroccan who fought in Afghanistan and became a Bosnian citizen before heading off to Canada, he has been convicted in France for charges related to passing fraudulent passports to al Qaeda members in Europe.[15]

Ayub, Fauzi Mohammed. Another Hezbollah operative, he allegedly was recruited by the terrorist group in Canada in the early

1990s. After training in Lebanon, he entered Israel in 2000 to set up storage sites for weapons and explosives. He settled in Canada in 1988 and his family remains there.[16]

Bagri, Ajaib Singh. A member of Babbar Khalsa International (BKL) who resides in British Columbia, he was placed on trial for the 1985 Air India bombing. BKL is a Sikh terrorist group that seeks to establish an independent Khalistan within the Punjab region of India. Despite the prosecution's preponderance of evidence, he was found not guilty in one of the lengthiest and most controversial trials in Canadian history.[17]

Bhullar, Davinder Pal Sing. A former leader in the Khalistan Commando Force, he is fighting extradition from Surrey, British Columbia, to India, where a death sentence awaits him for a bomb attack that killed nine people.[18]

Boumezbeur, Adel. A Montreal Salafist and Algerian, he has been convicted of terrorist-related offenses in France.[19]

Boussora, Faker. A wanted al Qaeda member, who is believed to be hiding in Montreal, he was born in Tunisia and trained in Afghanistan. He was unknown to Canadian authorities until a videotape surfaced in which he pledged commitment to serve as a suicide bomber in the war against the Great Satan. He, along with Adnan el-Shukrijumah, became the subject of a BOLO (be-on-the-look-out) issued by FBI director Robert Mueller and Attorney General John Ashcroft on March 21, 2004. He is believed to be a key planner in the American Hiroshima. A $5 million bounty has been placed on his head.[20]

Daher, Kassen. An al Qaeda member, he lived in Canada before being arrested in Lebanon.[21]

Dbouk, Mohammed Hassan. The former leader of Hezbollah in Vancouver, he is Ali Amhaz's brother-in-law and terrorist partner. His value to Hezbollah was so great that his application to become a martyr was rejected five times.[22] Recently, he has fled to southern Lebanon to aid Hezbollah in its struggles against the Israeli army.

Farahat, Hassan (aka Abdul Jaber). Accused of being a senior member of Ansar al-Islam, he has been arrested by Kurdish guerrillas in northern Iraq. From 1997 to 2002 he served as imam of the radical Salaheddin Mosque in Toronto.[23]

Haouari, Mokhtar. An Algerian who arrived in Montreal via France, he provided false documentation to Canadian recruits for the great jihad against the United States. He provided assistance to Ahmed Rassam in the plot to blow up the Los Angeles International Airport on January 1, 2000.[24]

Hardeep, Singh. A leading member of the Khalistan Commando Force (KCF), he was deported from Canada in 1995—the same year the KCF was mounting a major recruiting campaign here and in the United Kingdom.[25]

Al-Husseini, Mohammed Hussein. An alleged hijacker, he lived on welfare in Montreal while coordinating reconnaissance for Hezbollah on potential targets inside Canada.[26]

Ikhlef, Mourad. A refugee from Algeria, where he became a ringleader of the Armed Islamic Group (GIA), he helped to establish the Salafist cell in Montreal. The Salafists represent a breakaway faction of the GIA. They are aligned with al Qaeda. He helped to plan the attempted bombing of the Los Angeles International Airport.[27]

Jabalah, Mahmoud. A member of the Egyptian Islamic Jihad, he worked for Osama bin Laden's construction and development projects in Sudan in the early 1990s. This Toronto resident has been jailed since August 2001, after being deemed a national security risk. He arrived in Canada as a refugee claimant and received public welfare. He has managed to escape deportation by claiming that he would be tortured and killed if sent back to Egypt.[29]

Jabarah, Abdul Rahman. An immigrant to Canada from Kuwait in 1994, he settled in St. Catherine's, Ontario. Recruited by al Qaeda in 1990, he was killed in Saudi Arabia in July 2003 when police moved in on his terrorist cell after a series of truck bombings.[28]

Jabarah, Mohamed Mansour. Abdul's younger brother was raised in St. Catherine's, Ontario. He led an al Qaeda cell in Singapore that was planning a massive bomb attack (with twenty-one tons of improvised explosives) before he was arrested in Oman in 2002.[30]

Al-Jiddi, al-Rauf bin al-Habib bin Youssef (aka Abderraouf Jdey). The leader of the al Qaeda cell in Montreal, Jdey's involvement in al Qaeda was unknown until a videotape of him making a pledge to martyrdom turned up in Afghanistan. He was last seen with Adnan el-Shukrijumah while eating a chicken sandwich in a Denny's restaurant in Avon, Colorado (see the previous chapter).[31]

Kamel, Fateh. Another arrival from Algeria and former member of the GIA, he served as the leader of the Montreal Salafist Cell during the 1990s. He has been convicted in France for passing black market passports to Islamic militants and for organizing the Groupe Roubaix, a Canadian and French group of radicals who pledged their allegiance to bin Laden.[32]

Labsi, Mustapha. An Algerian, he came to Montreal, where he served as an active member of the Salafist cell and the roommate of Ahmed Ressam, who attempted to blow up the Los Angeles International Airport. He entered Canada with a fake passport and gained refugee status. In 1999 he spent eleven months with Ressam at an al Qaeda training camp in Afghanistan. In 2001 he was arrested for recruiting, fund-raising, and planning attacks in London.[33]

Mahjoub, Mohamed Zeki. A Toronto-area convenience store clerk and senior "fixer" for Vanguards of Conquest, one of al Qaeda's sister agencies, he managed a large farm for bin Laden in Sudan and helped to train new recruits for the jihad. In 1995 he came to Canada with a doctored passport and assisted in the planning of the attempted Los Angeles International Airport bombing. At this writing, he is fighting deportation to Egypt on the grounds that he will face persecution and death.[34]

Malik, Ripudaman Singh. A resident of British Colombia and senior fund-raiser for the BKL, he is on trial for his involvement in the Air India bombing.[35]

Marzouk, Hessam Mohamed Hafez. An Egyptian al Qaeda member, he lived in Surrey, British Colombia, and was arrested in Azerbaijan before facing charges in Egypt.[36]

Mohamed, Samir Ait. He lived in Vancouver, Montreal, and Toronto, and is currently awaiting extradition to the United States. In 1996 he facilitated Ahmed Ressam's acquisition of a handgun with a silencer and, in 1999, he provided Ressam with a fake ID and a counterfeit credit card so that Ressam could carry out his plans to blow up the Los Angeles International Airport.[37]

Muhammad, Saeed Sobrhatolla. A computer expert of Ansar al-Islam, he was arrested by Kurdish guerrillas in northern Iraq for launching insurrections against the US invasion and occupancy. He arrived in Toronto in 1995 and became affiliated with the radical Scarborough Islamic Center. He is believed to have served a key role in establishing ties between al Qaeda and Saddam Hussein's Iraqi regime.[38]

Nadarajah, Muralitharan. A senior fund-raiser for the Liberation Tigers of Tamil Eelam (LTTE), and a member of an assassination cell, he arrived in Canada as a refugee claimant from Switzerland in 1998 and was ordered deported in 2002—but remains free upon appeal. LTTE is one of the most violent terrorist organizations in the world.[39]

Nawar, Nizar Ben Muhammed Nasr. Nasr is one of some thirteen hundred Tunisian students who entered Montreal in 1999 (and one of one hundred who dropped out of sight after the WTC attacks). He recruited for the jihad against the United States and delivered a suicide attack on a historic synagogue in Tunisia in early 2002 that killed nineteen people.[40]

Ouzghar, Abdellah. Born in Algeria, he was an associate of the al Qaeda Salafist cell in Montreal in the 1990s, before moving to Hamilton, Ontario, where he raised funds for the Armed Islamic Group. He was convicted in absentia of producing fake passports for an Algerian terrorist group by a French court and sentenced to five years in prison. He didn't spend much time in jail. Ontario judge Ian Nordheimer released him on bail, saying that Ouzghar didn't represent a threat since he was married to a Canadian.[41] He has appealed the extradition order and, in the meantime, rallies for his release have been launched in Hamilton.

Reyat, Inderjit Singh. A BKL member and resident of British Colombia, he has been convicted in the United Kingdom for charges related to the Air India bombing. He is fighting his extradition order.[42]

Sabanayagam, Loganathan. One of the six founders of the LTTE, he was involved in the group's 1975 assassination of the mayor of Jaffna. He was convicted in 1994 of a number of fraud-related charges pertaining to passport forging. He entered Canada from the United States as a refugee claimant in 1988.[43]

El-Sayed, Omar. A Hezbollah member, he lived in Edmonton with a phony Canadian ID after entering Canada in 1998 with a fake Dutch passport. He was arrested after the Royal Canadian Mounted Police discovered that Germany wanted him to face charges relating to heroin and cocaine trafficking, selling firearms, and threatening a police officer. An Alberta judge ordered him released on bail in 2002, and he has since disappeared.[44]

Al-Sayegh, Hani. A Shiite Saudi who is suspected of being involved in the murder of nineteen US personnel in a 1996 truck bombing in Khobar, Saudi Arabia (an al Qaeda operation), he was arrested in 1997 at his home in Canada. He made a plea bargain with American officials, agreeing to plead guilty to conspiracy to kill Americans in exchange for a reduced ten-year sentence. Extradited to Canada, he withdrew his plea agreement, and, in the absence of corroborative evidence, the charges were dropped.[45] He was finally deported to Saudi Arabia, where he awaits trial.

Saygili, Aynur. A PKK (Kurdistan Workers' Party) member, she entered Canada under a false name in May 1996 and quickly became involved in the Kurdish Cultural Association of Montreal. She was arrested under a Canadian Immigration Security Certificate in November 1996. The Canadian Security Intelligence Service discovered that Saygili, along with Hanan Ahmed Osman, had been sent to Canada to gain control of the general Kurdish community for the PKK's own financial and strategic purposes.[46]

Singh, Iqbal. Iqbal arrived in Canada in 1991 as an undocumented refugee (after hopping through several countries with false documentation). He was a member of the Babbar Khalsa International and the Sikh Students Federation. He was ordered to be deported to Belize from Toronto in 2001 after a lengthy legal battle, but he appealed the ruling. At present, he lives in his comfortable Mississauga home (on the outskirts of Toronto) on a corner lot with a fenced yard.[47]

Slahi, Mohamedou Ould. An al Qaeda member, he went to Montreal for two years after fleeing Germany, where he was wanted for welfare fraud. In 1999 he carried a message from bin Laden to Ahmed Ressam, sanctioning the plans for the attack on the Los Angeles International Airport.[48]

Suresh, Manickavasagam. A senior LTTE leader who arrived in Canada in 1990 to take command of the group's front organizations, he has been fighting deportation since 1995. The case has set a number of important legal precedents, including a dismissal of arguments that fund-raising and propagandizing for terrorist groups in Canada is a form of free expression and free association.[49]

Tobbichi, Adel. An Algerian, he was extradited from Montreal to the Netherlands in 2002 to stand trial with six al Qaeda operatives who were planning a series of attacks in France and Belgium. He allegedly also altered passports and other documents to allow members of the terrorist group to travel throughout Europe.[50]

Vignarajah, Kumaravelu. A onetime LTTE combatant, he also worked for the Royal Canadian Mounted Police as a wiretapping translator, before the Mounties discovered he had concealed his part in the murder of Indian troops in Sri Lanka and was stealing highly sensitive intelligence documents. He entered Canada in 1989 as a political refugee.[51]

THE TORONTO PLOT

On June 2 and 3, 2006, police and security agencies in Ontario conducted raids in greater Toronto that resulted in the arrest of seventeen members of an Islamic terrorist cell. Canadian authorities and law enforcement agencies maintain that the suspects had been planning a series of major attacks, including the detonation of truck bombs at at least two locations in southern Ontario and raids on various buildings such as the Canadian Broadcasting Corporation, the CSIS central headquarters in Toronto, and Parliament. The members of the group also intended to behead Prime Minister Stephen Harper and other leading political figures.[52]

Fifteen of the suspects appeared in court on the afternoon of June 3, under heavy security. Their names were revealed as follows:

Qayyum Abdul Jamal, forty-three. Born and bred in Mississauga, a suburb of Toronto, he has been described as an active member of the mosque who frequently led prayers and made incendiary speeches. He migrated from Karachi, Pakistan, at an unknown date.

Shareef Abdelhaleem, thirty. He was born in Egypt and migrated with his family to Canada at the age of ten.

Steven Vikash Chand, alias Abdul Shakur, twenty-five. He is a recent convert to Islam and a former Canadian soldier.

Yasim Abdi Mohamed, twenty-four. Born in Somalia, he migrated to Canada with his family.

Jahmaal James, twenty-three. He is a native of Toronto.

Mohammed Dirie, twenty-two. He was born in Somalia and migrated to Canada with his family.

Fahim Ahmad, twenty-one. Born and bred in Toronto.

Asad Ansari, twenty-one. Born and bred in Mississauga.

Ahmad Mustafa Ghany, twenty-one. He was born in Canada. His family had migrated from Trinidad and Tobago.

Zakaria Amara, twenty. Born and bred in Mississauga.

Amin Mohamed Durrani, nineteen. He is a native of Toronto.

Saad Khalid, nineteen. He was born in Pakistan. He migrated with his family to Canada at the age of eight.

The names of the five minors were not released in accordance with Canada's Youth Criminal Justice Act.[53] Two members of the group were already serving time in a Kingston, Ontario, prison on weapons possession charges. According to the FBI, two other men, Syed Ahmed and Ehsanul Sadequee, who were recently arrested in Georgia in the United States on terrorism charges, are connected to the case.[54]

The arrests sparked several comments by US politicians regarding Canada's threat to national security. Congressman Peter King of New York said: "There's a large al Qaeda presence in Canada . . . because of their very liberal immigration laws, because of how political asylum is granted so easily." Congressman John Hostettler of Indiana added: "South Toronto, like those parts of London that are host to the radical imams who influenced the 9/11 terrorists and the shoe bomber, has people who adhere to a militant understanding of Islam."[55]

More sparks came when Mike McDonell of the Royal Canadian Mounted Police described the arrested people as representing a "broad strata" of Canadian society and the *Toronto Star* claimed that it is "difficult to find a common denominator" among the individuals who were taken into custody, even though all were Muslims and many attended the Al-Rahman Islamic Center for Islamic Education in Mississauga. Andrew C. McCarthy of *National Review* described such statements as an effort by the Canadian police and national media to whitewash a role of militant Islam in the terrorist plot and to ignore an elephant in a room.[55]

The problem with terrorists in Canada is troublesome in Toronto, monstrous in Montreal, out-of-control in Ottawa, and venomous in Vancouver, where Imad Mugniyah, until very recently, has presided over a virulent cell of Hezbollah.[56] Concerning the threat from America's neighbor to the north, Walter Todd Huston writes:

> *Al Qaeda understands well that Canada happily creates the conditions by which those attacks can be planned and fostered. Islamofascist operatives worldwide understand that Canada offers a rich bounty of social programs, a lax law enforcement culture and a visceral hatred of the USA that is growing with every year, all verdant soil in which to plant the hatred of Islamofascism.*
>
> *Al Qaeda knows that if one of their operatives is arrested in*

Canada it is pretty sure that no prosecution or even deportment will result. Further they know that even if arrested once, this does not eliminate the possibility of an operative carrying on his efforts as many are arrested and released multiple times before anything more stringent is applied to them.

One of the first things an Al Qaeda operative does when they enter a Western nation is get on the dole so that they have a supporting income as they go about their evil business. Canada offers one of the least restrictive and least accountable such systems and terrorists have a ready base because of it.

And, last but certainly not least, Canada has developed an institutional hatred of the USA that fosters a further laxity on matters of terror within its government which is reflected in its law enforcement branches as described above. Terrorists know that this anti-US bias gives them cover that they otherwise might not have. With the prevailing feeling among many Canadian Pols that the U.S. might deserve what they get, looking for terror suspects within their own borders is not the highest priority.[57]

How scary is the situation in Canada?
Turn the page for a few horror stories.

CHAPTER THIRTEEN
CANADIAN CAMPFIRE
A COUPLE OF SCARY TALES

With the possible exception of the United States, there are more international terrorist organizations active in Canada than anywhere in the world. This situation can be attributed to Canada's proximity to the United States which currently is the principal target of terrorist groups operating internationally; and to the fact that Canada, a country built upon immigration, represents a microcosm of the world. It is therefore not surprising that the world's extremist elements are represented here, along with peace-loving citizens. Terrorist groups are present here whose origins lie in regional, ethnic and nationalist conflicts, including the Israeli Palestinian one, as well as those in Egypt, Algeria, Sudan, Afghanistan, Lebanon, Northern Ireland, the Punjab, Sri Lanka, Turkey and the former Yugoslavia.

Anti-Defamation League, January 2004

There have been a number of instances where Canadians or individuals based here have been implicated in terrorist attacks or plans in

other countries, at least a half dozen or more in the last several years. There are several graduates of terrorist training camps, many of whom are battle-hardened veterans of campaigns in Afghanistan, Bosnia, Chechnya and elsewhere who reside here. . . . Often these individuals remain in contact with one another while in Canada or with colleagues outside of the country, and continue to show signs of ongoing clandestine activities, including the use of counter-surveillance techniques, secretive meetings, and encrypted communications.
Jim Judd, Canadian Security Intelligence Service Director,
March 2005

Canada has tried to smother terrorism with kindness. . . . Its most valuable contribution to the war on terrorism may well be its terrorists.
Stewart Bell, *Cold Terror: How Canada Nurtures and Exports Terrorism to the World,* 2004

SCARY STORY NUMBER 1: AHMED RESSAM

In 1994 Ahmed Ressam, an Algerian who served with the Armed Islamic Group, arrived in Montreal with a fake passport. When questioned by customs, he admitted that his passport was a fake and asked for political asylum. The request should have been denied immediately since Ressam had been convicted of weapons smuggling in Algeria and a host of other crimes in Europe.[1] In accordance with standard immigration procedure, the Canadian officials granted him a date for a hearing, permitted him to enter the country with no questions asked, and placed him on public welfare. Ressam, of course, never showed up for the hearing.

Since he failed to appear in court, Ressam's request for asylum was denied. A few months later, he was taken into custody, and again made a request for political asylum, and again he was granted another hearing date, and again he failed to make an appearance in court. This Canadian legal version of the Mad Hatter's tea party took place four times in two years. Ressam would commit a crime, get arrested, request asylum, gain a hearing date, secure release, and fail to attend the hearing. He never spent a day in jail and never was ordered deported by an immigration judge.[2]

By 1996 Ressam became affiliated with the radical Assuna Annabawiyah Mosque in Montreal, where he fell under the spell of Abderraouf Hannachi. Hannachi had been trained as a jihadist at Osama bin Laden's Khalden camp in Afghanistan, where he learned to fire handguns, AK-47s, and rocket-propelled grenade launchers.[3] In his Friday night addresses to the congregation of fifteen hundred worshipers, Hannachi urged the young men to follow his lead and to head off to Afghanistan to join up with the *mujahadeen.*

The mosque also sold tapes that implored believers to take up arms in the holy war against the West. In one such tape, Sheik Abu Abdul Aziz—a leader of jihad in Bosnia and Kashmir—gave the following recruitment message: "Come to Afghanistan! Only pay the fare for tickets. I am not asking you to get rid of your vacation or retire from your job or get rid of your business. I suggest that you come to vacation for training, and next year, second vacation, you come for *jihad.* If you are real believers, Allah is expecting you to do an extra job."[4]

Hundreds, including Ressam, answered the call that rang forth from the Montreal mosque. In order to raise money for the trip to Afghanistan, the industrious Algerian began stealing passports and other items from tourists, which he peddled in Montreal's thriving underworld.

With cash in hand, Ressam had another problem. He needed a new identity. If he were a Canadian with a passport, instead of an Algerian without one, he could move around the world with ease. He found the solution by stealing a blank baptismal certificate from a local Roman Catholic parish. Ressam visited the local library, discovered the name of a priest who had been the rector of the church in 1970 (which became his new year of birth), and signed the priest's name to the blank certificate. In this way, Ahmed Ressam, Algerian Muslim, became a French Canadian by the name of Benni Antoine Noris.[5]

The baptismal certificate, along with a photograph, was all Ressam needed to get a genuine Canadian passport. He didn't even have to take the forged certificate to the passport office himself. He simply shelled out three hundred dollars for one of his buddies at the mosque to pick it up for him.[6]

On March 16, 1998, Ressam bid adieu to his roommates and boarded a bus to Toronto. Using his new name, he purchased an airline ticket and flew from Toronto to Frankfurt, Germany. There, he met with al Qaeda contacts before flying on to Pakistan, where he was greeted by Abu Zubaydah, one of bin Laden's leading henchmen.[7]

In January 1999, after months of training at an al Qaeda camp, Ressam returned to Montreal with a notebook, twelve thousand dollars in cash, and a case of marijuana to raise additional funds. His assignment was to rent a safe house in Canada, purchase weapons, and build a bomb to blow up a major airport in the United States.[8]

For the next few months, Ressam used his Canadian passport to scout locations throughout the United States for the perfect site to mount the attack. He finally settled on the Los Angeles International Airport. Upon meeting with fellow members of the terrorist cell in Montreal, Ressam (now Benni Antoine Noris) headed off with three fellow jihadi to Vancouver, where he rented a room in a fleabag motel.

At the motel, the group proceeded to manufacture a bomb by brewing a batch of HMTD, an unstable mixture of hexamine, citric acid, and hydrogen peroxide in order to create (with hexamine and hydrogen peroxide) the military-grade explosive found in C-4 plastique.[9]

The bomb, unfortunately for Ressam and his tiny crew of conspirators, emitted such toxic fumes that they had to keep the windows of their motel room opened despite the subfreezing temperature and were compelled to suck on zinc lozenges to dull the pain from their raw throats. By December 14, Ressam's three companions were so sick that he was obliged to pack the bomb in the trunk of his rented Chrysler sedan and venture forth by himself to complete the monumental mission.[10]

When Ressam arrived in Port Angeles, Washington, Diana Dean, a US customs officials, sensing his nervousness, asked him to fill out a declaration form in order to stall for time. Inspector Danny Clem came to her assistance and began to inspect the car. In the spare-tire compartment, Clem discovered several green bags filled with white powder, four black boxes, two pill bottles, and two jars of a brown liquid. When Clem proceeded to shake one of the jars, Ressam took off like a jackrabbit. He was collared by other customs officials and taken into custody. The brown liquid, as it turned out, was highly unstable nitroglycerine.[11]

On March 13, 2001, Ressam was found guilty of nine criminal counts, including conspiracy to commit an act of international terrorism, in a federal court in Los Angeles. Faced with 150 years in prison, the terrorist transformed into a canary and began to sing in order to obtain the relatively light sentence of twenty-four years. Ressam's testimony eventually led to the arrests of numerous other al Qaeda agents, including Zacarias Moussaoui (a fellow Algerian with whom Ressam had trained in Afghanistan). It also exposed a virulent cell of al Qaeda in Montreal with sixty members; and shed light on the activities of the al-Kanadi family (see "Scary Story Number 2").[12]

Ressam's arrest, however, did little to alleviate fears concerning al Qaeda's ability to descend from the north in order to wreck destruction throughout the United States. He represented a minor player within the Montreal cell of the terrorist organization, which boasted sixty members. Of much greater significance was Abderraouf Jdey. Jdey was one of the four al Qaeda operatives who reportedly received training in nuclear technology at McMaster University in Hamilton, Ontario. Jdey and his cohorts, including Adnan el-Shukrijumah, reportedly stole over 180 pounds of radioactive material from the university for use in the long-planned American Hiroshima.[13] The radiological bomb that Jdey and his fellow jihadists could be in the process of making and delivering to a strategic site within a major American city might make Ressam's homemade bomb appear as harmless as a Fourth of July firecracker.

Also alarming is the fact that Ressam, despite his record of arrests and his affiliation with radical Islam, was not under surveillance by the CSIS or the FBI. The only thing that saved the Los Angeles International Airport from the attack was Diana Dean, a middle-aged border patrol officer, who noticed that Ressam was acting "hinky.")[14]

Ressam, a petty crook, was sloppy in his thinking and planning. The four-thousand-mile separation of Canada from the United States remains the largest border in the world. Ressam could have made the crossing by boat or by private plane. Crossing by car should have represented no great feat since there remain 225 unguarded roads between the two countries.[15]

Moreover, Ressam could have built his bomb in the United States, where the necessary materials were readily available at hundreds of hardware and agrosupply stores and where he could have made use of a garage, a warehouse, or a safe house in a rural area rather than a poorly vented motel room in Vancouver.

SCARY STORY NUMBER 2: THE KHADR FAMILY

The terrorist, who became known throughout the Arabian world as "al-Kanadi," or "the Canadian," was Ahmed Said Khadr, who left his native Egypt for the land of the maple leaf in 1975. In Ottawa, he established the Human Concern International (HCI), an organization with the purported aim of "alleviating human suffering" but a record of promoting militant Islam.[16] Khadr's "charity" prospered, attracting millions from radical mosques and extremist Islamic groups, along with gifts of $325,000 from the Canadian government.[17]

Flush with charitable funds, Ahmed traveled to Afghanistan, where he fought against the Soviets, developed a close friendship with Osama bin Laden, and set up his own training camp for jihadi recruits near Jalalabad.[18] In 1995 Ahmed supplied additional cash from the HCI coffers to fund the bombing of the Egyptian embassy in Islamabad that killed seventeen people.[19] In 1996 Ahmed was arrested in Pakistan for fostering terrorist acts and would have been put to death, save for a state visit by Canadian prime minister Jean Chrétien, who pleaded with the government of Benazir Bhutto for Ahmed's release and obtained it.[20]

Upon his return to Canada, Ahmed Khadr set up Health and Education Project International, another bogus charity. The success of this venture enabled him to head back to Afghanistan for a prolonged family vacation among the Taliban. During this hiatus, Zaynab, Ahmed's daughter, met and married an al Qaeda agent. Present at the nuptials were Osama bin Laden and other leaders of al Qaeda. One year later, Zaynab gave birth to a daughter and said: "If I was to choose for my daughter to live a life with no meaning or to die a martyr, I would choose for her to die a martyr. . . . I'd love to die a martyr. It's a desire that I believe every Muslim would have or should have."[21]

On 9/11, as soon as the planes crashed into New York's World Trade Center towers, Ahmed Khadr, like many other jihadis, vanished into the thin air. Several days later, Ahmed's wife, Maha Elsamnah, took her four sons to Pakistan in order to enroll them at an al Qaeda training camp. Insisting that such a camp was the best place for her children, Elsamnah was quoted in the *Toronto Globe and Mail* as saying: "Would you like me to raise my child in Canada to be, by the time he's 12 or 13 tears old, to be on drugs or having some homosexual relationship? Is it better?"[22]

Abdul Rahman, twenty-one, the second eldest, didn't last long as a jihadi. In November 2001 he was captured by Northern Alliance troops in Kabul and became one of the first terrorists to arrive at the US detention camp in Guantanamo Bay, Cuba. The incarceration set off a diplomatic spat between Ottawa and Washington, which resulted in Abdul Rahman's release on November 25, 2003.[23]

Upon his return to Ottawa, Abdul Rahman filed for the right to a Canadian passport. His application was approved by Canadian Federal Justice Michael Phelan, who ruled: "The court is mindful of the applicant's admitted conduct; he would not necessarily qualify as a model citizen, but that fact does not disentitle him to the application of fairness and natural justice to his passport application."[24]

Abdul Rahman proved to be thrice blessed. Not only did he receive his freedom and his passport but he also managed to sell the film rights of his life as a jihadist to Paramount Pictures for half a million dollars. A producer for the studio expressed his hope that Johnny Depp would star in the leading role.[25]

Not all of the Khadrs fared as well. On July 27, 2002, Omar Khadr, at the tender age of sixteen, was collared by US military forces after he tossed a hand grenade at a medical facility in Afghanistan and killed Sergeant 1st Class Christopher J. Speer.[26] Omar, who lost an eye in the incident, was sent to Guantanamo Bay for detention. His new surroundings, however, were not to his liking. Omar soon issued legal demands to the US government for unspecified monetary damages, claiming that he had been forced to use a bucket for a toilet and had not been provided with "basic hygienic facilities."[27]

In October 2003 Abdul Karim Khadr, fourteen, the youngest of the sons, was left half-paralyzed from gunshot wounds sustained when Pakistani forces raided an al Qaeda camp near the Pakistan-Afghanistan border. Among the dead, the troops found the badly deteriorated body of a portly man with a long white beard. The DNA matched that of Ahmed Khadr, the patriarch of the clan.[28]

Elsamnah, the dutiful mother, transported her injured son back to Toronto so that Abdul Karim could take full advantage of the Canadian healthcare system. She appeared in full burqa before the throng of reporters who gathered outside her home in Scarborough to say: "We've just been to the [Ontario Health Insurance Plan] office. That's it. They said we have to fill out forms. I'm proud of what we are and I'm proud we're in Canada now. Believe me; I will not force myself on anyone as a Canadian citizen. I'm demanding for my kids? Is that wrong? Is that a crime?"[29] The Canadian government obviously thought not. Ontario health minister George Smitherman confirmed that Abdul Karim and other members of the Khadr family were, indeed, entitled to all benefits of Canada's publicly funded healthcare program.[30]

On December 7, 2005, Abdullah Khan, twenty-four, the eldest of the sons, showed up in Toronto as a free man after spending some time in a Pakistani lockup. His whereabouts had been the subject of much speculation since his mother placed him under the care of al Qaeda. Abdullah, however, had been accused of killing a Canadian peacekeeper in Kabul and of operating a training camp for new recruits to the holy war.[31]

Before his return to Toronto, Abdullah granted an interview to correspondents from the PBS news program *Frontline*. A portion of the exchange is as follows:

What was your reaction to Sept. 11?

Like, I think itself was very amazing. It was very wild to see a person seeing a building in front of him and he's going 900 kilometers per hour straight in the building. That was very hard to believe. If you believe in something very hard you can do that . . .

So you felt admiration for the people who did this?

Yes. Because they did some things that stunned the entire world. Everybody for entire, like months, was only talking about that. I was watching TV and they brought some person from China, I think. China, Taiwan, something like that. And they asked him, he said that this is good for America to know that it is not always the superpower that can hit, that weak people have ways too to call the world for the world to listen to them, what they are saying, what do they want.

Once again, almost 2,500 people were killed in the World Trade Center, almost entirely civilians.

I feel sorry for those killed. But Americans kill civilians in Afghanistan. Nobody said anything to them. They killed about 100 persons in a wedding caravan and other place they had they killed about same thing, 100, 115 in a wedding. Nobody blamed them for doing it. And they have I think the most advanced technology in missiles and controls. So you cannot say they missed because they knew they knew what they're hitting. If their planes couldn't see it, the satel-

lites couldn't see it, then it's not a superpower, they shouldn't start hitting everybody. Accusing everybody of anything if they can't see.

What were your impressions of Osama bin Laden? I guess you saw him for the first time as a young boy. What were your impressions of him?

He was very quiet person. He would eventually get his respect. You would respect what he says. If he talks, he talks slowly. He never jokes, very quiet person, very polite. He can be a saint, something like a saint.[32]

Eight days after his return to hearth and home in Scarborough, Abdullah was taken into custody on the basis of a provisional warrant issued by the US Department of Justice. The warrant alleged that Abdullah had purchased munitions and explosives for al Qaeda and had participated in a plot to assassinate Pakistani president Pervez Musharraf.[33] At the preliminary hearing for extradition in July 2006, Prime Minister Paul Martin weighed in for Abdullah's rights by saying: "The family came in many, many years ago and they obtained Canadian citizenship many years ago. They have Canadian citizenship. We don't have two classes of citizens."[34] Abdullah's fate, at this writing, has yet to be determined.

The saga of the Khadr family should cause all Americans to shudder. It illustrates the fact that the Canadian government remains reluctant to address the problem of Islamic terrorism even when radical Muslims perform egregious acts. Terrorists from Canada, even those who have killed members of the US-led coalition forces (including fellow Canadians) and vow to create death and destruction throughout America, retain the right to political asylum, public welfare, and Canadian passports to travel freely. Why, therefore, would any self-respecting terrorist feel compelled to wade through the Rio Grande?

There is a codicil to the story. In a recent interview, Abdullah Khadr recalled meeting Prime Minister Jean Chrétien in 1996. "Once I was a son of a farmer," Chrétien told the young Abdullah, "and I became a prime minister. Maybe one day you will become one."

Certainly it is a stretch to believe that Abdullah will become Canada's prime minister.

But he could very well become the mayor of Islamberg, New York.

CHAPTER FOURTEEN

WELCOME TO ISLAMBERG

We dhikr [pray] *to the beat of a submachine gun.*
Sheikh Mubarak Gilani, founder of Jamaat-ul-Fuqra

"Come join my troops and my army,"
Says our Sheikh Gilani,
"A true believer is never dear.
Say, 'Victory is in the air!'
The kafir's [unbeliever's] *blood will not be spared."*
A poem by Sheikh Gilani

National unity is the basis of national security.
Supreme Court Justice Felix Frankfurter,
Fort Minersville School District v. Gobitis, 1940

Hancock, New York, is located at the base of Point Mountain, where the east and west branches of the Delaware River converge to form the headwaters that flow through Pennsylvania and New Jersey to the Atlantic Ocean. Two and a half hours from the hustle and bustle of New York City, Hancock is a sleepy little town with a population of 1,526. The downtown appears to have served as the backdrop for a Frank Capra movie. It contains a credit and loan, a commercial bank, a candy store, and a movie theater with a marquee. Two can wine and dine at one of the best eateries in town for less than forty dollars.

The streams and lakes that surround Hancock are teaming with brook and brown trout, perch, pickerel, bass, bullhead, and eels, and provide what many outdoorsmen believe to be "the best fishing in the country." In November hundreds of hunters descend on the area for the large-game season. The thick forests remain heavily populated with white tail deer and black bear, along with packs of coyotes and a few bobcats.

The two industries in Hancock are timber and stone. Oak, maple, ash, cherry, and other fine hardwoods are shipped from here to places throughout the world, where they are fashioned into stairways, tables, chairs, bookcases, and baseball bats, including the famed Louisville slugger. Bluestone from the local quarries graces the patios and fireplaces of elegant estates and the entranceways to such American landmarks as the Statue of Liberty and the Empire State Building.

THE MUSLIM MILITARY COMPOUNDS IN AMERICA

But Hancock no longer typifies small-town Americana. On the outskirts stands an encampment called Islamberg. The primary entrance is an unmarked road that leads to guard shacks, where armed black men stand guard to ward off any strangers or unwelcome visitors.

Located on seventy acres, Islamberg remains home to members of

Jamaat-ul-Fuqra ("community of the impoverished"), a group formed by Pakistani cleric Sheikh Mubarak Ali Gilani in 1980. Gilani, who refers to himself as "the sixth Sultan Ul Faqr," stated that the purpose of his group is to "purify" Islam through violence.[1] Gilani's gated "communities" were set up to serve as havens where young Muslims—primarily inner-city black men who became converts in prison—could begin a new life. In addition to the seventy-acre site in Hancock, the sheikh established "Hamaats" in Deposit, New York; Hyattsville, Maryland; Red House, Virginia; Falls Church, Virginia; Macon, Georgia; York, South Carolina; Dover, Tennessee; Buena Vista, Colorado; Talihina, Oklahoma; Tulane County, California; Commerce, California, and Onalaska, Washington.[2]

Before becoming a citizen of Islamberg or the other Fuqra communes, the Fuqra recruits are compelled to sign an oath that says: "I shall always hear and obey, and whenever given the command, I shall readily fight for Allah's sake."[3]

SHEIKH GILANI'S GROUP

Gilani also instituted the International Quranic Open University as an educational arm of Jamaat-ul-Fuqra. Every year, the university sends scores of American Muslims to Pakistan reportedly for guerrilla training. They are granted this degree of higher education with the stipulation that they return to the "Hamaats" (Gilani's term for the encampments) in order to provide the same training to others. In one of Gilani's works, published by the university, he writes that the foremost duty of all students is to wage jihad against "the oppressors of Muslims."[4]

Over the years, numerous members of Jamaat-ul-Fuqra have been convicted in US courts of such crimes as conspiracy to commit murder, firebombing, gun smuggling, and workers' compensation fraud. Others remain leading suspects in criminal cases throughout the country, including ten unsolved assassinations and seventeen firebombings between 1979 and 1990.[5] The criminal charges against the group and the criminal convictions are not things of the past. In 2001 a resident of the California compound was charged with first-degree murder in the shooting of a sheriff's deputy; another was charged with gun smuggling; and twenty-four of the Red House community were convicted of firearms violations.[6] By 2004 investigators uncovered evidence that purportedly linked both the DC "sniper killer" John Allen Muhammad and "Shoe Bomber" Richard Reid to the group and reports surfaced that *Wall Street Journal* reporter Daniel Pearl was captured and killed in the process of attempting to obtain an interview with Sheikh Gilani in Pakistan.[7]

LIFE WITHIN ISLAMBERG

The complex at Islamberg is constructed like a boot camp with trailers for recruits, a firing range, and a military-training area, replete with an obstacle course. It also contains two central structures for religious training, education, and community gatherings.[8]

Individuals from Hancock and its environs have complained about the activities taking place within the Muslim encampment. "We see children—small children running around over there when they should be in school," one local resident told Douglas Hagmann, director of the Northeast Intelligence Network, a multi-state-licensed private investigative firm that serves many Fortune 500 clients, and a member of the International Counter-Terrorism Officers' Association. "We hear bursts of gunfire all the time and we know that there is military-like training going on there. Those people are armed and dangerous."[9]

"We don't even dare to slow down when we drive by," another resident said. "They own this mountain and they know it, and there is nothing we can do about it but move, and we can't even do that. Who wants to buy a property next to that?"[10] Hagmann said that the residents did not wish to be identified for fear of reprisal from the inhabitants of the compound.

THE INVESTIGATIVE FINDINGS

Hagmann summarized his findings concerning Islamberg as follows:

- *The encampment has been in operation for at least 20 years and appears to maintain a steady level of occupancy. Each source confirmed the existence of at least one armed guard at the main entrance, especially during "special events" that result in a significant number of visitors by vehicle. The events appear to be meetings or religious services held within the compound.*
- *Nearly every weekend, [the] sound of gunfire can be heard from the camp. According to one neighbor who stated he's a combat veteran of the Vietnam War, some of the weapons obviously are "automatic" and large-caliber. On at least two occasions last summer, area residents heard small explosions.*
- *The occupants won't allow anyone not affiliated with their organization to enter the encampment. All of the residents stated they've never observed a marked law enforcement vehicle enter the compound at any time.*
- *Visitors to the compound are numerous and frequent. All visitors appear to be black males operating late-model vehicles, mostly SUVs, and many possess license plates from Michigan, Ohio, South Carolina, and Tennessee.*
- *At least once each week, private deliveries of unknown items are made to the camp by unmarked box-style trucks. The trucks, usually at the compound for two to three hours at a time, are operated by black males or men who appear to be of Middle Eastern origin.*
- *Men of Middle Eastern origin appear to be "frequent guests" of the encampment, many in traditional Islamic attire. Some appear to stay at the encampment for three to four days or longer. During the visits, activity and security at the compound is heightened noticeably.*[11]

In the course of his investigation, Hagmann also discovered that some residents of Islamberg work for the New York State Thruway, as tollbooth operators in the New York City area, while others are employed at a nearby center that processes credit card transactions and maintains vital confidential financial records.[12]

SAFE FROM SCRUTINY

Even though Jamaat-ul-Fuqra has been involved in serious terror attacks (and sundry criminal activities), recruits thousands of members, and may be operating paramilitary facilities for militant Muslims, it has never been placed on the official US Terror Watch List. On the contrary, it continues to operate as a legitimate nonprofit, tax-deductible organization.[13]

MATTERS OF REFLECTION

How can such compounds function as training sites for the jihad under the noses of the Federal Bureau of Investigation? Why do federal law enforcement officials remain reluctant to pursue these sites? Why has the current administration remained reluctant to adopt the necessary steps to prevent the next terrorist attack on US soil—the long-planned American Hiroshima?

These questions beg answers.

THE MIR WARNING IGNORED

In 2006 Hamid Mir—the only individual to interview bin Laden and al-Zawahiri in the wake of 9/11 and one of the world's leading journalists—issued this warning to the American people concerning the nuclear threat from al Qaeda:

As far as I know, they smuggled three suitcase nukes from Russia to Europe. They smuggled many kilos of enriched uranium inside America for their dirty bomb projects. They said in 1999 that they must have material for more than six dirty bombs in America. They tested at least one dirty bomb in the Kunar province of Afghanistan in 2000. They have planned an attack bigger than 9-11, even before 9-11 happened. Osama bin Laden trained 42 fighters to destroy the American economy and military might. Nineteen were used on 9-11, 23 are still "sleeping" inside America waiting for a wake-up call from bin Laden.[14]

David Dastych, an award-winning journalist from Poland and former CIA operative, testified that, in addition to the suitcase nukes that had been forward-deployed to the United States, another had arrived in Italy.[15] Despite their alarming reports, neither Mir nor Dastych were interviewed by the CIA, the US Department of Defense officials, or any other American official.

LOSING THE WAR

Will the United States of America—the richest and most powerful nation on earth—lose a war against the hordes of Islamic fanatics, who promote genocide, murder civilians, and behead captives? The thought of such an outcome seems incomprehensible. After all, al Qaeda and its sister organizations do not possess a standing army, lack sophisticated weaponry (including aircraft), operate on limited budgets, possess (save Hezbollah) no state sponsorship, and manifest a medieval view of reality replete with *jinn* (mischievous spirits) and jihad. The leaders of these groups are not educated in military science and the tactics of modern warfare. Moreover, the objective of these groups to establish a universal caliphate and to impose shariah (Islamic law) on the Western world seems not only preposterous but laughable.

But, five years after 9/11, the terrorists appear to be prevailing, thriving, and, yes, winning. They have mounted spectacular attacks in Tunisia, Bali, Mombasa, Riyadh, Istanbul, Jakarta, Madrid, Sharm el-Sheik, and London. In 2005 the number of "significant terrorist attacks" by radical Islamic groups mounted to 11,111, a fourfold increase over the previous year and the highest since the US State Department began gathering such figures over two decades ago.[16] A third of these attacks occurred in Iraq, President Bush's "central front on the war on terror," where the number of "high fatality incidents"— those resulting in ten or more deaths—rose from 65 in 2004 to 150 in 2005.[17] Instead of standing as the "shining example of democracy" that the White House had promised, Iraq became a grotesque advertisement against the US invasion and occupation.

Within Afghanistan in 2006, the United States witnessed the resurgence of the Taliban and received intelligence that one-eyed Mullah Omar and his army of radical Islamic students remain in control of all the rural and mountain areas of Afghanistan, including Khost, Paktia, Paktika, Ghazni, Zabul, Helmand, and Oruzgan, as well as a vast expanse of the eastern and southern provinces including sections of Kandahar.[18] The same intelligence confirmed that the Taliban has become the central governing body in South and North Qaziristan and other tribal territories of Pakistan.[19]

Interestingly, President Bush had earlier assured the nation that the terrorist groups had been severely impaired. "Nearly two-thirds of al Qaeda's known leaders have been captured or killed," he announced in his State of the Union Address.[20] And yet, Osama bin Laden, Ayman al-Zawahiri, and other al Qaeda leaders continued to make regular appearances on Al-Jazeera, the Arabian news network, to announce their victories, to restate their ideology, and to urge their fellow jihadis to make more audacious and more lethal attacks. Indeed, the widespread support of bin Laden throughout the Muslim world testifies to the fact that al Qaeda had become al Qaeda-ism, transmogrifying from a small conspiratorial group of Afghan Arabs into a worldwide political movement with millions of adherents.[21]

EPILOGUE

THE DAY OF ISLAM

Let me inform you about your inability to stop them [nuclear attacks on US soil] *before they are carried out. The reason is simple; you cannot uncover or stop them except by letting them be carried out. Furthermore, the best you could do would be to accelerate the day of carrying out the operations. In other words, if we schedule the operation to take place tomorrow, the best you could do is to make it happen today.*

This indeed is a sweet situation to be in. It is a win-win all the way for us. It is the ultimate control and the most stunning way to stop an operation (accelerating it with the same impact). What we are saying is this: You will have a choice of either let us carry it out on our own schedule and with our own hands or allow your own intelligence apparatus to cause it to happen. This second choice will cause a level of dissatisfaction (with your decision makers) to reach its highest level. Therefore, your Homeland Security Agencies would have no choice but to surrender and wait for the inevitable to happen.

I will not give any more clues; this is enough as a wake-up call.
Perhaps the American people will start thinking about the magni-
tude of the danger that is coming their way.

Rakan bin Williams, al Qaeda commander, March 2006

T he saga of the world, according to the Koran, is "play, idle talk, and pageantry" (57:20). The plot of the production concerns the struggle between the House of Islam (*dar al-Islam*), where Muslims rule and the law of Islam prevails, and the House of War (*dar al-Harb*), which consists of the rest of the world.[1] It is a vast spectacle with heroes and villains, believers and heretics—a multitudinous drama in which the only certainty is death.

From a human perspective, the dramatic work is all but incomprehensible. Glorious victory leads to ignoble defeat. High hope becomes deep despair. Brilliant light transforms into stygian darkness. The struggle of the Muslim people against the militant *kafirs* often seems futile, even farcical. Events unfold upon events in rapid succession without apparent rhyme or reason. And no one, not even the wisest imam, knows when the last act will begin or when the final curtain will fall.

But Allah, the supreme author, knows such things. Everything occurs according to his perfect design. He writes the words that the characters speak and he charts the linear action. Nothing can be changed. As Omar Khayyam, the twelfth-century Arabian poet, observed:

The Moving Finger writes, and, having writ,
Moves on: nor all your Piety nor Wit
Shall lure it back to cancel half a Line,
Nor all your Tears wash out a word of it.[2]

Belief in destiny is a cardinal precept of Islam: "Allah verily sends whom he will astray, and guides whom he will" (Koran 35:8). All is determined and nothing can change. The play is really a puppet show: "Allah has created you and what you do" (37:96). For this reason, wise men and true believers know they have no choice except to bow before the will of Allah five times a day. "Islam" means "submission"; and a Muslim is "one who surrenders to *taqdir* ("divine providence)."³

Behind the scenes of the spectacle are angels, who serve as Allah's messengers and secretaries, and *jinn*, who are made of fire and lead men into temptation. The leader of the *jinn* is Iblis, the great Satan, whose present abode is the United States of America.

The conflict between the House of Islam and the House of War will continue until the Day of Islam when all of creation will bow before the throne of Allah to utter the *shahadah* ("I testify that there is no God but Allah and Muhammad is his prophet"). The following signs, according to a number of Muslim fundamentalists, will signal the dawning of this day:

a. There will be an increase in war and bloodshed.
b. Mankind will become consumed by materialism.
c. Religious knowledge will decrease.
d. Women will outnumber men.
e. Rain will fall like acid from the heavens.
f. Illegitimate children will be widespread.
g. Homosexuality will be rampant.
h. Men will obey their wives and ignore their mothers.
i. Female singers will be commonplace.
j. People will dance long into the night.
k. Builders will compete with each other to build taller and taller buildings.
l. Women will enter the workforce out of love of the world.
m. Family ties will be cut.
n. Men will look like women and women like men.
o. Many women of childbearing years will not give birth.
p. Earthquakes will increase in number.
q. Time will be shortened so that a year will seem like a month.
r. Smog will appear in cities.
s. People will pass by graves and wish to change places with the dead.⁴

When these things come to pass, *Dajjal*, the "Antichrist" will appear. He will be one-eyed and red-faced; his unruly hair will stick up; and his voice will be so loud that all the earth will hear him. *Dajjal* will ride a white ass that will cross great distances within short expanses of time. His father will be tall and thin with a nose like a beak, while his mother will be fat with two long hands.[5]

While some Islamic scholars have identified the Antichrist as former US president Bill Clinton, a growing number now concur that President George W. Bush fits the bill of the apocryphal figure.[6] The one eye of *Dajjal*, this group insists, refers to President Bush's vision of a new world order with a global system of economics; the red face and unruly hair to his bellicose and (in their opinion) incoherent foreign policy, including his invasions and occupations of Muslim nations and his support for Israel; the loud voice to his access to the international media; and his white ass (the donkey) to Air Force One, the presidential jetliner.[7]

Dajjal will lead the world—with the sole exception of stalwart Muslim believers—astray. Almost everyone will become subject to his tyrannical rule. But before *Dajjal* succeeds in annihilating the pious remnant of Islam, Jesus (*'Isa*) will descend from heaven and appear at a mosque in Damascus. He will kill all pigs and break all crosses, and thereby confirm that Islam is the only true religion.[8]

Jesus will be joined by the Mahdi, "the enlightened one," who will arise from Arabia and, by popular acclamation in Mecca, receive the commission to lead the *mujahadeen* in the final conflict. With Jesus by his side, the Mahdi and the holy Muslim warriors will engage the forces of *Dajjal*, the *Dabbah* or "Beast," and the rapacious hordes of Gog and Magog at 'Aqabat Afiq in Syria, according to some accounts, or the Ludgate in Jerusalem, according to others.[9] At this time, Jesus will kill *Dajjal*; the kingdom of Gog and Magog will sink and be swallowed up by the hungry earth; and the great jihad will come to a glorious conclusion.

In the aftermath of the great battle, Jesus and the Mahdi will establish a universal caliphate in which *shariah* becomes the prevailing law for all nations. They will redistribute wealth from the rich to the poor on a global scale and every man will become a pious Muslim, every woman a modest figure in full burqa, and every child a model of obedience. *Kafirs* and apostates no longer will be permitted to exist. The Sunni Manual of Islamic Law states: "After His ['*Isa's*] final coming, nothing but Islam will be accepted from them, for taking the poll tax is only effective until Jesus's descent (upon Him and our Prophet be peace, which is the divinely revealed law of Muhammad. The coming of Jesus does not entail a separate divinely revealed law, for He will rule by the law of Muhammad."[10]

Many al Qaeda detainees at Guantanamo Bay and in the CIA "ghost prisons" throughout Eastern Europe claim that Osama bin Laden is the Mahdi, the realization of fourteen hundred years of Islamic history. They point out that the emir bears the correct facial physiognomy (a distinct forehead, a prominent nose, a gap between his teeth, and even the telltale black mole); that he is, as the sacred hadiths foretold, of Arabian origin and a direct descendent of Fatima, the Prophet Muhammad's daughter; that he possesses a generous and altruistic nature, exemplified by his desire to distribute the oil wealth of the Arabian peninsula among the disadvantaged Muslim masses; and that he was called from a cave in Afghanistan to serve as the leader of the *mujahadeen*.[11] Moreover, bin Laden acts like the Mahdi. He speaks of President Bush as al-Dajjal, of the United States as *Dabbah* the beast he must slay, and of the American people as the nation of Gog and Magog that he must destroy. Moreover, in his edicts and official correspondence, he no longer signs his name as Osama bin Laden but as Osama bin Mohammed bin Laden.[12]

After the arrival of the Day of Islam, other events will take place: a blast from a trumpet will resound throughout the earth; the sun will go out, the stars will fall, the skies will melt, mountains will explode into rubble, and the seas will burst into flame. With the second blast from the trumpet, all living creatures—*jinn*, angels, and men (save for a favored few) will be annihilated. At the third blast, the dead will arise to stand in judgment before the throne of Allah.[13]

The vast majority of mankind will be cast into hell, where they will experience burning heat or biting cold for all eternity. Their drink will be boiling water mixed with excrement. The blessed will enter one of the seven levels of heaven. The highest level will be reserved for the holy martyrs who have fought and died in the jihad against the Great Satan. The martyrs will be dressed in resplendent gowns and adorned with gems. They will eat from trees bowing down with succulent fruit and drink from rivers of milk, honey, and wine (forbidden on earth). Every blessed martyr will be granted seventy-two *houris*— virgins with "dark beautiful eyes," "swelling breasts," and "modest gaze")—as brides, who will cater to their every whim.[14]

In the wake of 9/11, FBI agents discovered letters in the luggage of the terrorists who had piloted three of the four doomed flights. The letters had been written by Mohammed Atta, who had distributed them to his fellow jihadists during their last meeting in Las Vegas. At the close of one letter, Atta wrote: "Know that the Gardens of Paradise are beautiful with its best ornaments and its inhabitants are calling you." After the death of a suicide bomber, members of al Qaeda and other terrorist groups hold a joyous celebration and speak of the martyr's death as a "wedding." In one of Atta's suitcases that had failed to make it aboard American Airlines Flight 11, inspectors found a perfectly pressed white wedding suit with a sapphire blue necktie.[15]

Atta, radical Muslims believe, is in the highest level of Paradise with his seventy-two brides. He will partake of pleasure for all eternity. This is in keeping with the immutable will of Allah. So, too, is the inevitable triumph of Islam over the United States of America and all of creation. The moving fingers of Allah have written the script of human history, and a flood of tears cannot "wash out a word of it."

APPENDIX A

THE NUCLEAR FATWA

AS ISSUED BY NASIR BIN HAMID AL-FAHD AND SIGNED BY OTHER SAUDI CLERICS, GRANTS AL QAEDA PERMISSION TO KILL TEN MILLION AMERICANS WITH NUCLEAR WEAPONS FOR THE SAKE OF PARITY

A TREATISE ON THE LEGAL STATUS OF USING WEAPONS
OF MASS DESTRUCTION AGAINST INFIDELS
by
NASIR BIN HAMD AL-FAHD
Rabi'I 1424 [May 2003]

QUESTION

Peace be with you and God's mercy and blessings!

Everyone knows what has been published in the media about al Qaeda's intention to strike America with weapons of mass destruction. Perhaps the so-called weapons of mass destruction are calamities of modern times. We have found no contemporary who has spoken about them.

What then is the legal ruling on their use by Muslims engaged in jihad? If one upholds the permissibility, are they permissible unconditionally? Or are they permissible for compelling necessity, for example, if the enemy's evil can be repelled only by their means? Are such weapons antithetical to humanity's purpose of making the earth prosper? Do such weapons fall under God's pronouncement: "And when he turns his back, he hastens about the earth to do corruption there and to destroy the tillage and the stock" (Koran 2:205). Or is the verse wrongly brought to bear upon the action, like the verses that occur condemning killing and the like?

ANSWER

The question that you have raised, noble brother, is one that deserves a full treatise that gathers up scholarly arguments and pronouncements; a treatise in which one records positions about questions such as the abode of war, ways of repelling assailants, the jihad of defense, the meaning in law of "destroying the tillage and the stock," and other matters. Perhaps, God willing, I can gather together what is at hand.

Know, generous brother, that the phrase "weapons of mass destruction" is inexact. By it they mean nuclear, chemical, or biological weapons, and no others. If anyone should use any of these weapons and kill a thousand people, they would launch accusations and media wars against him, saying that he had used "internationally banned weapons." If he had used high explosive bombs weighing seven tons apiece and killed three thousand or more because of them, he would have used internationally permitted weapons.

Surely, the effect of several kilograms of TNT can be considered mass destruction if you compare it to the effect of a catapult stone of old. An RPG [rocket-propelled grenade] or mortar projectile can be considered mass destruction if you compare it to the shooting of arrows of old. Certainly, the infidels of our time have made these so-called weapons of mass destruction (deterrence weapons) only to frighten others. America's threat to Iraq to use these weapons should Iraq attack Israel is not remote from us. What, then, allows them to America and the infidels and forbids them to Muslims? If a Muslim group should assault life or honor and could be repelled only by killing all its members, it would be permissible to kill them, as scholars have mentioned in chapters on repelling an assailant. How much more permissible is it when it comes to an infidel assailing the faith, life, honor, the intellect, and the homeland!

If the infidels can be repelled from the Muslims only by using such weapons, their use is permissible, even if you kill them without exception and destroy their pillage and stock. All this has its foundation in the Prophet's biography, the Prophet's sayings about jihad, and the pronouncements of scholars, may God have mercy on them.

FIRST PRELIMINARY

That Proscription Belongs to God Almighty, and to None Other Than He, Such as Humans

God has said: "And do not say, as to what your tongues falsely describe, 'This is lawful, and this is forbidden,' so that you may forge against God falsehood; surely those who forge against God falsehood shall not prosper" (Koran 16:116).

Ibn Kathir says (2:591): "God Almighty has forbidden following the path of the polytheists, who declared lawful or unlawful merely because they described something and gave a term to it by their own judgment, such as the *bahirah*, the *sa'ibah*, the *wasilah*, the *hami* [classes of cattle liberated in honor of idols and reverenced by the pagan Arabs], and other things that were law for them and that they invented in their time of ignorance."

I hold that things in the infidels' laws today belong in the same category. For example, they call something "internationally banned," "contrary to legitimate international authority," "forbidden by international law," "in violation of the Charter of Human Rights," or "in violation of the Geneva Convention," and so forth. The subject of this treatise belongs to the same category, insofar as they use the term "internationally banned weapons."

All these terms have no standing in Islamic law, because God

Almighty has reserved judgment and legislation to Himself. As He has said: "Judgment belongs only to God; He has commanded that you shall not serve any but Him" (Koran 12:40). God has said: "Or have they associates who have laid down for them as religion that for which God gave not leave?" (Koran 42:21). And God has said: "Verily, His are the creation and the command" (Koran 7:54).

This is a matter so obvious to Muslims that it needs no demonstration.

This having been established, you will realize that their words "internationally banned weapons" have no value. In judging these weapons, one looks only to the Koran, the Sunnah, and the statements of Muslim scholars. I would call attention here to the following two points:

Point One: When they say "weapons of mass destruction," they mean nuclear, biological, and chemical weapons. They hold that using any of these weapons is a violation of international law. If one state should strike another with tons of "conventional" bombs, killing tens of thousands, this use of weapons would be allowed internationally. If another state should use a small number of so-called weapons of mass destruction, killing only a few hundred, this use of weapons would be forbidden internationally. Thus it is evident that they do not wish to protect humanity by these terms, as they assert; rather, they want to protect themselves and monopolize such weapons on the pretext of "banning them internationally."

Point Two: Those who speak so pretentiously about combating the spread of weapons of mass destruction, America and Britain, for example, were the first to have used these weapons: Britain used chemical weapons against the Iraqis in World War I; America used nuclear weapons against Japan in World War II; and their arsenals—and those of the Jews—are full of such weapons!

SECOND PRELIMINARY

The Basic Rule in Killing Is to Do It in a Good Manner

An authentic tradition in the *Sahih* from Shaddad ibn Aws, a companion of the Prophet, says: "God has enjoined benevolence on everything. If you kill, kill in a good manner. If you slaughter animals, slaughter in a good manner; let the slaughterer sharpen his blade and put his victim at ease."

Al-Nawawi said in his commentary on the *Sahih* of Muslim (13:107): "The Prophet's words, 'Kill in a good manner,' include every animal slaughtered, every killing in retaliation or execution, and similar things. This hadith is one that sums up the foundations of Islam."

Ibn Rajab said in *Jami'* al *'Ulum wa-al-Hikam*, p. 152: "Doing good with regard to such humans and animals as may lawfully be killed is to take the life as swiftly, easily, and desirably as possible, without inflicting excessive pain. The easiest way to kill a human being is by striking the neck. God has said, referring to unbelievers, 'When you meet the unbelievers, smite their necks'" (Koran 47:4). And He has said: "I shall cast into the unbelievers' heart terror; so smite above the necks, and smite every finger of them" (Koran 8:12).

It has been established that whenever the Prophet sent out a raiding party, he said to them: "Do not mutilate, and do not kill a young child." Both Abu Dawud and Ibn Majah transmit a hadith from Ibn Mas'us, a companion of the Prophet, that the Prophet said: "The most restrained people in killing are the people of faith." Al-Bukhari transmits as part of the hadith from 'Abdallah ibn Yazid, a companion of the Prophet, that the Prophet said: "Mutilation has been forbidden." The traditions concerning this are many. All indicate that the basic rule is to kill in a good manner any such as may lawfully be killed and not to be excessive. However, this basic rule has exceptions. These exceptions are the subject of the third preliminary consideration.

THIRD PRELIMINARY

Distinguishing between the Possible and the Impossible

An established rule in Islamic law is to distinguish between the possible and the impossible. This is indicated in God's words: "So fear God as far as you are able" (Koran 64:16). This is a constant throughout the topics of Islamic law, whether in matters of worship or in matters of interpersonal relations. A well-established tradition transmitted in the *Sahih* from Abu Hurayrah, a companion of the Prophet, is that the Prophet said: "If you give a command, perform it as far as you are able." Al-Nawawi commented on the hadith as follows (Sharh Sahih Muslim, 9:102): "This is one of the important foundations of Islam and one of the comprehensive maxims that were given to the Prophet. Innumerable judgments fall under it. Prayer, for example, in all its kinds: if one cannot fulfill some of its principles or conditions, one fulfills the remaining ones. If one cannot wash all the limbs in the ablutions or in the full washing of the body, one washes what one can."

Scholars have deduced from these and similar texts the rule that there is no obligation when there is inability; there is no prohibited thing when there is necessity. The relevance of this rule here is that any obligations that fall under the category jihad depend on ability. Any obligation that is impossible lapses, as in any other category.

1. One kills in a good manner only when one can. If those engaged in jihad cannot do so, for example, when they are forced to bomb, destroy, burn, or flood, it is permissible.
2. One avoids killing women and children only when one can distinguish them. If one cannot do so, as when the infidels make a night attack or invade, they may be killed as collateral to the fighters.
3. Similarly, killing a Muslim is forbidden and not permitted; but if those engaged in jihad are forced to kill because they cannot

repel the infidels or fight them otherwise, it is permitted, as when the Muslim is being used as a living shield.

ARGUMENTS FOR THE PERMISSIBILITY OF USING WEAPONS OF MASS DESTRUCTION

I mentioned in the previous section that the rule is to kill in a good manner, that killing infidels falls under this rule, but that this can take place only when one has the ability to do so. The infidels might be in such a position that they cannot be resisted or repelled from Islamic territory and Muslims are spared their violence unless they are bombed with what are called weapons of mass destruction, as people with experience in jihad affirm. If people of authority engaged in jihad determine that the evil of the infidels can be repelled only by their means, they may be used. The weapons of mass destruction will kill any of the infidels on whom they fall, regardless of whether they are fighters, women, or children. They will destroy and burn the land. The arguments for permissibility of this in this case are many. They fall into two divisions.

First Division: Arguments relating to a particular time period and a particular enemy. For example, with regard to America at this time, the matter of striking her with these weapons is permissible without mentioning the arguments of the second section (arguments of general legitimacy). This is because God has said: "Whoso commits aggression against you, do you commit aggression against him like as he has committed against you" (Koran 2:194). And God also said: "And the recompense of evil is evil the like of it"(Koran 42:40). Anyone who considers America's aggression against Muslims and their lands during the past decades will conclude that striking her is permissible merely on the basis of the rule of treating as one has been treated. No other arguments need be mentioned. Some brothers have totaled the number of Muslims killed directly or indirectly by their weapons and come up with a figure of merely ten million. As for the lands that their bombs, explosives, and missiles have burned only God can compute them. The most recent events we have witnessed are those in Afghanistan and Iraq, and this is in addition to the uprooting that their wars have caused for many Muslims. If a bomb that killed ten million of them and burned as much of their land as they have burned Muslims' land were dropped on them, it would be permissible, with no need to mention any other argument. We might need other arguments if we wanted to annihilate more than this number of them!

Second Division: General arguments for the legitimacy of this action universally if required by jihad in the way of God. These are texts that indicate the permissibility of using such weapons if those engaged in jihad decide that there is benefit in using them. The arguments for this are many. I shall mention three of them.

First Argument

The Permissibility of Attacking the Polytheists by Night, Even If Their Children Are Injured

Among them is a hadith transmitted in both *Sahihs* from al-Sa'b ibn Jaththamah, a companion of the Prophet, who said that the Prophet was asked about some Muslims who had raided the polytheists at night, wounding some of their women and children. He replied, "They are of them." Also in both *Sahihs* is a hadith from Ibn 'Umar, a companion of the Prophet, who says: "The Prophet, may God bless him and grant him peace, attacked the Banu al-Mustaliq while they were off guard among their cattle. He killed the fighters and took the children captive." Also, Ahmed [ibn Hanbal] and Abu Dawud relate a hadith from Salamah ibn al-Akwa', who said: "The Messenger of God, may God bless him and grant him peace, appointed Abu Bakr to be our commander, and we raided a group of polytheists. We lay wait for them at night to kill them. Our slogan that night was 'Kill! Kill!' with my own hand that night I killed seven high-ranking polytheists." It has been established that the Prophet forbade the killing of women and children. However, if you put these hadiths together, it will become apparent that the prohibition is against killing them intentionally. If they are killed collaterally, as in the case of a night attack or an invasion when one cannot distinguish them, there is nothing wrong with it. Jihad is not to be halted because of the presence of infidel women and children.

Al-Bayhaqi devoted a chapter of Al-Sunan al-Kubra (9:78) to al Sa'b's hadith, entitling it: "On Unintentionally Killing Women and Children in a Night Raid or Attack, Hadiths Transmitted Permitting Night Attacks." He cites this hadith and then quotes al-Shafi, who said, "In our view, and God alone knows best, the meaning of the prohibition on killing women and children is on intentionally seeking to kill them when they can be recognized and distinguished from those who have been ordered to be killed. The meaning of the Prophet's words, 'They are of them' is that they unite two traits: they do not have the legal factor of faith, which spares one's blood, nor do they live in an abode of faith, which prevents an attack on that abode."

The Imam Ahmad [Ibn Hanbal] said, as stated in Al-Mughni (9: 230): "There is nothing wrong with night attacks. The attack on the Byzantines was nothing but a night attack. We know of no one who finds it reprehensible to attack the enemy at night."

Al-Tahawi mentions the reports relevant to the prohibition on killing women and children. Then he mentions the hadith of al-Sa'b ibn Jaththamah about the night raid and says (Sharh Ma'ani al-Athar, 3:222): "Since the Messenger of God, may God bless him and grant him peace, had not yet forbidden them from incursions, and in them they used to injure children and women whose intentional killing is forbidden, this indicates that what he permitted in these traditions was for some other reason than the one for which he forbade what he forbade in the first traditions; that what he forbade in the first traditions was the intent to kill women and children; and that what he allowed was the intent against polytheists, even if that involved harm to the others whom it is not allowed to hurt intentionally. In this way, these traditions related from the prophet are sound and not to contradict each other. The Messenger of God commanded an attack on the enemy. In many traditions he attacked others—these we have mentioned in the chapter on prayer before fighting. He was not prevented from this by what we know, namely, that he knew that children and women would not be safe from harm. He allowed the attack because the intent on the attackers was not to harm them. This agrees with my interpretation of the hadith of al Sa'b. Thus, he has enjoined us to fight the enemy, but he has forbidden us to kill their women and children. It is a sin for us to intend to do what he has forbidden us to do, but it is permitted for us to intend to do what has been permitted for us, even if it involves harming others whom we have been forbidden to harm and for whom we are not responsible." Therefore, the situation in this regard is that if those engaged in jihad establish that the evil of the infidels can be repelled only by attacking them at night with weapons of mass destruction, they may be used even if they annihilate all the infidels.

Second Argument

The Permissibility of Burning the Enemy's Lands

The great mass of scholars held the view that burning and devastating are permissible in enemy territory. Ibn 'Umar's hadith proves that Muslims may employ any stratagems that will sap their polytheist enemy's strength, weaken their cunning, and facilitate victory over them. They may cut down their crops, divert their water, and besiege them. Those who permitted this were the Kufans, Malik, al-Shafi'i, Ahmed [ibn Hanbal], Ishaq, al-Thawri, and Ibn al-Qasim. The Kufans said that their trees could be cut down, their land devastated, and their cattle slaughtered or hamstrung if they could not be dislodged. This hadith is clear in its indication that setting fire to enemy territory is permissible if the fighting requires it.

Third Argument

The Permissibility of Striking the Enemy with Weapons That Cause Mass Destruction

Abu Dawud and others transmit the following hadith with a broken chain of transmission: that the Prophet, may God bless him and grant him peace, set up a catapult to attack the people of al Ta'if. Al-Bay-haqi and others relate that 'Amr ibn al 'As, a companion of the Prophet, set up a catapult to attack the people of Alexandria. Al-Bay-haqi also relates that Yazid ibn Abi Habib reported that at the conquest of Caesaria in the days of 'Umar ibn al-Khattab they bombarded the city every day with sixty catapults. That was how the Muslims conducted their military campaigns. Sa'id ibn Mansur related from Safwan ibn 'Amr that Junadah ibn Abi Umayyah al-Azdi, 'Abdallah ibn Qays al Fazari, and other sea captains and their men—it was in the time of Mu'awiyah—would bombard the Byzantines and other enemies with fire and burn them, with each side doing it to the other. He said that Muslims never ceased doing so. Sa'idibn Mansur also related from 'Alqamah that they attacked during the days of Mu'awiyah and used a catapult during their attack.

Scholars have agreed that it is permissible to bombard the enemy with catapult and similar things. As everyone knows, a catapult stone does not distinguish between women, children, and others; it destroys anything that it hits, buildings or otherwise. This proves that the principle of destroying the infidels' lands and killing them if the jihad requires it and those in authority over the jihad decide so is legitimate; for the Muslims bombarded these countries with catapults until they were conquered. No one reports that they ceased for fear of annihilating their infidels or for fear of destroying their territory.

God alone knows best.

APPENDIX B

EXAMPLES OF TERRORISM CONVICTIONS SINCE SEPTEMBER 11, 2001

(US DEPARTMENT OF JUSTICE)

Hassan Moussa Makki (Eastern District of Michigan)—In September 2003 Hassan Makki pleaded guilty to racketeering charges and providing material support to Hezbollah in conjunction with the Mohammed Hammoud case in Charlotte, North Carolina. Makki was sentenced to fifty-seven months in prison.

Richard Reid (District of Massachusetts)—British national Richard Reid was sentenced to life in prison following his guilty plea in January 2003 on charges of attempting to ignite a shoe bomb while on an airplane from Paris to Miami. Reid was subdued by passengers on the December 22, 2001, American Airlines flight before he could ignite the explosives.

John Walker Lindh (Eastern District of Virginia)—Lindh pleaded guilty in July 2002 to one count of supplying services to the Taliban and a charge that he carried weapons while fighting on the Taliban's front lines in Afghanistan against the Northern Alliance. Lindh was sentenced to twenty years in prison.

Lackawanna Six: Shafal Mosed, Yahya Goba, Sahim Alwan, Mukhtar al-Bakri, Yasein Taher, Elbaneh Jaber (Western District of New York)—Six defendants from the Lackawanna, New York, area pleaded guilty to charges of providing material support to al Qaeda, based on their attendance at an al Qaeda terrorist training camp. The defendants were sentenced to terms ranging from seven years to ten years in prison.

Portland Cell: Maher "Michael" Hawash, October Martinique Lewis, Habis Abdullah al-Saoub, Patrice Lamumba Ford, Ahmed Ibrahim Bilal, Muhammad Ibrahim Bilal, Jeffrey Leon Battle (District of Oregon)—The defendants in the so-called Portland Cell case pleaded guilty to criminal charges ranging from laundering money to conspiracy to supply goods to the Taliban to seditious conspiracy. Ford and Battle were each sentenced to eighteen years in prison. The charges resulted from an investigation into the defendants' training for preparation to fight violent jihad in Afghanistan.

Earnest James Ujaama (Western District of Washington)—Pursuant to a cooperation agreement, Earnest James Ujaama was sentenced to two years in jail in February 2004 following his guilty plea on a charge of conspiring to supply goods and services to the Taliban in violation of the International Emergency Economic Powers Act.

Sayed Mustajab Shah, Ilyas Ali, Muhammed Abid Afridi (Southern District of California)—In April 2006 Muhammed Abid Afridi was sentenced to fifty-seven months in prison on one count of conspiracy to distribute heroin and hashish and one count of providing material support to terrorists. Afridi was arrested in September 2002 and indicted by a federal grand jury in October 2002 along with codefendants Sayed Mustajab Shah and Ilyas Ali for their involvement in an international drugs-for-weapons program. Shah's sentencing is scheduled for June 2006. Ali was sentenced to fifty-seven months in prison.

Carlos Ali Romero Valera, Uwe Jensen, Edgar Fernando Blanco Puerta, Elkin Alberto Arroyave Ruiz, Carlos Adolfo Romero-Panchano, Fanny Cecilia Barrera de Amaris, Adriana Gladys Mora (Southern District of Texas)—As part of Operation

White Terror, Carlos Ali Romero Valera, Uwe Jensen, Edgar Fernando Blanco Puerta, and Elkin Alberto Arroyave Ruiz were convicted on charges of supplying material support to a terrorist organization (the United Self-Defense Forces [AUC] of Colombia) through a weapons-for-drugs deal. In December 2005 Fanny Cecilia Barrera de Amaris and Carlos Adolfo Romero-Panchano were convicted on charges of conspiracy to provide material support and resources to a foreign terrorist organization. Both were extradited in 2004 and pleaded guilty. Barrera de Amaris was sentenced to five years and one month in prison while Romero-Panchano was sentenced to three years. Adriana Gladys Mora was convicted in January 2004 of conspiring to provide material support to a terrorist organization and distributing cocaine.

Iyman Faris (Eastern District of Virginia)—In October 2003 Iyman Faris was sentenced to twenty years in prison for providing material support and resources to al Qaeda and conspiracy for providing the terrorist organization with information about possible US targets for attack. Faris pleaded guilty in May 2003.

Virginia Jihad: Masoud Ahmad Khan, Seifullah Chapman, Hammad Abdur-Raheem (Eastern District of Virginia)—In the Virginia Jihad case, Masound Ahmad Khan was convicted in March 2004 of eight charges including conspiracy to levy war against the United States; providing support to the Taliban and conspiracy to provide support to Lashkar-e-Toiba (LET); and gun violations. He was later sentenced to life in prison. Hammad Abdur-Raheem was convicted on three charges of providing material support to LET, firearms and conspiracy charges, and later sentenced to fifty-two months in prison on each count. Seifullah Chapman was convicted on five counts, including conspiracy to provide material to LET and weapons charges, and later sentenced to 780 months in prison.

Virginia Jihad: Aatique Mohammed, Donald Thomas Surratt, Khwaja Mahmood Hasan, Yong Ki Kwon, Randall Todd Royer, Ibrahim Ahmed al-Hamdi (Eastern District of Virginia)—Also in the Virginia Jihad case, these six defendants pleaded guilty to various charges, including conspiracy to commit an offense against the United

States and weapons violations, and were sentenced to terms ranging from forty-six months to twenty years in prison.

Virginia Jihad: Ali al-Timimi (Eastern District of Virginia)—Al-Timimi was convicted in April 2005 on all ten charges brought against him in connection with the Virginia Jihad case. Al-Timimi, a spiritual leader at a mosque in Northern Virginia, encouraged other individuals at a meeting to go to Pakistan to receive military training from Lashkar-e-Toiba, a designated foreign terrorist organization, in order to fight US troops in Afghanistan. Al-Timimi was sentenced to life in prison.

Abdurahman Alamoudi (Eastern District of Virginia)—In October 2004 Alamoudi was sentenced to twenty-three years in prison for his activities in the United States and abroad with nations and organizations that have ties to terrorism. In September 2003 Alamoudi was arrested at Dulles International Airport and pleaded guilty in July 2004 to three federal offenses: violating the International Emergency Economic Powers Act; false statements made in his application for naturalization; and a tax offense involving a long-term scheme to conceal from the IRS his financial transactions with Libya and his foreign bank accounts and to omit material information from the tax returns filed by his charities.

Hamant Lakhani (District of New Jersey)—British national Hamant Lakhani was convicted by a federal jury on charges of attempting to sell shoulder-fired missiles to what he thought was a terrorist group intent on shooting down US airliners. Lakhani was sentenced to forty-seven years in prison.

Mohammed Junaid Babar (Southern District of New York)—In June 2004 Mohammed Junaid Babar, a naturalized American originally from Pakistan, pleaded guilty to five counts of conspiring to provide material support to al Qaeda. He is awaiting sentencing.

Lynne Stewart, Mohammed Yousry, Ahmed Abdel Sattar (Southern District of New York)—In February 2005 a federal jury in Manhattan convicted attorney Lynne Stewart, Mohammed Yousry, and Ahmed Abdel Sattar on charges including providing, and concealing the provision of, material support or resources to terrorists. The defendants were associates of Sheikh Abdel-Rahman, leader of the terrorist organization Islamic Group (IG), who is serving a life sentence for his role in terrorist activity, including the 1993 bombing of the World Trade Center.

Rafil Dhafir, Osameh al-Wahaidy, Ayman Jarwan (Northern District of New York)—In February 2005 a federal jury convicted Dhafir of participating in a conspiracy to unlawfully send money to Iraq and money laundering. Dhafir was sentenced to twenty-two years in prison. Al-Wahaidy and Jarwan pleaded guilty to charges in the same case.

Mohammad Ali Hasan al-Moayad and Mohammed Moshen Yahya Zayed (Eastern District of New York)—In March 2005 a federal jury convicted al-Moayad, a Yemeni cleric, and Zayed on charges of providing and conspiring to provide material support and resources to al Qaeda and Hamas. Al-Moayad was sentenced to seventy-five years in prison; Zayed was sentenced to forty-five years in prison.

Zacarias Moussaoui (Eastern District of Virginia)—In April 2005 Zacarias Moussaoui pleaded guilty to six charges against him related to his participation in the September 11th conspiracy. In May 2006 Moussaoui was sentenced to life in prison.

Basman Elashi, Bayan Elashi, Ghassan Elashi, Hazim Elashi, Ihsan Elashi (Northern District of Texas)—In April 2005 a federal jury convicted Basman, Bayan, and Ghassan Elashi, and the Infocom Corporation, on charges of conspiracy to deal in the property of a specially designated terrorist and money laundering. The activities were related to Infocom, an Internet service provider believed to be a front for Hamas. Hazim and Ihsan Elashi were also convicted in the same case and were sentenced to sixty-six months and seventy-two months in prison, respectively.

Mark Robert Walker (Western District of Texas)—In April 2005 Walker was sentenced to two years in prison for aiding a terrorist organization. He was indicted in December 2004 and pleaded guilty to two counts of attempting to make a contribution of goods and services to a designated terrorist organization (Al-Ittihad al-Islami in Somalia).

Carlos Gamarra-Murillo (Middle District of Florida)—In August 2005 Gamarra-Murillo was sentenced to twenty-five years in prison for engaging in the business of brokering and exporting defense articles without a license and providing material support to a foreign terrorist organization (FARC). Gamarra-Murillo was charged in April 2004 and pleaded guilty in February 2005.

Ahmed Omar Abu Ali (Eastern District of Virginia)—In November 2005 a federal jury convicted Ali on all counts of an indictment charging him with terrorism offenses, including providing material support and resources to al Qaeda, conspiracy to assassinate the president of the United States, conspiracy to commit air piracy, and conspiracy to destroy aircraft. Ali was sentenced to thirty years in prison.

Uzair Paracha (Southern District of New York)—Paracha was convicted in November 2005 on charges of providing material support to al Qaeda. Evidence at trial demonstrated that Paracha agreed with his father and two al Qaeda members to provide material support to al Qaeda by, among other things, trying to help an al Qaeda member reenter the United States to commit a terrorist act.

Hamid Hayat (Eastern District of California)—On April 25, 2006, a federal jury in Sacramento convicted Hamid Hayat of Lodi, California, of one count of providing material support or resources to terrorists and three counts of lying to the FBI in a terrorism investigation. The jury found that Hayat provided material support to terrorists by attending a jihad training camp overseas, and that he attempted to conceal his training from the FBI. Hayat faces up to thirty-nine years in prison; sentencing is scheduled for July 2006.

Ali Asad Chandia and Mohammed Ajmal Khan (Eastern District of Virginia)—On June 6, 2006, Ali Asad Chandia was found guilty on charges of conspiracy to provide material support to Lashkar e Toiba (LET). This case resulted from the continuation of the Virginia Jihad investigation. All four counts of the indictment rested upon the premise that Chandia and Mohammed Ajmal Khan conspired to provide, and did provide, material support to LET both before and after it was designated as a foreign terrorist organization. Chandia met Khan, a senior official and procurement officer for LET, at an office of that organization in Pakistan in late 2001. Khan traveled to the United States in 2002 and 2003 to acquire equipment for Lashkar-e-Toiba, and Chandia assisted him in these efforts both times. A jury found Chandia guilty of three of the four counts of the indictment.

NOTES

CHAPTER 1

1. Mark Fineman and Stephen Braun, "Life Inside Al Qaeda: A Destructive Devotion," *Los Angeles Times*, September 24, 2001.

2. Testimony of Jamal Ahmed al-Fadl, *The United States of America v. Osama bin Laden, et al.*, US District Court, Southern District of New York, February 6, 2001.

3. Ibid.

4. Testimony of Jamal Ahmed al-Fadl, *The United States v. Osama bin Laden, et al.*, February 8, 2001. See also Gordon Thomas, "Los Malerines de Osama," *El Mundo* (Spain), September 23, 2001.

5. Testimony of Jamal Ahmed al-Fadl, February 6, 2001.

6. Ibid.

7. Jason Williams and Andrew Brent, "The World Comes to Atlantic Avenue," *Street Level*, School of Journalism, New York University, July 15, 2003, http://journalism.nyu.edu/publiczone/streetlevel/atlanticave/world/money.htm.

8. Carl Limbacher, "Mosque Linked to '93 World Trade Center Bombing Funded by Bin Laden," *Newsmax*, November 26, 2003, http://www.newsmax.com/archives/ic/2003/11/26/123312.shtml.

9. Peter Lance, *100 Years of Revenge* (New York: Regan Books, 2003), pp. 38–42.

10. Abdullah Azzam, quoted in Peter L. Bergen, *Holy War, Inc.: Inside the Secret World of Osama bin Laden* (New York: Simon & Schuster, 2002), p. 136.

11. Daniel Pipes, *Militant Islam Reaches America* (New York: Norton, 2003), p. 137.

12. Testimony of Jamal Ahmed al-Fadl, February 6, 2001.

13. Ibid.

14. Ibid.

15. Ibid.

16. Lawrence Wright, "The Man behind Bin Laden," *New Yorker*, September 16, 2002.

17. Ibid.

18. Robert Young Pelton, *The World's Most Dangerous Places*, 5th ed. (New York: Harper Resource, 2004), p. 430.

19. Ibid., p. 377.

20. Wright, "The Man behind Bin Laden."

21. Testimony of Jamal Ahmed al-Fadl, February 6, 2001.

22. Wright, "The Man behind Bin Laden."

23. Peter L. Bergen, *The Bin Laden I Know* (New York: Simon & Schuster, 2006), p. 81.

24. Ibid.

25. Testimony of Jamal Ahmed al-Fadl, February 6, 2001.

26. Dan Darling. "Revisionist History," *Weekly Standard*, November 11, 2005.

27. Roland Jacquard, *In the Name of Osama Bin Laden: Global Terrorism and the Bin Laden Brotherhood* (Durham, NC: Duke University Press, 2002), p. 14.

28. Ibid., pp. 22–23.

29. Pelton, *The World's Most Dangerous Places*, p. 347.

30. Robert Windrem, "CIA Is Looking for a Few Good Doctors," NBC News, December 29, 2004.

31. "Bin Laden Alive as of Late December Report," Reuters, June 30, 2002 (7:11 PM EST).

32. Pepe Escobar, "Osama Is in Kunar but U.S. Can't Get Him," *Asia Times*, August 29, 2002.

33. "Bin Laden Tape," BBC, January 19, 2006.

34. "Who Is Ayman al-Zawahiri?" MSNBC, March 25, 2004.

35. Bergen, *The Bin Laden I Know*, p. 66.

36. "Pakistan Rally against US Strike," BBC, January 15, 2006.

37. Bergen, *The Bin Laden I Know*, p. 255.

38. "Pakistan Says Al Qaeda Spy Chief Wasn't Killed," Associated Press, March 30, 2004.

39. Dan Darling, "Al-Libbi: Still Not #3: But No Mistaken Identity," *Weekly Standard*, May 8, 2003, http://www.windsofchange.net/archives/006799.php.

40. Christina Lamb and Mohammad Shehzad, "Captured Al Qaeda Kingpin Is a Case of Mistaken Identity," *Sunday Times* (London), May 8, 2005.

41. Ibid.

42. Ibid.

43. Ibid.

44. Joe Trento, "Pakistan and Iran's Scary Alliance," *Public Education Center*, National Security and National Resources News Services, August 15, 2003, http://www.publicedcenter.org/stories/trento/2003-08-15. See also Paul L. Williams, *The al Qaeda Connection: International Terrorism, Organized Crime, and the Coming Apocalypse* (Amherst, NY: Prometheus Books, 2005), p. 131.

45. Faye Bowers, "Iran Holds Al Qaeda's Top Leaders," *Christian Science Monitor*, July 28, 2003.

46. Ibid.

47. Bergen, *The Bin Laden I Know*, p. 82. See also Testimony of Jamal Ahmed al-Fadl, February 6, 2001.

48. Ibid.

49. "Al Qaeda: Killed or Captured," MSNBC and NBC News, June 22, 2005.

50. Testimony of Jamal Ahmed al-Fadl, February 6, 2001.

51. Howard Chua-Eoan, "Is He Osama's Best Friend?" *Time*, November 12, 2001. See also Testimony of Jamal Ahmed al-Fadl, February 6, 2001.

52. Indictment of Mamdouh Mahmud Salim, US Attorney's Office, Southern District of New York, January 6, 1999.

53. Viola Gienger, Cam Simpson, and Laurie Cohen, "Chicagoan Accused of Aiding Fugitive," *Chicago Tribune*, August 7, 2002.

54. Indictment of Mamdouh Mahmud Salim.

55. Gienger, Simpson, and Cohen, "Chicagoan Accused of Aiding Fugitive."

56. *The 9/11 Commission Report: Final Report of the National Commission on Terrorist Attacks upon the United States*, authorized ed. (New York: Norton, 2004), p. xv.

57. Benjamin Weiser, "Trial Poked Holes in Image of Bin Laden's Terror Group," *New York Times*, May 31, 2001.

CHAPTER 2

1. Kimberly McCloud and Matthew Osborne, "Chart: Al Qaeda's WMD Activities," Center for Nonproliferation Studies, Monterey Institute of International Studies, May 2005, http://cns.miis.edu/pubs/other/sym.cht.htm.

2. Peter L. Bergen, *The Osama bin Laden I Know* (New York: Free Press, 2006), p. 349.

3. Osama bin Laden, quoted in Simon Reeve, *The New Jackals: Ramzi Yousef, Osama Bin Laden, and the Future of Terrorism* (Boston: Northeastern University Press, 1999), p. 170.

4. Jane Corbin, *Al Qaeda: In Search of a Terror Network That Threatens the World* (New York: Thunder's Mouth Press/Nation Books, 2002), p. 27.

5. Mark Danner, "Taking Stock of the Forever War," *New York Times Magazine*, September 11, 2005.

6. Yossef Bodansky, *Bin Laden: The Man Who Declared War on America* (New York: Random House, 1999), p. 29.

7. Phil Gasper, "Afghanistan, the CIA, bin Laden, and the Taliban," *International Socialist Review*, November/December 2001, http://www.third worldtraveler.com/Afghanistan/Afghanistan_CIA_Taliban.html\.

8. Osama bin Laden, "Jihad against Jews and Christians," appendix B in Paul L. Williams, *Osama's Revenge: The Next 9/11* (Amherst, NY: Prometheus Books, 2005).

9. Daniel Benjamin and Steven Simon, *The Age of Sacred Terror* (New York: Random House, 2002), pp. 107–108.

10. Reeve, *The New Jackals*, p. 72.

11. Robert Young Pelton, *The World's Most Dangerous Places*, 5th ed. (New York: HarperCollins, 2003), p. 915.

12. Corbin, *Al-Qaeda*, p. 31.

13. Testimony of Jamal al-Fadl, *The United States of America v. Osama bin Laden, et al.*, United States District Court, Southern District of New York, February 6, 2001.

14. Peter L. Bergen, *Holy War, Inc.: Inside the Secret World of Osama bin Laden* (New York: Simon & Schuster, 2002), p. 84.

15. Ibid., p. 83.

16. Corbin, *Al-Qaeda*, pp. 35–36.

17. Testimony of Jamal al-Fadl, February 6, 2001.

18. Ibid.

19. Ibid.

20. Michael Barletta and Erik Jorgensen, "Weapons of Mass Destruction in the Middle East," Center for Nuclear Nonproliferation Studies, Monterey Center for International Studies, Monterey, CA, April 1999.

21. Testimony of Jamal al-Fadl, February 7, 2001.

22. Ibid.

23. "Suburban Chicago-Based International Charity and Its Director Charged with Perjury Relating to Alleged Terrorist Activity," Office of International Information Programs, US Department of State, April 30, 2002.

24. Ibid.

25. Daniel Eggen and Manuel Roig-Franzia, "FBI on Global Hunt for Al Qaeda Suspect," *Washington Post*, March 21, 2003.

26. "Islamic Charity Director Charged with Lying about Ties to Bin Laden," Fox News, May 1, 2002, http://www.foxnews.com/printer_friendly _story/0,3566,51559,00.html.

27. Testimony of Jamal al-Fadl, February 7, 2001.

28. Ibid.

29. Ibid.

30. Larry C. Johnson, op-ed, *New York Times*, July 10, 2001.

31. Pelton, *The World's Most Dangerous Places*, p. 928.

32. Gordon Thomas, "Los Malerines de Osama," *El Mundo* (Spain), September 23, 2001.

CHAPTER 3

1. Paula De Masi and Vincent Koen, "Anatomy of the Russian Inflation," World Bank Group, May/June 1995.

2. Robert Young Pelton, *The World's Most Dangerous Places*, 5th ed. (New York: HarperCollins, 2004), pp. 873–74.

3. "Poverty in Russia: An Assessment," World Bank Group, December 1995.

4. Pelton, *The World's Most Dangerous Places*, p. 870.

5. Ibid., p. 858.

6. "The Rise and Rise of the Russian Mafia," BBC News, November 21, 1998.

7. "So Who Are the Russian Mafia?" BBC News, April 1, 1998.

8. "The Rise and the Rise of the Russian Mafia."

9. "So Who Are the Russian Mafia?"

10. Pelton, *The World's Most Dangerous Places*, p. 870.

11. "So Who Are the Russian Mafia?"

12. Chechen Anthem, in Pelton, *The World's Most Dangerous Places*, p. 441.

13. Eric Margolis, "The Savage War in Chechnya," *Foreign Correspondent*, October 2002, http://www.ericmargolis.com/archives/2002/10/index.php.

14. Wayne Anderson, "Chechnya, Russia Unable, Unwilling to Compromise," International Center for Psychosocial Trauma, November 12, 2002.

15. "Chechnya's Special Weapons," Global Security, October 2001, http://www.globalsecurity.org/wmd/wond/chechnya/.

16. Anup Shah, "Crisis in Chechnya," *Global Issues*, September 4, 2004, http://www.geoglobalissues.org/Geopolitics/Chechnya.asp.

17. Margolis, "The Savage War in Chechnya."

18. Ibid.

19. Pelton, *The World's Most Dangerous Places*, p. 230.

20. Ibid., p. 862.

21. Ibid., p. 438.

22. Graham Allison, *Nuclear Terrorism: The Ultimate Preventable Catastrophe* (New York: Henry Holt, 2004), p. 70.

23. Pelton, *The World's Most Dangerous Places*, p. 783.

24. Allison, *Nuclear Terrorism*, p. 70.

25. Ibid., p. 61.

26. William C. Potter, "Nuclear Profiles of the Soviet Successor States," Center for Nonproliferation Studies, Monterey Institute of International Studies, Monterey, CA, September 14, 1993.

27. Rensselaer Lee, *Smuggling Armageddon: The Nuclear Black Market in the Former Soviet Union* (New York: St. Martin's, 1998), pp. 135–36.

28. Oleg Bukharin and William Potter, "Potatoes Were Guarded Better," *Bulletin of Atomic Scientists*, May/June 1995.

29. "The Rise and Rise of the Russian Mafia."

30. Ibid.

31. "Chechnya's Secret Weapons."

32. Patrick J. Buchanan, *The Death of the West* (New York: St. Martin's, 2002), p. 18.

CHAPTER 4

1. David Filipov, "New Fears Chechens May Seek Nukes," *Boston Globe*, December 2, 2002.

2. "Chechnya's Special Weapons," FAS: Weapons of Mass Destruction, WMDs Around the World, no date, http://www.fas.org/nuke/guide/chechnya/index.html.

3. George Kenney, "Spy or Savior?" *Nation*, July 26, 1999.

4. Phil Williams and Paul Woessner, "The Real Threat of Nuclear Smuggling," *Scientific American*, January 1999.

5. Scott Parish, "Are Suitcase Nukes on the Loose?" Center for Nonproliferation Studies, Monterey Institute of International Studies, November 1997, http://cns.miis.edu/pubs/reports/lebedlg.htm.

6. Andrew Cockburn and Scott Cockburn, *One Point Safe* (New York: Doubleday, 1998), pp. 101–103.

7. David Smigielski, "A Review of the Nuclear Suitcase Bomb Controversy," Policy Update, Russian-American Nuclear Security Council (RANSAC), September 2003, http://www.ransac.org/Documents/suitcase nukes/ 090102.pdf.

8. Stanislav Lunev, "Do the Russians Know Where Their Nuclear Weapons Are?" *Prism* 1, no. 22 (October 20, 1995).

9. Jeffrey M. Bale, "The Chechen Resistance and Radiological Terrorism," Center for Nonproliferation Studies, Monterey Institute of International Studies, April 2004, http://www.nti.org/e_research/e3_47a.htm.

10. "Chechnya's Special Weapons."

11. Malcolm Gray, "Chechen Leader Killed," *MacLean's*, May 6, 1996.

12. Rensselaer Lee, *Smuggling Armageddon: The Nuclear Black Market in the Former Soviet Union and Europe* (New York: St. Martin's, 1998), pp. 135–36.

13. Simon Saradzhyan, "Russia: Grasping Reality of Nuclear Terror," BCSIA Discussion Paper, 2003–02, Belfer Center for Science and International Affairs, John F. Kennedy School of Government, Harvard University, March 2003.

14. Bill Nichols, Mimi Hall, and Peter Eisler, "Dirty Bomb Threatens U.S. with Next Terror Attack," *USA Today*, June 11, 2002.

15. Ibid.

16. "Dirty Bombs: Response to a Threat," Public Information Report, *Journal of the Federation of American Scientists*, March/April 2002.

17. Rohan Gunaratna, *Inside Al Qaeda: Global Network of Terror* (New York: Berkley Books, 2002), p. 179.

18. Daniel Benjamin and Steven Simon, *The Age of Sacred Terror* (New York: Random House, 2002), p. 113.

19. Claire Sterling, *Octopus: How the Long Reach of the Sicilian Mafia Controls the Global Narcotics Trade* (New York: Simon & Schuster, 1996), p. 162.

20. Roland Jacquard, *In the Name of Osama bin Laden: Global Terrorism and the bin Laden Brotherhood* (Durham, NC: Duke University Press, 2002), p. 137.

21. Kakharov's remarks were reported in the *Washington Post*, September 7, 2001.

22. Robert Young Pelton, *The World's Most Dangerous Places*, 5th ed. (New York: HarperCollins, 2004), p. 432.

23. Riyad 'Alam al-Din, untitled report, *Al-Watan Al-Arabi*, November 13, 1998, pp. 20–21.

24. Fareed Zakaria, "The New Rules of Engagement," *Newsweek*, December 6, 2001.

25. US Department of Health and Human Services, "National Household Survey on Drug Abuse," SAMHSA (Substance Abuse and Mental

Health Services Administration), Office of Applied Studies, http://www
.oas.samhsa.gov/nhsda.htm#NHSDAinfo.

26. Rachel Ehrenfeld, quoted in James Rosen, "Drug Trade Filled Coffers of Taliban, bin Laden Group," *Minneapolis Star Tribune*, September 30,
2001.

27. Nimrod Raphaeli, "Ayman Muhammad Rabi al-Zawahiri: The Making
of an Arch Terrorist," *Terrorism and Political Violence* (Winter 2002): 1–22.

28. "Report Links bin Laden, Nuclear Weapons," *Al-Watan Al-Arabi*,
November 13, 1998.

29. Ibid. See also Yossef Bodansky, *Bin Laden: The Man Who Declared
War on America* (New York: Random House, 1999), p. 330.

30. Marie Calvin, "Holy War with U.S. in His Sights," *Times* (London),
August 16, 1998; news brief, *Jerusalem Report*, October 25, 1999; "Report
Links bin Laden, Nuclear Weapons"; Emil Torabi, "Bin Laden's Nuclear
Weapons," *Muslim Magazine*, Winter 1998; "Al-Majallah Obtains Serious
Information on al Qaeda's Attempts to Acquire Nuclear Weapons," *Al-
Majallah*, September 8, 2002.

31. "Bin Laden Endorses 'The Nuclear Bomb of Islam,'" *Fact Sheet:
The Charges against Osama bin Laden*, US Department of State, December
15, 1999, http://usinfo.state.gov/topical/pol/terror/99129502.htm.

32. "Interview with bin Laden," *Time*, December 23, 1998.

33. John Miller, "Interview with bin Laden," ABC News, May 24, 1998.

34. Hamid Mir, "If US Uses Nuclear Weapons, It Will Receive Same
Response," interview with Osama bin Laden, *Dawn* (Pakistan), November
10, 2001. See also Evan Thomas, "The Possible Endgame and the Future of
al Qaeda," *Newsweek*, November 26, 2001.

35. Ibid.

36. Michael Scheuer, interviewed by Tim Russert, *Meet the Press*, NBC
News, November 4, 2004.

37. "Bin Laden's Nuclear Weapons," *Insight*, November 2, 2001.

CHAPTER 5

1. Tom Clancy, *The Sum of All Fears* (New York: Berkley Books,
1992), p. 918.

2. John McEwen, *The Republican*, September 26, 1997; Gabriel Biel, *The Spectator*, October 2, 1997.

3. Rose Gottemoeller, quoted in Richard Miniter, *Disinformation: 22 Media Myths That Undermine the War on Terror* (Washington, DC: Regnery Publishing, 2005), p. 140.

4. Ibid., p. 141.

5. Ibid., p. 148.

6. "U.S. Nuclear Weapons Cost Study Project," Atomic Audit, Brookings Institute, 1775 Massachusetts Avenue, NW, Washington, DC 20036.

7. Ibid.

8. Ibid.

9. A photo of the world's largest nuke can be seen at the following Web site: www.atomicmuseum.com/tour/np6.cfm.

10. "Suitcase Nukes: A Reassessment," Center for Nonproliferation Studies, Monterey Institute of International Studies, September 30, 2002, http://cns.miis.edu/pubs/week/020923.htm.

11. Graham Allison, *Nuclear Terrorism: The Ultimate Preventable Catastrophe* (New York: Henry Holt, 2004), p. 49.

12. "Mi Hermano bin Laden," *El Mundo* (Spain), September 16, 2001, http://www.elmundo.es/2001/09/16/cronica/1047765.html.

13. Stephen Schwartz, ed., *Atomic Audit: The Costs and Consequences of U.S. Nuclear Weapons Since 1940* (New York: Brooklings Institution Press, 1998), p. 49.

14. Miniter, *Disinformation*, pp. 140–41.

15. National Resources Defense Council, "Estimated Russian Stockpile," *Bulletin of Atomic Scientists*, September 1995.

16. Barry Farber, "The Case of Keith Idema," Newsmax.com, July 22, 2004, http://www.newsmax.com/archives/2004/7/22/105010.shtml. Idema's exploits are chronicled in Robin Moore, *The Hunt for Bin Laden* (New York: Random House, 2003).

17. David Smigielski, "A Review of the Nuclear Suitcase Bomb Controversy," Policy Update, Russian-American Nuclear Security Council (RANSAC), September 2003, http://www.ransac.org/Documents/suitcase nukes/90103.pdf.

18. General Alexander Lebed, quoted in Scott Parish, "Are Suitcase Nukes on the Loose? The Story behind the Controversy," Center for Nonpro-

liferation Studies, Monterey Institute of International Studies, November 1997, http://cns.miis.edu/pubs/report/lebedlg.htm.

19. Ibid.

20. Ibid.

21. "The Perfect Terrorist Weapon," interview with Gen. Alexander Lebed, *60 Minutes*, CBS News, September 7, 1997.

22. Lt. Gen. Igor Valynkin, quoted in Parish, "Are Suitcase Nukes on the Loose?"

23. Ibid.

24. Tatyana Samolis, quoted in ibid.

25. Vladimir Kryuchkov, quoted in ibid.

26. Physicians for Social Responsibility, *Fact Sheet*, Institute for Energy and Environmental Research (Takoma Park, MD), March 20, 1996.

27. Valynkin, quoted in "Suitcase Nukes: A Reassessment," Center for Nonproliferation Studies, Monterey Institute of International Studies, September 23, 2002, http://cns.miis.edu/pubs/week/020923.htm.

28. Vladimir Denisov, quoted in Parish, "Are Suitcase Nukes on the Loose?"

29. Georgi Kaurov, quoted in ibid.

30. Aleksey Yablokov, quoted in ibid. See also Paul L. Williams, *The al Qaeda Connection: International Terrorism, Organized Crime, and the Coming Apocalypse* (Amherst, NY: Prometheus Books, 2005), p. 90.

31. Carey Sublette, "Are Suitcase Bombs Possible?" Nuclear Weapon Archive, May 18, 2001, http://nuclearweaponarchive.org/News/DoSuitcase NukesExist.html.

32. Vincent Morris, "Pol Fears Soviets Hid A-Bombs Across U.S.," *New York Post*, November 7, 1999.

33. Congressman Curt Weldon, quoted in ibid.

34. Testimony of Col. Stanislav Lunev, House Committee on Government Reform, *Russian Threats to U.S. Security in Post–Cold War Era*, 106th Congress, 6th session, January 4, 2000.

35. Testimony of Vasili Mitrakhin in ibid.

36. Steve Goldstein, "Nukes on the Loose: The Black Market in Weapons Components," *Philadelphia Inquirer*, January 10, 1999.

37. Ibid.

38. Roland Jacquard, *In the Name of Osama Bin Laden* (Durham, NC: Duke University Press, 2002), p. 142.

39. Testimony of Col. Stanislav Lunev, National Security Committee, *Hearing on Russian Threats*, January 2000.

40. Bill Keller, "Nuclear Nightmares," *New York Times Magazine*, May 26, 2002.

41. "Nuclear Center Worker Caught Selling Secrets," BBC, December 21, 1998.

42. Miniter, *Disinformation*, p. 144.

43. Jeffrey St. Clair, "The Case of the Missing A-Bomb," *In These Times*, August 20, 2001.

44. Ibid.

45. GAO Report, "Nuclear Nonproliferation," May 2002.

46. Steve Rodan, "Iran Has Up to 4 Nuclear Bombs," *Jerusalem Post*, April 9, 1999; William C. Potter, "Nuclear Profiles of the Soviet Successor States," Center for Nonproliferation Studies, Monterey Institute of International Studies, September 14, 1993.

47. Rensselaer Lee, *Smuggling Armageddon: The Nuclear Black Market in the Former Soviet Union and Europe* (New York: St. Martin's, 1999), pp. 135–38.

48. Miniter, *Disinformation*, p. 145.

49. Robert Friedman, "The Most Dangerous Mobster in the World," *Village Voice*, May 22, 1998. Also see Ryan Mauro, "Terrorist Possession of Weapons of Mass Destruction," *World Threats*, Monthly Analysis, February 2003, http://www.worldthreats.com/monthly%20Analysis/MA%202003.htm.

50. Oleg Bukharin and William Potter, "Potatoes Were Guarded Better," *Bulletin of Atomic Scientists*, May/June 1995.

51. Miniter, *Disinformation*, p. 146.

52. Lyudmila Zaitseva and Friedrich Steinhausler, "International Dimensions of Illegal Trafficking in Nuclear and Other Radioactive Material," Center for International Security and Cooperation, Stanford University, 2002.

53. Keller, "Nuclear Nightmares."

54. Ibid.

55. Daniel Benjamin and Steven Simon, *The Age of Sacred Terror* (New York: Random House, 2002), p. 398.

56. Ibid.

57. Keller, "Nuclear Nightmares."

CHAPTER 6

1. Frank Gardner, "Al Qaeda 'Was Making Dirty Bomb,'" BBC, January 31, 2003.

2. Eliza Manningham-Butler, quoted in Jane Corbin, *Al Qaeda: In Search of the Terror Network That Threatens the World* (New York: Thunder Mouth's Press/Nation Books, 2003), p. 366.

3. Abdel Bari Atwan, quoted in Gardner, "Al Qaeda 'Was Making Dirty Bomb.'"

4. Richard Sale, "Israel Finds Radiological Backpack Bomb," United Press International, October 14, 2002.

5. Richard Sale, "U.S. Investigating Whether Nukes in Country," United Press International, December 20, 2001.

6. Congressman Christopher Shays, quoted in ibid.

7. Ibid.

8. Naveed Miraj, "Al Qaeda Nukes May Already Be in the U.S.," *Frontier Post* (Islamabad), November 11, 2001.

9. Barton Gellman, "Fears Prompt US to Beef-Up Nuclear Terror Detection," *Washington Post*, March 3, 2002. Also, "N-Weapons May Be in US Already," *Daily Telegraph* (Sydney), November 14, 2001. The *Telegraph* article not only substantiates Miraj's finding but also provides additional information about the nukes that were forward-deployed to the United States.

10. Gellman, "Fears Prompt US to Beef-Up Nuclear Terror Detection."

11. Shaykh Hisham Kabbani, "Islamic Extremism: A Viable Threat to the U.S. National Security," US Department of State, January 7, 1999; Dave Eberhart, "Muslim Moderate Kabbani Firm on Terrorist Nuclear Threat," United Press International, Newsmax.com, November 19, 2001, http://www.newsmax.com/archives/articles/2001/11/16/172201.shmtl.

12. Sale, "U.S. Investigating Whether Nukes in Country."

13. Ibid.

14. Stephen Flynn, quoted in ibid.

15. "The Strange Case of the 'Palermo Senator,'" *Debka*, September 14, 2002, http://www.debka.com/article.pjp?aids=162.

16. Ibid.

17. "Navy SEALs Inspecting Radioactive Ship Off New Jersey," Fox News, September 12, 2002, http://www.foxnews.com/story/0,2933,62897,00.html.

18. "The Strange Case of the 'Palermo Senator.'"

19. "New U.S. Terror Alert Linked to Nuke Fear," *Debka*, December 5, 2001, http://www.ki4u.com/loose_nukes.htm.

20. Ibid.

21. "Live from Afghanistan: Was Al Qaeda Working on a Super-Bomb?" CNN, January 24, 2002.

22. David Albright, "Al Qaeda's Nuclear Program: Through the Window of Seized Documents," Nautilis Institute (Washington, DC), November 6, 2002, http.//www.nautilis.org/archives/fora/Special-Policy -Forum147_Albright.html.

23. Graham Allison, *Nuclear Terrorism: The Ultimate Preventable Catastrophe* (New York: Times Books, 2005), p. 96.

24. Ibid.

25. Albright, "Al Qaeda's Nuclear Program."

26. Barbie Dutter and Michael Smith, "Inside Bin Laden's 'Nuclear Arsenal,'" *Daily Telegraph*, December 24, 2001, http://www.telegraph.co .uk/core/Content/displayPrintable.jhtml?xml=/news/2001/12/24/wb.

27. Ibid.

28. Ibid.

29. Barbie Dutter and Ben Fenton, "Uranium and Cyanide Found in Drums at Bin Laden Base," *Daily Telegraph,* December 24, 2001, http:// www.telegraph.co.uk/core/Content/displayPrintable.jhtml?xml=/news/2001/ 12/24/wb.

30. Albright, "Al Qaeda's Nuclear Program."

31. Jeffrey Kluger, "Osama's Nuclear Quest," *Time*, November 12, 2001.

32. Allison, *Nuclear Terrorism*, p. 99.

33. Kevin Whitelaw, "A Tightening Noose," *U.S. News & World Report*, March 17, 2003.

34. "Al Qaeda Names Match Those under U.S. Surveillance," CNN, March 5, 2003.

35. Elaine Shannon and Michael Weisskopf, "Khalid Sheikh Mohammad Names Names," *Time*, March 24, 2003; James Gordon Meek, "Officials Fear Al Qaeda Nuclear Attack," *New York Daily News*, March 14, 2003.

36. Meek, "Officials Fear Al Qaeda Nuclear Attack."

CHAPTER 7

1. David Albright and Holly Higgins, "Pakistani Nuclear Scientists: How Much Nuclear Assistance to Al Qaeda?" Institute for Science and International Security (ISIS), August 30, 2002, http://www.exportcontrols.org/print/pakscientists.html.

2. John J. Curtis, "Pakistan's Bomb Maker," OnlineColumnist.com, January 5, 2003, http://www.onlinecolumnist.com/01503.htm.

3. Graham Allison, *Nuclear Terrorism: The Ultimate Preventable Catastrophe* (New York: Times Books, 2004), p. 99.

4. Ibid., pp. 99–100,

5. David E. Sanger and William J. Broad, "From Rogue Nuclear Programs: Web of Trails Leads to Pakistan," *New York Times*, January 4, 2004.

6. Rajesh Kumar Mishra, "Pakistan as a Proliferator State: Blame It on Dr. A. Q. Khan," South Asia Analysis Group, paper no. 567, December 20, 2002, http://www.saag.org/papers7/paper601,html.

7. B. Rahman, "Lashkar-e-Toiba: Its Past, Present, and Future," Institute of Topical Studies, Chennai, India, December 25, 2003.

8. Ibid.

9. Ben Fenton and Ahmid Rashid, "US Hails Capture of Bin Laden's Deputy," *Daily Telegraph* (Sydney), February 4, 2002.

10. Eric Stakelbeck, "Terror's South American Front," *FrontPage*, March 19, 2004, http://www.frontpagemag.com/Articles/ReadArticle.asp?ID=12643.

11. Kauhik Kapisthalam, "Pakistan's Forgotten Al Qaeda Nuclear Link," *Asia Times*, June 3, 2004.

12. Alexandra Marks, "Are Terrorist Cells Still in the US?" *Christian Science Monitor*, August 10, 2005.

13. Sultan Mahmood and Muhammad Nasim, "CTBT: A Technical Assessment," *Pakistan Link*, January 7, 2000, http://Pakistanlink.com/Opinion/2000/Jan/07/02.htm.

14. Arnaud de Borchgrave, "Pakistan's Nuclear Oddballs," *Washington Times*, April 26, 2005.

15. Albright and Higgins, "Pakistani Nuclear Scientists."

16. Dr. Mahmood, quoted in ibid.

17. Ibid.

18. Julian Borger, "Pakistan's Nuclear Experts Advise Bin Laden," *Guardian* (Islamabad), December 13, 2001.

19. David Albright and Holly Higgins, "A Bomb for the Ummah," *Bulletin of Atomic Scientists*, March/April 2003.

20. Albright and Higgins, "Pakistani Nuclear Scientists."

21. Peter Baker, "Pakistani Scientist Who Met with Bin Laden Failed Polygraphs, Renewing Suspicion," *Washington Post*, March 3, 2002.

22. Dr. Sultan Bashiruddin Mahmood, quoted in Robert Sam Anson, "The Journalist and the Terrorist," *Vanity Fair*, August 2002.

23. Ibid.

24. Ibid.

25. Dr. Sultan Bashiruddin Mahmood, quoted in Arjad Bashir Siddiqi, "I Never Thought Meeting Osama, Omar Would Spell Trouble for Me," *The News* (Pakistan), March 19, 2002, http://www.jang.com.pk.

26. Baker, "Pakistani Scientist Who Met Bin Laden Failed Polygraphs."

27. Peter Baker and Kamran Khan, "Pakistan to Forego Charges against Two Nuclear Scientists," *Washington Post*, January 30, 2002.

28. Bertil Lintner, "Myanmar Gets a Russian Reactor," *Wall Street Journal*, January 3, 2002.

29. Ian Bremer, quoted in "Nuclear Energy: Is Burma/Myanmar the New Iran?" *Democratic Voice of Burma*, March 11, 2006, http://english.dvb.no/news.php?id=6634.

30. Kaushik Kapisthalam, "Pakistan's Forgotten Al-Qaeda Nuclear Link," *Asia Times*, June 3, 2004.

31. William J. Broad and David E. Sanger, "The Bomb Merchant: Chasing Dr. Khan's Network; As Nuclear Secrets Emerge More Are Suspected," *New York Times*, December 26, 2004.

32. B. Rahman, "A. Q. Khan and Osama Bin Laden," *Kashmir Herald* 3, no. 10 (March/April 2004), http://www.kashmirherald.com/featuredarticle/khanandbinladen.html.

33. Allison, *Nuclear Terrorism*, pp. 61–63.

34. Robert Gallucci, quoted in Seymour Hersh, "The Deal: Why Is Washington Going So Easy on Pakistan's Nuclear Black Marketers," *New Yorker*, March 3, 2004.

CHAPTER 8

1. Christopher Clary, "A. Q. Khan and the Limits of the Non-proliferation Regime," 2005 NPR Review Conference, Washington, DC, http://www.unid.org/pdf/artcles/pdf-art2188.pdf.

2. Ibid.

3. John J. Curtis, "Pakistan's Bomb Maker," Online Columnist.com, January 5, 2003, http://www.onlinecolumnist.com/01503.htm.

4. Gary Sick, "The Iran-Iraq War," in *Iran: The World's Hot Spot*, ed. Mikko Canini (San Diego: Greenhaven Press, 2005), p. 40.

5. David Albright and Corey Hinderstein, "Documents Indicate A. Q. Khan Offered Nuclear Weapons Designs to Iraq in 1990," Institute for Science and International Security (ISIS), February 4, 2004, http://www.isis-online.org/publications/southasia/khan_memo.html.

6. Ibid.

7. Michael Laufer, "A. Q. Khan Nuclear Chronology: Proliferations Brief," *Carnegie Endowment for International Peace* 8, no. 8 (2006), http://www.CarnegieEndowment.org/static/npp/Khan_chronology.pdf.

8. "Pakistan Scientist Brokered North Korea Deal," NBC News, October 18, 2002. See also Rajesh Kumar Misha, "Nuclear Scientific Community of Pakistan: Clear and Present Danger to Nonproliferation," South Asia Analysis Group, paper no. 601, July 2, 2003, http://www.onlinecolumnist.com/0153.html.

9. Leonard S. Spector, "How to Be Weapon-Ready NPT Members," *Yale Global* (Yale University), August 16, 2005, http://yaleglobal.yale.edu/display.article?id=6153.

10. "Khan's Nuclear Chronology," Center for Nonproliferation Studies, Monterey Institute for International Studies, 2006, http://cns.miis.edu/research/korea/nuc/yonbyon.htm.

11. Ibid.

12. Wisconsin Project on Nuclear Arms Control, "Libya's Nuclear Update," *Risk Report* 10, no. 2 (March/April 2004), http://www.wisconsinproject.org/countries/libya/libya-nuc.htm.

13. William J. Broad and David E. Sanger, "The Bomb Merchant: Chasing Dr. Khan's Network; As Nuclear Secrets Emerge, More Are Suspected," *New York Times*, December 26, 2004.

14. Ibid.

15. Bernard-Henri Levy, "Pakistan Must Provide Proof of Reforming the ISI," *South Asia Tribune*, September 14, 2003.

16. Ibid.

17. Mishra, "Nuclear Scientific Community of Pakistan."

18. Nigel Hawkes, "The Nuclear Threat: Pakistan Could Lose Control of Its Nuclear Arsenal," *Times* (London), September 20, 2001.

19. Ibid.

20. Musharraf, quoted in Rajesh Kumar Mishra, "Pakistan as a Proliferator State: Blame It on Dr. A. Q. Khan," South Asia Analysis Group, paper no. 601, July 2, 2003, http://www.saag.or/papers7/paper601.html.

21. Ash-har Quraishi, "U.S. Supports Nuclear Pardon," CNN, February 5, 2004.

22. Ibid.

23. Seymour Hersh, "The Deal," *New Yorker*, March 8, 2004.

24. "Profile: Abdul Qadeer Khan," BBC News, December 20, 2003, http://news.bbc.co.ul/1/hi/world/south_asia/3343621.stm.

25. Ludwig De Braeckeleer, "Why Did the CIA Resist the Arrest of Dr. Abdul Qadeer Khan?" *Canada Free Press,* March 23, 2006, http://www.canadafreepress.com/phprint.php.

26. Dr. A. Q. Khan, quoted in ibid.

27. Robert Young Pelton, *The World's Most Dangerous Places*, 5th ed. (New York: Harper Resource, 2003), p. 328.

28. De Brarckeleer, "Why Did the CIA Resist the Arrest of Dr. Abdul Qadeer Khan?"

29. Anwar Iqbal, quoted in ibid.

30. Ruud Lubbers, quoted in ibid.

31. Adam Ereli, quoted in ibid.

32. Ibid.

33. Judge Anita Lesser, quoted in ibid.

34. Jody Warrick, "Pakistan's Expanding Nuclear Program," *Washington Post*, July 24, 2006.

35. Erick Stakelbeck, "Terror's South America Front," *FrontPage*, March 19, 2004, http://www.frontpagemag.com/articles/2004-03-19.

36. Ibid.

37. Luiz Inácio Lula da Silva, quoted in Robert Burbach, "Brazil's Lula:

Confounding Friends and Foes," Redress Information Analysis, June 18, 2003, http://www.redressbtinternet.co.uk/rburbach20.htm.

38. Deroy Murdock, "A Latin American Axis," *National Review*, October 4, 2002.

39. Ibid.

40. Gary Milhollin and Liz Palmer, "Brazil's Nuclear Program," *Science*, October 2004.

41. George Jahn, "Brazil Has Tentatively Agreed to Let U.N. Atomic Watchdog View Parts of Its Equipment to Enrich Uranium," Associated Press, October 6, 2004.

42. Ibid.

43. Henry Sokolski, quoted in Louis Charbonneau, "Did Brazil Buy a Black Market Nuke?" Reuters, September 30, 2004.

44. Craig Unger, "Saving the Saudis," *Vanity Fair*, October 2003.

45. Martin Edward Anderson, "Al-Qaeda Across America," *Insight*, November 2, 2001. See also Peter Hudson, "There Are No Terrorists Here," *Newsweek*, November 19, 2001.

46. Hudson, "There Are No Terrorists Here."

47. Ibid.

48. "Terrorist and Organized Crime Groups in the Tri-Border Area of South America," Federal Research Division, Library of Congress under an Interagency Agreement with the director of the Central Intelligence Crime and Narcotics Center, July 2003.

49. Unger, "Saving the Saudis."

50. David Kalish, "Charming and Well-Connected: Bin Laden Family Spans the Globe," Associated Press, October 4, 2001.

CHAPTER 9

1. William L. Cleveland, *A History of the Modern Middle East*, 3rd ed. (Boulder, CO: Perseus Books, 2004), p. 479.

2. Daniel Pipes, "Heroes and Knaves of the Kuwait Crisis," in *A Restless Mind: Essays in Honor of Amos Perimutter*, ed. Benjamin Frankel (London: F. Cass, 1999). The material here comes from the prepublished version of Pipe's article, which can be found at http://www.danielpipes.org/article/985.

3. Paul Johnson, *Modern Times: From the Twenties to the Nineties*, rev. ed. (New York: HarperCollins, 1992), p. 769.

4. Ibid.

5. Ibid.

6. Ibid.

7. "Prince Sultan's Air Base," Global Security, 2006, http://www.globalsecurity.org/militaryfacility/princesultan.htm.

8. Ibid.

9. Ibid.

10. Yaroslav Troflimov, *Faith at War: A Journey on the Frontlines of Islam from Baghdad to Timbuktu* (New York: Henry Holt, 2005), pp. 13–14.

11. Osama bin Laden, "Jihad against Jews and Christians," World Islamic Statement, appendix B in Paul L. Williams, *Osama's Revenge: The Next 9/11* (Amherst, NY: Prometheus Books, 2004), p. 215.

12. Daniel Benjamin and Steven Simon, *The Age of Sacred Terror* (New York: Random House, 2002), pp. 107–108.

13. Simon Reeve, *The New Jackals: Ramzi Yousef, Osama Bin Laden, and the Future of Terrorism* (Boston: Northeastern University Press, 2002), p. 172.

14. Peter Bergin, *Holy War, Inc.: Inside the Secret World of Osama Bin Laden* (New York: Simon & Schuster, 2002), pp. 86–87.

15. Robert Young Pelton, *The World's Most Dangerous Places*, 5th ed. (New York: Harper Resource, 2003), p. 917.

16. Lenny Ben-David, "Sunni and Shiite Terrorist Networks: Competition or Collusion?" *Jerusalem Issue Brief* (Jerusalem Center for Public Affairs), no. 12, December 18, 2003.

17. Hassan Abdallah al-Turabi, quoted in Yossef Bodansky, *Bin Laden: The Man Who Declared War on America* (New York: Random House, 1999), p. 36.

18. Ibid.

19. Matthew Levitt, "New Arena for Iranian-Sponsored Terrorism: The Arab-Israeli Heartland," *Policy Watch*, February 22, 2002.

20. Jeffrey Goldberg, "In the Party of God," *New Yorker*, October 10, 2001.

21. Ibid.

22. Yael Shahar, "Al Qaida's Links to Iranian Security Services," Inter-

national Policy Institute for Counter-Terrorism," Herzlia, Israel, January 20, 2003.

23. Dana Priest and Douglas Farah, "Terror Alliance Has U.S. Worried; Hezbollah, Al Qaeda Seen Joining Forces," *Washington Post*, June 30, 2002.

24. Yael Shahar, "Al Qaida's Links to Iranian Security Services."

25. Pelton, *The World's Most Dangerous Places*, p. 703.

26. Priest and Farah, "Terror Alliance Has U.S. Worried."

27. Lt. Col. John R. Lawson III, "Barracks Bombing: 18 Years Ago," press release, US Marine Corps Headquarters, October 18, 2001.

28. Ibid.

29. Ibid.

30. Priest and Farah, "Terror Alliance Has U.S. Worried,"

31. Bodansky, *Bin Laden: The Man Who Declared War on America*, p. 157.

32. Ibid.

33. Martin Edwin Andersen, "Al-Qaeda Across America," *Insight*, November 2, 2001.

34. Erick Stakelbeck, "Terror's South America Front," *FrontPage*, March 19, 2004, http://www.frontpagemag.com/articles/2004-03-19.

35. Harris Whitbeck and Ingrid Arneson, "Terrorists Find Haven in South America," CNN, November 7, 2001.

36. Marc Perelman, "Brazil Connection Links Terrorist Groups," *Forward*, March 21, 2003.

37. Henry Orrego, "Bin-Laden's Trail Grows Cold on South America's Triple Frontier," Al-Jazeera, May 20, 2003.

38. Perelman, "Brazil Connection Links Terror Groups." Also see James Robbins, "Ambassadors of Terror," *National Review*, April 10, 2003.

39. Jim Bronskill, "Terrorists Eyed Ottawa Targets," *Ottawa Citizen*, February 8, 2004.

40. Ibid.

41. Stakelbeck, "Terror's South America Front." See also "A Global Overview of Narcotics-Funded Terrorist and Other Extremist Groups," Federal Research Division, Library of Congress under an Interagency Agreement with the Department of Defense, May 2002.

42. John C. K. Daly, "The Latin Connection," *Terrorism Monitor* (Jamestown Foundation) 3 (October 10, 2003).

43. Ibid.

44. "A Global Overview of Narcotics-Funded Terrorist and Other Extremist Groups."

CHAPTER 10

1. Peter Hudson, "There Are No Terrorists Here," *Newsweek,* November 19, 2001.

2. Ibid.

3. Marc Perelman, "Feds Call Chile Resort a Terror Hot Spot," *Forward,* January 2, 2003.

4. "Al-Qaeda South of the Border," *G-2 Bulletin* (World Net Daily), February 18, 2004, http://www.worldnetdaily.com/news/article/asp?Article_ID=37133.

5. Joseph Farah, "Terrorist Base South of Border," World Net Daily, December 1, 2003, http://www.wnd.com/news/printer-friendly.asp?ARTICLE_ID=35881.

6. Martin Argostegui, "Search for Bin Laden Looks South," United Press International, October 12, 2001.

7. Ibid.

8. "Narco-News Editorial on Citigroup and White Collar Terrorism," *Narco News,* October 12, 2001, http://www.narconews.com/issue14/whitecollarterror1.html.

9. "Peru Announces Arrest in U.S. of Suspects in Crime Network," *Washington Post,* news brief, October 2, 2004.

10. Terror-Linked Migrants Channeled into U.S.," Associated Press, July 3, 2005, http://www.foxnews,com/printer_friendly_story/0,3566,161473,00.html.

11. "Report Evaluates Al-Qaeda Risks World Wide," *USA Today,* November 11, 2003.

12. "Texaco Faces $1 Billion Lawsuit," BBC, October 22, 2003. See also "U.S. Lawyers Say Chevron Texaco Fear Lawsuit," *San Jose Mercury News,* October 24, 2003.

13. Ibid.

14. Arostegui, "Search for Bin Laden Looks South."

15. Chris Zambelis, "Al Qaeda in the Andes: Spotlight on Colombia," *Terrorism Monitor*, April 6, 2006, http://www.jamestown.org/terrorism/news/article.php?articleid=2369952.

16. "Latin America Security Challenges," http://www.nwc.navy.mil/press/npapers/np21/np21.pdf.

17. Ivan G. Osorio, "Chavez's Bombshell," *National Review*, January 8, 2003.

18. Ibid.

19. Arostegui, "Search for Bin Laden Looks South."

20. Ibid.

21. Dale Hurd, "Terrorism's Western Ally," Christian Broadcasting Network, April 22, 2003.

22. Patrick Goodman, "Chavez Plans to Meet with North Korea's Kim Jung il," CNS News, Cybercast News Service, June 26, 2006, http://www.cnsnews.com/viewForeignBureaus.asp?Page=/ForeignBureaus/archives/200606/in120060626c.html. See also Bruce McQuain, "Venezuela and North Korea: Arms for Oil," Qando Blog, July 6, 2006, http://www.qando.net/details.aspx?Entry=4185.

23. Christopher Brown, "The Other Iranian Nuclear Crisis," *FrontPage*, March 22, 2006, http://frontpagemag.com/Articles/Printable.asp?ID=21690.

24. Ibid.

25. "Latin America on Alert for Terror," *USA Today*, August 21, 2004.

26. Joseph Farah, "Islam on March South of Border," World Net Daily, June 7, 2005, http://www.wund.com/news/printer-friendly.asp?ARTICLE_ID=44636.

27. Patricia Guillermo and Ryan Wolf, "Border on Alert for Al Qaeda Terrorists," KGBT-TV, Brownsville, TX, aired on September 2, 2004, http://www.team4news.com/Global/story.asp?S=2254265; "Terror-Linked Migrants Channeled into U.S.," Fox News, Associated Press, July 3, 2005.

28. Investigators on Eyewitness New 4, "Terrorist Alley: Illegals from Terrorist Nations Are Crossing the Border into Arizona," KVOA-TV, Tucson, AZ, aired August 13, 2004.

29. Emma Perez-Trevino, "Potential Terrorists Released Due to Lack of Jail Space, Congressman Says," *Brownsville (Texas) Herald*, July 23, 2004.

30. Steve McCraw, quoted in ibid.

31. Donald Barlett and James Steele, "Who Left the Door Open?" *Time*, September 20, 2004.

32. Walter Ewing, "Border Insecurity: U.S. Border-Enforcement Policies and National Security," Immigration Policy Center, American Immigration Law Foundation, Washington, DC, Spring 2006.

33. Investigators on Eyewitness New 4, "Terrorist Alley: Illegals from Terrorist Nations Are Crossing the Border into Arizona."

34. Jon Dougherty, "Al Qaida Evidence along U S. Border?" World Net Daily, November 26, 2005, http://www.wnd.com/news/printer-friendly.asp?ARTICLE_ID=47589.

35. "Newly Obtained OTM and Special Interest Alien Information," press release, Office of Congressman Tom Tancredo, Colorado's Sixth District, August 10, 2004.

36. Julian Corman, "Border Incident," *Daily Telegraph* (London), August 14, 2004.

37. Congressman Tom Tancredo, quoted in "Al-Qaeda Coming Through," *National Review*, August 24, 2005.

38. "51 Terror Suspects Nabbed Trying to Enter U.S. Illegally," World Net Daily, December 15, 2005, http://www.wnd.com/news/printer-friendly.asp?ARTICLE_ID=47914.

39. Perez-Trevino, "Potential Terrorists Released Due to Lack of Jail Space, Congressman Says."

40. Congressman Solomon Ortiz, quoted in ibid.

41. Sheriff D'Wayne Jernigan, quoted in Karen Gleason, "Sheriff's Protests Delays Release," *Del Rio (Texas) New Herald*, July 12, 2004.

42. Jerry Seper, "Sensitivities 'Key' in Future Arrests," *Washington Times*, July 4, 2004.

43 "Woman with Altered Passport Detained," CNN, July 28, 2004.

44. Michelle Malkin, "Homeland Insecurity Files," August 1, 2004, http://michellemalkin,com/archives/00325.htm.

45. Robert Young Pelton, *The World's Most Dangerous Places*, 5th ed. (New York: Harper Resource, 2003), pp. 167–68.

46. Ibid.

47. Susan E. Reed, "Certifiable: Mexico's Corruption, Washington's Indifference," *New Republic*, March 17, 1997.

48. Pelton, *The World's Most Dangerous Places*.

49. Reed, "Certifiable: Mexico's Corruption, Washington's Indifference."

50. Author's interview with a federal official. See also, Keach Hagey, "Jamaica Man Pleads Guilty to Giving Al-Qaeda Money and Supplies," *Queens Chronicle*, August 19, 2004; and Elaine Shannon and Tim McGirk, "What Is This Man Planning?" *Time*, August 23, 2004.

CHAPTER 11

1. Andy Newan and Daryl Khan, "Brooklyn Mosque Becomes Terror Icon," *New York Times*, March 9, 2003.

2. Daniel Eggen and Manuel Roig-Franzia, "FBI on Global Hunt for Al Qaeda Suspect," *Washington Post*, March 21, 2003.

3. Sofian Abdelaziz Zakout, quoted in "Texas and Arizona on Alert for Dirty Bomber Wannabe Shukrijumah, Officials Warn of Border Crossing," *Militant Islam Monitor*, August 18, 2004, http://www.militantislammonitor .org/article/id/249.

4. Kelli Arena and Kevin Bohn, "Link between Wanted Saudi Man and 'Dirty Bomb' Suspect," CNN, March 22, 2003.

5. "Texas and Arizona on Alert for Dirty Bomber Wannabe Shukri-jumah, Officials Warn of Border Crossing."

6. Chitra Ragavan, "A Hunt for 'The Pilot,'" *U.S. News & World Report*, June 15, 2003.

7. Ibid.

8. "FBI Manhunt Targets Al Qaeda Suspects," CBS News, March 26, 2004.

9. FBI Alert, March 20, 2003.

10. James Gordon Meek, "Officials Fear Al-Qaeda Nuclear Attack," *New York Daily News*, March 14, 2003.

11. "One-Man 'Dirty Bomb' Cell Sought in US and Canada," Debka file, issue 132, November 7, 2003, http://www.debka-net-weekly.com/issue .pl? username=iunmber-132.

12. Ibid.

13. Ibid.

14. Ibid. See also Bill Gertz, "Al Qaeda Pursued a Dirty Nuke," *Washington Times*, October 16, 2003, http://www.washtimes.com/national/2003 1016-110337-4698r.htm.

15. Christine Cox, "Terror Fears Suspend Tours of Mac Reactor," *Hamilton Spectator*, October 15, 2001. See also "Board Suspends Hospital License," *McMaster News* (the news outline for McMaster University), March 1998, http://www.mcmaster.ca/us/opr/courier/mar998/news.html.

16. "One-Man 'Dirty Bomb' Cell Sought in US and Canada."

17. "Most Wanted: The Next Atta," *60 Minutes*, CBS News, March 26, 2004.

18. Ragavan, "A Hunt for 'The Pilot.'"

19. Ibid.

20. Meek, "Officials Fear Al-Qaeda Nuclear Attack."

21. Ibid.

22. "One-Man 'Dirty Bomb' Cell Sought in US and Canada."

23. "FBI Seeking Public Assistance in Locating Individuals Suspected of Terrorist Activities," FBI National Press Office, March 20, 2004. Also see Evan Thomas, David Klaidman, and Michael Isikoff, "Enemies among Us," *Newsweek*, June 7, 2004.

24. Jim Kirksey, "Two Suspected Al Qaeda Agents Dropped In for Meal, Says Denny's Manager," *Denver Post*, May 28, 2004.

25. Ibid.

26. Ibid.

27. Monique Kelso, quoted in ibid.

28. Elaine Shannon and Tim McGirk, "What Is This Man Planning?" *Time*, August 23, 2004.

29. Interview with Steve Emerson, *Hannity and Colmes*, Fox News, April 24, 2006.

30. "Al Qaeda Said to Recruit in South America," Associated Press, August 22, 2004.

31. Sherrie Gossett, "Police Searching for Next Muhammad Atta," World Net Daily, May 27, 2004, http://www.worldnetdaily.com/news/article.asp?ARTICLE=39237.

32. "Texas and Arizona on Alert for Dirty Bomber Wannabe Shukrijumah, Officials Warn of Border Crossing."

33. "Border Breach Stirs Fears," *Dallas Morning News*, August 14, 2004.

34. Michael Marizco, "Sonora on Alert for #1 Al Qaeda Suspect," *Arizona Daily Star*, August 18, 2004.

35. "Al-Qaeda Wants to Smuggle N-Materials to US," *Nation*, November 17, 2004.

36. Anna Clearley and Ornell R. Soto, "Reason for Plane Theft Worrisome," *San Diego Union Tribune*, November 7, 2004.

CHAPTER 12

1. Alex Roslin, "Canada's Nuke Tie to Taliban," *NOW Magazine* (Toronto), December 12, 2001.

2. Pervez Hoodbhoy, quoted in ibid.

3. Ibid.

4. Center for Nonproliferation Studies, Monterey Institute of International Studies, "Pakistan's Nuclear-Related Facilities," *Nonproliferation Review* 4 (1994).

5. Roslin, "Canada's Nuke Tie to Taliban."

6. John Sommerville, quoted in ibid.

7. James Bissett, "Learning from Canada's Mistakes: Terror along the Border," *Chronicles Magazine*, October 2005, http://www.chronicles magazine.org/www./Chronicles/2005/October2005/Bissett.html.

8. Ibid.

9. Ibid

10. Ibid.

11. Ibid.

12. Ibid.

13. "In-Depth: Hassan Almrei," Canadian Broadcasting Corporation, November 27, 2003.

14. John Thompson, "Other People's Wars: A Review of Overseas Terrorism in Canada," Mackenzie Institute, 2003, http://www.mackenzie institute.vom/2003/other_peoples_war//htm.

15. Ibid.

16. Ibid.

17. "Air India Suspects Are Not Guilty," BBC News, March 16, 2005.

18. Thompson, "Other People's Wars."

19. Ibid.

20. "FBI Seeking Public Assistance in Locating Individuals Suspected of Terrorist Activities," FBI National Press Office, March 20, 2004.

21. Thompson, "Other People's Wars."

22. Stephen Brown, "Canada—Terror Haven," *FrontPage*, December 9, 2002, http://frontpagemag.com/Articles/Printable.asp?ID=5007.

23. Thompson, "Other People's Wars."

24. "Homegrown Terrorist Plot Thwarted," *MacLeans*, June 19, 2006.

25. Thompson, "Other People's Wars."

26. Ibid.

27. Hal Benton et al., "'The Mission,' the Terrorist Within: The Story behind One Man's Holy War against America," *Seattle Times*, chapter 10 in a thirteen-part series, July 4, 2002.

28. Thompson, "Other People's Wars."

29. "Security Certificates and Secret Evidence," Canadian Broadcasting Corporation, June 23, 2006.

30. Thompson, "Other People's Wars."

31. Jim Kirksey, "Two Suspected Al Qaeda Agents Dropped In for Meal, Says Denny's Manager," *Denver Post*, May 28, 2004.

32. Bruce Crumley, "Fighting Terrorism: Lessons from France," *Time*, September 24, 2001.

33. John Hooper and Nick Hopkins, "Al Qaeda Cell in UK Planned Attack," *Guardian*, October 26, 2001.

34. Thompson, "Other People's Wars."

35. Ibid.

36. Ibid.

37. Lorraine Passchier, "Canadian Terror Cell Background," *New Republic*, June 3, 2006, http://www.freerepublic.com/focus/f-news/1642905/posts.

38. Michelle Shepherd, "Canadian Detained in Iraq," *Toronto Star*, May 25, 2004.

39. Stewart Bell, "Threat to Canadians," *National Post*, June 6, 2001.

40. Thompson, "Other People's Wars."

41. "Ontario Judge Grants Convicted Terrorist Bail," Canadian Broadcasting Corporation, November 30, 2001.

42. Thompson, "Other People's Wars."

43. Ibid.

44. Ibid.

45. Linda Kozaryn, "U.S. Indicts Arabian for Terrorism," Armed Forces Press Services, US Department of Defense, January 14, 2003.

46. Stewart Bell, "A Conduit for Terrorists," *National Post*, September 13, 2002.

47. Stewart Bell, "Accused Terrorist's Low-Key Life," *National Post*, October 29, 2005.

48. Thompson, "Other People's Wars."

49. "Canada: Fear of Forcible Return/Fear of Torture, Manickavasagam Suresh," Amnesty International, December 21, 2001.

50. Thompson, "Other People's Wars."

51. Ibid.

52. Michelle Shephard and Isabel Teotonio, "RCMP behind Bomb Material," *Toronto Star*, June 4, 2006.

53. Anthony De Palma, "Six of 17 Arrested in Canada's Antiterror Sweep Have Ties to Mosque Near Toronto," *New York Times*, June 5, 2006.

54. Ibid.

55. Andrew C. McCarthy, "The Elephant in the Room," *National Review*, June 25, 2006.

56. Stephen Brown, "Canada—Terrorist Haven," *FrontPage*, December 9, 2002, http://frontpagemag.com/Articles/ReadArticle.asp?ID=5007.

57. Walter Todd Huston, "Canada/Al-Qaeda—More Dangerous Than Mexico," *ChronWatch*, October 20, 2005, http://www.cronwatch.com/content/contentDisplay.asp?aid=17607&catcode=13.

CHAPTER 13

1. Rohan Gunaratna, *Inside Al Qaeda: Global Network of Terror* (New York: Berkley Books, 2002), pp. 147–48.

2. *The 9/11 Commission Report: Final Report of the National Commission on Terrorist Attacks upon the United States* (New York: Norton, 2004), pp. 177–78.

3. Hal Benton et al., "'Joining Jihad,' the Terrorist Within: The Story behind One Man's Holy War against America," *Seattle Times*, chapter 7 in a thirteen-part series, June 30, 2002.

4. Sheik Abu Abdul Aziz, quoted in ibid.

5. Ibid.

6. Hal Benton et al., "'Going to Camp,' the Terrorist Within: The Story

behind One Man's Holy War against America," *Seattle Times*, chapter 8 in a thirteen-part series, July 2, 2002.

7. Ibid.

8. Ibid.

9. Ibid.

10. Hal Benton et al., "'The Ticking Bomb,' the Terrorist Within: The Story behind One Man's Holy War against America," chapter 11 in a thirteen-part series, July 5, 2002.

11. Hal Benton et al., "'The Crossing,' the Terrorist Within: The Story behind One Man's Holy War against America," chapter 12 in a thirteen-part series, July 6, 2002.

12. Patrick Poole, "Terror from the North," *FrontPage*, June 14, 2006, http://www.frontpagemag.com/Articles/ReadArticle,asp?ID=22809.

13. "One-Man 'Dirty Bomb' Cell Sought in US and Canada," Debka file, issue 132, November 7, 2003, http://www.debka-net-weekly.com/issue .pl?username=iunmber-132.

14. Ibid.

15. James Bissett, "Learning from Canada's Mistakes: Terror along the Border," *Chronicles Magazine*, October 2005, http://www.chronicles magazine.org/www./Chronicles/2005/October2005/Bissett.html.

16. Daniel Pipes, "Canada's First Family of Terrorism," *New York Sun*, March 16, 2004.

17. Ibid.

18. Hayder Mili, "Securing the Northern Front: Canada and the War on Terror," *Terrorism Monitor* 3 (July 28, 2005).

19. John Thompson, "Other People's Wars: A Review of Overseas Terrorism in Canada," Mackenzie Institute, 2003, http://www.mackenzie institute.vom/2003/other_peoples_war//htm.

20. Michelle Malkin, "While Jean Chrétien Golfs," *Townhall*, April 18, 2003, http://www.townhall.com/Columnists/MichelleMalkin/2003/04/18/ While_Jean_Chretien_Golfs.

21. Zaynab Khadr, quoted in Daniel Pipes, "The Khadrs, Canada's First Family of Terrorism," Daniel Pipes's Weblog, April 9, 2004, http://www .danielpipes.org/blog_pf.php?id=303.

22. Colin Freeze, "Khadr Matriarch Returning to Canada," *Toronto Globe and Mail*, April 9, 2004.

23. Colin Freeze and Gay Abbate, "U.S. Releases Canadian Detained in Guantanamo," *Toronto Globe and Mail*, November 25, 2003.

24. Pipes, "The Khadrs, Canada's First Family of Terrorism."

25. Dave McNary, "'Rwanda' Man Plots CIA Stint," *Variety*, June 5, 2005.

26. Jerry Seper, "Al Qaeda Operating in Canada," *Washington Times*, December 26, 2002.

27. Pipes, "The Khadrs, Canada's First Family of Terrorism."

28. "Canadians Believed Killed in Pakistani Shoot-Out," Canadian Broadcasting Corporation, October 14, 2006.

29. Kim Lunman and Colin Freeze, "Khadr's Citizenship Safe, PM Says," *Toronto Globe and Mail*, April 16, 2004.

30. Ibid.

31. "Son of Al Qaeda: Interview—Abdullah Khadr," *Frontline*, Public Broadcasting System, February 23, 2004.

32. Ibid. See also Michelle Shephard, "Al Qaeda Suspect Back in T.O.," *Toronto Star*, December 7, 2005.

33. Pipes, "The Khadrs, Canada's First Family of Terrorism."

34. Colin Freeze and Jill Mahoney, "Khadr Held as Suspect in Abetting Al-Qaeda," *Toronto Globe and Mail*, December 19, 2005.

CHAPTER 14

1. "Probe Finds Terrorists in U.S. 'Training for War,'" World Net Daily, February 17, 2006, http://www.worldnetdaily.com/news/printer-friendly .asp?ARTICLE_ID=48868. News of Islamberg came through the ground-breaking work of Douglas Hagmann, the chief investigative officer of the Northeast Intelligence Network.

2. "Identifying Links between White Collar Crime and Terrorism," A White Collar Crime Center Report, 2005, http://www.ncjrs.org/pdffiles1/ nij/grants/209520.pdf.

3. Mira L. Boland, "Sheikh Gilani's American Disciples," *Weekly Standard*, March 17, 2002.

4. "Jamaat-ul-Fuqra, Terror Group of Pakistan," Institute of Contact Management, 2001, http://www.satp.org/satorgtp/pakistan/terroristoutfits/ jamaar-ul-fuqra.htm.

5. Ibid.

6. Ibid.

7. "The Jamaat-al-Fuqra Threat," *Stratfor*, Security Consulting Intelligence Resources (a preminum intelligence gathering agency), June 3, 2005, http://www.stratfor.com/products/premium/print.php?storyid=249345.

8. "Probe Finds Terrorists in U.S. 'Training for War.'"

9. Douglas J. Hagmann, "Special Report: Jamaat ul-Fuqra Training Compound Inside the U.S.," Northeast Intelligence Network, February 28, 2006. In addition to serving as president of the Northeast Intelligence Network, Hagmann serves as a correspondent for *Canada Free Press*.

10. Ibid.

11. Ibid.

12. Ibid.

13. Patrick B. Briley, "Al-Fuqra: U.S. Islamic Terror Network Protected by FBI, US State Department," *Liberty Post*, July 28, 2006, http://www.libertypost.org/cgi-bin/readart.cgi?Artnum=15222.

14. Hamid Mir, interview with Ryan Mauro, "Osama's Biographer Says Nukes in U.S.," World Net Daily, May 24, 2006, http://www.worrldnetdaily.com/news/article.asp?Article_ID=50341.

15. Dastych confirmed this finding to the author. The news was relayed to FBI officials who failed to take appropriate action.

16. Karen De Young, "Terrorist Attacks Rose Sharply in 2005, State Dept. Says," *Washington Post*, April 29, 2006.

17. "President Addresses Nation, Discusses Iraq, War on Terror," Fort Bragg, NC, White House press release, June 28, 2005; DeYoung, "Terrorist Attacks Rose Sharply."

18. David Dastych and Paul Williams, "Real Bad News in Afghanistan," World Net Daily, April 18, 2006, http://www.worldnetdaily.com/news/article.asp?ARTICLE_ID=49807.

19. Ibid.

20. Michael Isikoff and Mark Hosenball, "Catching Al Qaeda," *Newsweek*, September 8, 2004.

21. Mark Danner, "Taking Stock of the Forever War," *New York Times Magazine*, September 11, 2005.

EPILOGUE

1. Bernard Lewis, *The Political Language of Islam* (Chicago: University of Chicago Press, 1988), p. 73.

2. "The Rubaiyat of Omar Khayyam," LXXI, trans. Edward Fitzgerald, in *Palgrave's The Golden Treasury* (New York: Random House, 1944), p. 412.

3. Thomas Patrick Hughes, *Dictionary of Islam* (New York: Houghton, 1886), http://muslim_canada.org/islam_hughes.html.

4. Gharm-Allah el-Ghamdry, "Signs of the Last Hour," Compendium of Muslim Texts, University of Southern California, undated, http://www .edu/dept/MSA/fundamentals/pillars/signsof last hour.html.

5. "The Anti-Christ," *Palestinian Philosopher*, July 14, 2006, http:// palestinianphilosopher.wordpress.com/tag/religion/.

6. David Cook, "America, the Second AD: Prophecies about the Downfall of the United States," Yale Research papers, Yale University, 2003, http://research.edu/ycias/database/files/mesv5-5.pdf.

7. Ibid.

8. Abu Aasiya, "Signs before the Day of Judgment," *Search 4 Truth*, Spiritual Fortress (Saudi Arabia), 2006, http://etori.tripod.com/jajjalsystem/ judgement.html.

9. Ibid.

10. Ahmad ibn Naqib al-Misri, *Reliance of the Traveler: A Classic Manual of Islamic Sacred Law*, ed. and trans. Nuh Ha Nim Keller (Beltsville, MD: Amana Publications, 1994), p. 603.

11. Ibid.

12. Timothy R. Furnish, "Bin Laden: The Man Who Would Be Mahdi," *Middle East Quarterly*, Spring 2002, http://www.meforum.org/pf.php ?id=159.

13. Will Durant, *The Age of Faith*, vol. 4, *The Story of Civilization* (New York: Simon & Schuster, 1950), p. 178.

14. *Quran: The Final Testament*, 55:70–71, Authorized English Version, trans. Rashad Kahlifa (New York: Islamic Productions, 2003).

15. Paul Sperry, "Airline Denied Atta Paradise Wedding Suit," World Net Daily, September 11, 2002, http:///www.worldnetdaily.com/news/article ,asp?ARTICLE_ID=28904.

INDEX